Essential Skills for Historians

Essential Skills for Historians

A Practical Guide to Researching the Past

*J. Laurence Hare, Jack Wells,
and Bruce E. Baker*

BLOOMSBURY ACADEMIC
LONDON • NEW YORK • OXFORD • NEW DELHI • SYDNEY

BLOOMSBURY ACADEMIC
Bloomsbury Publishing Plc
50 Bedford Square, London, WC1B 3DP, UK
1385 Broadway, New York, NY 10018, USA

BLOOMSBURY, BLOOMSBURY ACADEMIC and the Diana logo are
trademarks of Bloomsbury Publishing Plc

First published in Great Britain 2020

Cover design by Tjaša Krivec
Cover image © Illustration by Mojca Fo

A catalogue record for this book is available from the British Library.

A catalog record for this book is available from the Library of Congress.

ISBN: HB: 978-1-3500-0544-0
          PB: 978-1-3500-0545-7
      ePDF: 978-1-3500-0543-3
   eBook: 978-1-3500-0546-4

Typeset by Integra Software Services Pvt. Ltd.
Printed and bound in Great Britain

To find out more about our authors and books visit www.bloomsbury.com
and sign up for our newsletters.

CONTENTS

LIST OF FIGURES

PREFACE

This book has two origin stories. The first was the result of long discussions about the best ways to help history majors appreciate the unique challenges of our profession and to teach them the skills needed to meet those challenges. Methods training has an odd place in many history curricula. It too often appears at the end of a course of study, where it does little to impart meaningful experience with research, or it is treated as an optional course, perhaps for honors students, and thus fails to reach many students. What is needed, we have concluded, is a curricular solution that makes methods training a product of many courses working together within a history program. Skill training, in other words, should be inseparable from teaching about historical content.

The problem with this approach is that it stretches the reach of a historical methods book. There are several terrific texts out there, but some are oriented toward beginners and may not appeal to advanced undergraduate or graduate students. Others are intended for the advanced level, but their emphasis on theoretical or historiographical issues, while important, can be somewhat inaccessible for early undergraduates. What is needed is a book that can help history faculty integrate considerations of methods and skills at all levels, offering introductory research training while also connecting students to more advanced techniques.

Here lies the second point of origin for this book. One of the overwhelming concerns facing universities today is the problem of student success and retention. Administrators and faculty alike fret about how to help students meet the rigors of university study and complete their degree programs on time. A number of institutions have responded by creating summer bridge courses, perspectives courses, or first-year seminars aimed at teaching such crucial intellectual skills as critical thinking and active reading, along with essential habits like successful goal planning. These experiments, however well intentioned, often meet with resistance from students, who balk at the extra requirements of a transitional course and criticize their content. In my experience, students routinely complain that such training is wasted time, since they already have experience with the basics. I have the impression that incoming students prefer to think of the university as a place to learn something new and sophisticated. They are much less interested in practicing the basics or participating in general education. Yet, time and again, when students seem to struggle academically, they often do so precisely because of shortcomings with the fundamentals.

My own experience with student research offers some key examples. In 2007, I had just left graduate school to take a position at Emory & Henry College, where the first course I taught was an advanced lecture course on postwar European history. My syllabus included a short research paper assignment. As the semester wound on, I took great care with my course lectures, but I assumed my students were fine to work on their projects independently. When the due date for the paper arrived, however, I was shocked to learn that half of the class had no clear idea what a research paper was, and the result was a set of essays that included virtually no citations. A few years later, while teaching at the University of Arkansas, I had a similar experience. This time, I was a little wiser and was careful to interrogate my students about what they did and did not know about research. I was nonetheless surprised to learn that over a third did not know what I meant when I asked them to go to the reference section of the library. Another group had no experience inserting footnotes into a word processing document. These sorts of gaps in student learning extend all the way to the graduate level, where I have seen MA students heartily agree that they were equipped to practice critical thinking but then become confounded when asked to explain what that means in practice.

The challenge, then, is to give students enhanced training in the fundamental skills that attach to university learning while also maintaining student engagement. The solution, I would argue, lies with making the connections between the types of core learning found in general education curricula and the advanced skills taught in the academic major. Students often come to university eager to learn more about their major or focus area, and by tapping into that enthusiasm, I believe that we can lead them to see the value of the underlying habits and skills that serve as the foundation for our work in the discipline. This is certainly the case in history, where our historical thinking practices grow directly from the principles of critical thinking, and where our research techniques rest upon common information literacy practices.

Essential Skills for Historians has emerged from these two challenges. It is designed to introduce students to the methods of professional history by way of the skills they must learn to succeed at the university. In this way, the book aspires to serve students at a variety of levels, from the first-year student making that delicate transition to university learning, to the advanced undergraduate planning a senior thesis, to the beginning graduate student who may not only need a greater awareness of the roots of our disciplinary practices but also need to think about how best to teach their own students someday.

In many ways, this is a "nuts and bolts" book. There is a healthy dose of theory and historiography in here, but the focus is on practical research techniques, with samples that show students how to move from beginning to end in a project. It thus works as a companion to other historiography or theory readers in methods courses, but it can also serve as a component of a survey or advanced topical course, where students can use it to guide their term papers. It is meant to be a versatile guide that can serve students across the history curriculum, with advice at the end that may help them think about career planning and the ways their university learning can serve them long after graduation.

I have been very grateful for the opportunity to collaborate with Jack Wells and Bruce E. Baker on this project. Wells and I worked together at Emory & Henry College in Virginia on bringing our history program in line with a new core curriculum, and this book reflects the many conversations we had about how to help students succeed academically in the major and in general education. Baker and I were fellow graduate students at the University of North Carolina at Chapel Hill, and from his most recent position at Newcastle University, he has made it possible for us to speak to students both in the United States and in the United Kingdom.

The three of us would like to thank the many individuals who helped make this book possible. Emma Goode at Bloomsbury Press was instrumental in launching the project, while Dan Hutchins and Maddie Holder supported us every step of the way. We would also like to thank the Wally Cordes Center for Teaching and Faculty Support at the University of Arkansas, who supported the initial research through a Teaching Improvement Grant. Kelsey M. Lovewell at the University of Arkansas Libraries and Lauren Beyea at Ford's Theatre generously shared images for the text. My colleague at Arkansas, Jared Phillips, offered thoughtful advice on approaching oral history. And the final stages of this project were greatly enhanced by the work of Sarah Riva, who assisted us with critical research assistance and thoughtful comments. We would also like to thank Mojca Fo, whose beautiful original illustration graces the cover of this book. And, of course, we must express our gratitude to the many students in the Emory & Henry Transitions I program; the University of Arkansas Perspectives in History, Graduate Methods, and Honors Methods courses; and to all of the history undergraduate honors thesis researchers who helped us develop and test the techniques we describe in the pages of this book.

J. Laurence Hare
Fayetteville, Arkansas

Introduction

Historians can be a formidable bunch. This may not seem obvious at first, when we see them hunched over some weathered text in an archive or pontificating through a cloud of chalk dust in a classroom. But our impression changes markedly if we think beyond the physical places where historians work and consider instead the domain in which they study. This more figurative space is nothing short of the whole vastness of the human past. It includes thousands of years in which human beings kept written records and can encompass even more remote periods bearing the continual traces of human cultures. Indeed, some enterprising historians have gone further still, laying claim to immense swathes of time stretching back to the Big Bang and the beginnings of the universe.[1] Within these vast epochs are stories, both profound and mundane, told in hundreds of languages and inscribed as both text and art in written and oral traditions. They concern great civilizations, nation-states, and metropolises, but also small communities, families, and individual lives. As the nineteenth-century Swiss historian Jacob Burckhardt famously observed, if but one of these accounts is like a drop of water, then the aggregate of human history is akin to a "wide ocean," placid in its everyday moments and rolling in its more dramatic episodes.[2] It is because historians seem to plunge so fearlessly into these metaphorical seas that we often assume they must possess an immense range of knowledge and skill. And this is what makes historians seem so ... formidable.

The reality, of course, is that historians can also feel overwhelmed not only by the size of their field but also by its fluidity. What's more, they are not alone; everyone in some way swims in the seas of the past. History is part of our daily lives. We encounter it in books, classrooms, and museums, of course, but also in movies and video games, in parks, neighborhoods, and across our university campuses. So, what separates the professional historian from the rest of us? One obvious answer is experience. Historians simply spend more time reading the most extant sources, piecing together historical events, and thinking about how best to interpret them. A second difference comes from the structures in which they work, including their discipline, their academic organizations, and their institutions. And perhaps most importantly, historians set themselves apart by practicing a particular set of methods that guide their engagement with the past. If we may push our pelagic analogy just a bit further, we might say that with their methodology, historians have the techniques they need to swim faster and deeper than the average person. At times, the gap between casual historical encounters and scholarly research may seem like the difference between dog-paddling and scuba diving, but it is important to note that one must learn to do the former before accomplishing the latter.

This observation serves as the point of departure for *Essential Skills for Historians*. The book is designed to reveal how many of the fundamental lessons that students learn in college or university, whether it be critical thinking or active reading or effective numeracy, form the basis of the advanced techniques needed to plumb the depths of the past in the manner of professional historians. The purpose of this book is to show students the connections between the two and in so doing to help them learn how to improve their mastery of both the fundamental and advanced skills.

Of course, one might be tempted to think that there is little need to review the basics. After all, colleges and universities claim that mastery of core skills is a natural by-product of the general curriculum. Yet it is worth considering how university curricula actually teach core skills. Would an average student know how to respond if asked, "How does one think critically?" or "What is the best way to read a scholarly monograph?" Universities, of course, value these skills, but as sociologists Richard Arum and Josipa Roksa have argued, it is too often the case that "commitment to these skills appears more a matter of principle than practice."[3] In other words, universities tend to assume too much that fundamental learning and thinking skills come across in a diverse array of classes, which can sometimes leave students unaware of what they are able to do, unable to explain their skills to others, or otherwise unsure of how best to utilize their abilities.

It is also worth considering the difference between learning a skill and mastering a skill. Even if a student practiced critical thinking in a sociology survey, or worked with numbers in a math course, or went to the library to research a history paper, it stands to reason that the student could stand a refresher from time to time and that more practice leads to higher achievement. Furthermore, a strong foundation in core skills is indispensable to the more advanced techniques that help define professional work, though students could be forgiven for not always seeing the connections between the two. In the United States, the divide between so-called general education and more advanced learning is institutionalized in two separate curricular pathways that students must navigate in the university. The first leads to an encounter with a core curriculum, which often entails a so-called distribution model introducing a broad range of disciplines and cultivating both breadth of learning and fundamental skills. The second pathway, known in the United States as the academic major, explores a specific subject (e.g., history) in greater depth and is often designed to facilitate the development of professional-level skill competency. Recently, American higher education leaders have begun rethinking this model, partly because they recognize that students and professors alike tend to treat these pathways as discrete experiences, when in fact the skills for the latter are inevitably built upon the foundation of the former.[4]

These points illustrate how important it is for historians, history majors, and anyone else wishing to know more about the past to think about the links between advanced practices of historical research and the core skills that make historical research possible. Yet many approaches to teaching historical methodology miss precisely this point and target advanced undergraduate history majors or graduate students with jargon-laced discussions of historiography and historical theory. As a result, students encountering history at the university level often must either do without a rigorous introduction to methodology, because the content of the methods training is too advanced, or otherwise miss key opportunities to learn about how historians work with the past or how a proper understanding of history can serve as a cultural and social good. Even seasoned students of history sometimes struggle to link advanced practices with the lessons they learned in their early university years. Such concerns also apply to history instructors, who may miss an opportunity to cultivate program-specific curriculum goals for beginning students.

For these reasons, this book will help you make the connections between the activities that students do in their daily learning and the methods that historians use in their daily work. This means that the lessons in each chapter are appropriate for students at a variety of levels. Whether you are a relative newcomer to university enrolling in history courses as part of your broader curriculum, or a more advanced student embarking upon history as a major or principal area of study, or even a graduate student crafting a major research project and considering a career as a professional historian, this book will help you to situate the academic study of history and the work of professional historians within a broader popular encounter with the past while introducing you to the methods that form the contours of the historical discipline. In this way, the book functions as a practical guide both for new students learning university success skills and more advanced students studying historical methods, as a complement to content-based textbooks in survey courses, and as a companion to texts dealing with historiography or historical theory in advanced undergraduate or graduate seminars.

In order to achieve its aims, this book will not only show you how professional historians pursue their scholarship but will also guide you through the development of your own project. It will begin by framing the pursuit of history and explaining how the profession is organized as a discipline and within institutions. It will then move step by step through the process of finding a suitable topic in history for you to explore, designing an original research project to answer a well-defined historical question, and seeing it through to completion, from working in the library to evaluating sources to writing a finished product. In this way, you will be able to use this book to plan and carry out your own term paper, thesis, or even a doctoral dissertation. Along the way, you will learn about and practice a specific set of methodological techniques and understand how they emerge from more fundamental skills. You will see, for example, how historians practice specific types of "historical thinking" based upon the simple rules of good critical thinking or how the principles of active reading inform analyses of historical sources. Finally, the chapters in this book are designed to link the development of specific academic habits, which are essential to every successful university student, to the professional norms and practices of historians and other scholars. For instance, you will encounter how specific approaches to setting goals can help you manage both short-term assignments and long-term research projects, and you will see how the academic integrity rules that guide many universities and the professional ethics of such major organizations as the American Historical Association stem from a common set of scholarly values. In this way, you will learn not only techniques that shape solid historical scholarship but also the principles on which they are based and the best strategies for using them in your work.

To deliver these lessons, each chapter is divided into three parts. The first part features a reflection on a key aspect of historical practice, including such topics as the motives for studying history, changes in how historians find information, or the elements of historical writing. A second section focuses on discovering how general skills inform the advanced techniques used in historical research. Finally, a third section calls for you to apply what you have learned to build your own research project. Wherever possible, we have worked to align the skills you need with different stages of project development, so that you can learn and practice the different techniques while advancing your independent research. Along the way, we will model the lessons using two sample projects—one drawn from ancient Greco-Roman history and the other from US history—that act as unifying threads across each of the chapters. Since this book is designed to grow with students across their curriculum, the sample projects are aimed at different skill levels. The Greco-Roman example is geared toward undergraduates who may be completing a term paper, while the US example is aimed at more advanced students who may be thinking about writing an undergraduate or graduate thesis. These examples will serve as practical illustrations of the methods discussed in the chapters, and they will provide you with examples for your own research, leading you along the way through the process of developing an initial set of research questions, collecting and analyzing primary sources, situating your work within the academic literature, writing a persuasive argument, and presenting your finished research to an audience.

As you begin this text, we might suggest that your first step should be to approach its lessons with an open mind. For some readers, all of the material in this text may seem new, but others will find that they are reviewing core skills. The point is that everyone can benefit from reviewing the fundamentals and thinking about them in new ways. Second, ask yourself about your own interest in history. What do you see as the value of studying the past? What time periods, places, or historical figures first drew you to history? About which aspects of history would you like to know more? Such questions are important because they can help us identify and refine research topics and also because they can engender a deeper personal investment in a long-term scholarly project. The principle is simple: people tend to put forth more effort and be persistent when they feel connected to the work they are doing.

Finally, we would encourage you to think beyond the project. Too often when working with student researchers, we see that an otherwise laudable attention to the finer details can yield a tendency to forgo a larger perspective. For this reason, this book will conclude by placing individual research projects back into a larger context. It will discuss the implications of historical practice, including its role in mediating disputes about the past, its place in presenting the past to the public, and the ways in which proper historical thinking can illuminate a broad range of contemporary and social issues. It will also help you envision the wide array of possibilities for careers based on the skills afforded by the study of history. As you reach the end of this book and work through the steps to complete your own project, you will gain valuable experience with the essential skills needed to dive into the depths without losing sight of the "wider ocean" in which you are swimming.

Notes

1   David Christian, *Maps of Time: An Introduction to Big History* (Berkeley: University of California Press, 2004); Fred Spier, *Big History and the Future of Humanity*, 2nd ed. (Chichester: Wiley-Blackwell, 2015).

2   Jacob Burckhardt, *The Civilization of the Renaissance in Italy*, translated by S.G.C. Middlemore (London: Sonnenschein, 1904), 3.

3   Richard Arum and Josipa Roksa, *Academically Adrift: Limited Learning on College Campuses* (Chicago: University of Chicago Press, 2011), 35.

4   Scott Jaschik, "Distribution Plus," *Inside Higher Ed* (January 19, 2016), accessed July 1, 2018, https://www.insidehighered.com/news/2016/01/19/ survey-colleges-finds-distribution-requirements-remain-popular-new-features.

1

History as Discipline and Practice: From the "Why" to the "How" of Studying the Past

What we will do in this chapter:

➤ **REFLECT** on our motives for university study and for the study of history.
➤ **DISCOVER** historiography, the origins of historical scholarship, and the features of today's historical discipline.
➤ **APPLY** your own experiences with history to a potential research topic.

The "Why" of History

It all begins with a question. It is curiosity that sets us off on our journey and the questions that guide us along our path toward knowledge. This is true both for good research and for successful university study, and it applies equally to the questions we pose to the world and those that we ask of ourselves. Before setting out, the first question we ask should be the *why* question. From the first day of their first semester, students should consider why they wish to study at university and follow a certain curriculum. This too often goes unasked because students tend to assume that they already know the answer. Even student success guides sometimes skip this crucial point and instead leap directly into a discussion of the skills needed to succeed. Without this preliminary consideration, however, there can be no firm definition of success. University study at any level requires a great deal of work and commitment, and students who understand their motives tend to have a greater stake in their learning. Research has shown that self-awareness yields higher levels of engagement, better academic performance, and greater persistence in completing a curriculum.[1] The why question thus lies at the heart of successful goal planning.

REFLECTION EXERCISE

Discuss or write about your motivations for university study. What were your primary reasons for choosing your college or university and enrolling in your current degree program? Why did you choose to take a history course? And, finally, why do you think that universities should include history in their curricula?

The underlying why questions are no less important to the study of history. Unfortunately, our assumptions similarly obscure the answers. On the first day of many history classes, it is common for professors to ask their students why they are taking the course. Some respond that history is a suitable preliminary pathway to a career in law or civil service. Others see the courses merely as a way to meet a curricular requirement for a university degree. Such answers share an assumption that the purpose of studying history is a functional one, a means to a short-term end. Astute history professors will push the conversation toward larger questions about the purpose of history, but even here another set of assumptions comes into play. When pressed on the reasons why human beings bother to study history at all, very often the responses coalesce around a single cliché, which runs something along the lines of "we study the past so we do not repeat it."

The phrase sounds like a rather dire warning: Study history or else! One can imagine wary historians ever on the lookout for the next dictator or the next man-made catastrophe. In fact, the truth behind this saying is more complex ... and more revealing. It is drawn from the work of the philosopher George Santayana (1863–1952), whose original words, "those who cannot remember the past are condemned to repeat it," appeared in his 1905 work, *The Life of Reason*.[2] The original quote still sounds ominous, but Santayana was less concerned with the next catastrophe than he was with the notion of progress, which was an alluring ideal during the nineteenth and early twentieth centuries. In Western culture it represented a firm belief in the capacity of human societies to grow and improve steadily across the centuries. In his book, however, Santayana portrayed progress not as an inevitability but as something that demanded constant cultivation. His words were meant to suggest that the preservation of the past was essential to allowing humankind to move forward into the future. For contemporary believers of progress, not going forward meant risking a return to the less desirable state from whence their ancestors came. Today a belief in progress continues to inform our perception of ourselves and our place in time, but the experience of the twentieth century, with the devastation of two world wars, the horrors of modern genocide, and the threat of nuclear war, has left the notion with less credibility than it had a century earlier. Just as we now deem it unlikely that a particular historical moment will actually "repeat" itself, so too do we no longer conceive of history as a fixed track leading into the future.

It may thus seem odd that Santayana's expression continues to justify our study of the past. Part of the reason why it remains appealing is that it embodies two central assumptions that guide how we think about history. The first and most obvious is that the value of history lies in its negative examples. To caution that we might be doomed to fall into some trap suggests that we are best served to attend to the wrong turns in the past. In this way, it evokes a one-dimensional image of history replete with mistakes and terrors whose sum is less developed materially, politically, and morally than the world of the present. Here the specter of progress rattles its chains. The second assumption concerns the fundamental relationship between the past and the present. By warning us to keep a lookout for the encroachment of the past on the present, Santayana posits the two as inherently separate conceptions. It implies that as long as we remain alert to the errors of history, we can keep the past at bay.

Decades later, the German philosopher Walter Benjamin (1892–1940) offered a similar perspective in his "Theses on the Philosophy of History," in which he famously described the metaphorical "angel of history":

> His face is turned towards the past. Where we perceive a chain of events, he sees one single catastrophe which keeps piling wreckage upon wreckage and hurls it in front of his feet. The angel would like to stay, awaken the dead, and make whole what has been smashed. But a storm is blowing from Paradise; it has got caught in his wings with such violence that the angel can no longer close them. This storm irresistibly propels him into the future to which his back is turned, while the pile of debris before him grows skyward. This storm is what we call progress.[3]

Just as Santayana's quote is a common feature of the undergraduate classroom, so Benjamin's "angel of history" frequently appears in the graduate seminar. It strikes us as more poetic, more sophisticated, and thus more fitting for the budding doctoral student, but like Santayana, Benjamin harbors a distinctly twentieth-century view of the past that is characterized by its darker moments. The difference is that where Santayana's uncertainty about the future of progress leads to a sense of caution about history, Benjamin, who was writing while on the run from the Nazis during the

Second World War, articulates a tragic view of the past. Taken together, the two philosophers arrive at similarly negative assessments of history while also stressing its separation from the present. Santayana advises us to avoid resurrecting the past, while Benjamin's "angel" helplessly observes an irreparable gulf between past and present. If the former has since come to serve as a hackneyed rationale for historical study, the latter stands as a fatalistic denial of its utility.

In these instances, Santayana and Benjamin draw on particular perceptions of the past to reflect on their own times. A closer look at their writings, however, reveals that both held views that were far more complex than are evident in a few selected quotes. Santayana's warning fits within a work that was less an indictment of history than a nuanced view of progress, while Benjamin's other writings defend the value of tradition.[4] Yet by drawing their words out of context and treating them as axioms, we oversimplify their meaning and create a distorted view of the value of history. The lesson here is that we cannot hope to answer the "why" question on the first day of a history class with trite quotations; rather, we must seek to justify our studies through a more nuanced discussion and then carry it with us as we explore the past.

We can begin by scrutinizing the specious assumptions that arise from our two quotes. First, we must recognize their misleadingly bleak view of the past. At issue is not simply a negative slant that obscures the true breadth of historical experiences but also the temptation to see the sum of history as a single narrative, whether bracketed by the upward trajectory of linear progress or by the haunting futility of amalgamated wreckage. Contemporary historians have long rejected unified narratives of history and have come to see the diversity of history as one of the hallmarks of its inherent value. As Norman Cantor and Richard Schneider have explained, history is important because it provides "a road to self-knowledge and a means of understanding the motives and attitudes of people of disparate backgrounds."[5] This notion of diversity applies not only to the differences among cultures but also to different groups within societies, all of whom have their own unique perspectives and stories.

Second, we should rethink the boundaries between past and present. People in unique historical periods thought, spoke, acted, and perceived in ways alien to us today. As the novelist L.P. Hartley famously wrote in his 1953 novel, *The Go-Between*, "The past is a foreign country: they do things differently there."[6] With this idea in mind, one of the most important tasks for the historian is to find ways to render the past intelligible to the present. At the same time, however, the notion of history as hopelessly remote belies the degree to which it is deeply ingrained in the here and now. If the past is a "foreign country," the present is by no means virgin soil. In the words of R.G. Collinwood (1889–1943), "In a sense we are all historians nowadays."[7] To understand what this means, imagine yourself going through a normal day without encountering some relic of the past: a museum, an old building, a disused road, a weathered monument, or even a period drama playing at the cinema. It is virtually impossible; the vestiges of the past linger in our everyday. Even if students never managed to take a history course at university, they would by no means spare themselves from an encounter with history.

We become more acutely aware of the ephemeral nature of the present over the course of our lives, as our experiences accumulate and our own lives become a landscape imbued with a sense of the past. Here lies the tricky distinction between history and memory. In many ways, the two represent different orientations to the past. As Geoffrey Cubitt has explained, "Where the discourse of history poses the question of how the present can achieve knowledge of a past from which it is separated, the discourse of memory posits a more intimate or continuous connection between past experience and present consciousness."[8] In this interpretation, history represents the remote past that we can study objectively, while memory contains the elements that are more immediate and subjective, whether from the point of view of an individual or of an entire community (what we would refer to as collective or cultural memory). As Cubitt admits, however, the distinctions between history and memory are often hazy. Particularly in the case of the recent past, both history and memory cover the same terrain. They may approach it differently, with academic history representing a more objective perspective, but even here the two overlap a great deal. Memory, for example, is a key source of the historian's work, while the historian's personal recollections inform his or her approach to questions and method. History, in turn, lends the supporting voices and finer details that inform both personal and collective memory. The inevitable conflation of history and memory tends to cloud our perception of the past, even when dealing with events in our own lifetime. It means that historians must do more than build bridges between past and present; they must also draw out the realities of the past from the vagaries of memory.

By confronting the twin challenges of representing the diversity of human experience and managing its intimate connections with our present, we arrive at a more nuanced sense of the value of history. Humans have lived, died, thought, fought, loved, built, destroyed, and invented in myriad ways over the course of millennia. To explore the past is to inventory the possibilities for human ingenuity and achievement. At the same time, it is to understand how humans have encountered the same sorts of problems that we face today, such as managing a society, dealing with conflict, determining what is good, interpreting the world around us, and deriving meaning from existence. It not only brings us closer to historical cultures separated by thousands of years but also illuminates our own lives. But it demands that we question our assumptions and engage more deeply with convenient quotations taken out of context. If, for example, we investigate L.P. Hartley's line about the past as a "foreign country," we learn that he was not speaking of some lost civilization but was giving voice to the confusion of his protagonist, who discovers a diary from his youth and seeks to rediscover something of himself in its pages. Now an old man, the character looks with confusion at the pages from his school days: "It was a roll-call in reverse; the children of the past announced their names, and I said 'Here'. Only the diary refused to disclose its identity."[9] In the end, this story is not about the protagonist's search for a lost time but about his search for himself. This is one of the most important reasons that we study history. We explore the past because in its nearness to the present it forms a part of our vision of ourselves and our society today, and in its remoteness, it reveals how much more expansive that vision could be. Ultimately, history is vital because we cannot understand ourselves without it.

Historiography and the Genealogy of History

As we have seen, we embark on the study of history already deeply engaged in the past, both as individuals and as members of communities. For this reason, we can never hope to study history from a truly fresh perspective. There is no clean slate upon which we may write the story of the past or convey its value. Students and scholars alike engage the past with unfiltered assumptions and a body of personal experiences and memories. As a result, historians may agree that history has the power to tell us something about ourselves as human beings and about the present world in which we live. Yet they have not always shared the same idea about what those lessons might be. They have adopted different views on the finer details about the value of the past, and these differences have in turn informed different beliefs about how we should study the past.

The questions that we have been asking about the value of history thus serve as useful ways of thinking about **historiography**, which concerns the study of historical scholarship and writing. Historiography is concerned not with historical events themselves but with the changing ways in which historians have researched, interpreted, written about, and debated those events. According to the British historian Herbert Butterfield, "Ultimately it comprises the study of the development of man's sense for the past, and the manifold relationships between the living generations and their ancestors."[10] In other words, historiography refers to the ways in which historians have negotiated the dilemmas we described in this chapter: the diversity of past experience and the thorny connections between past and present. In its most general sense, historiography is important because it reveals how the practice of historical scholarship has changed over time. As Jeremy D. Popkin has explained, historiography tells us about "how historians of the past conceived of their projects and the methods they used."[11] It explains how past cultures framed the questions they asked of the past, how historical writers discovered and dealt with research problems, and how the academic discipline of history emerged and evolved over time.

Traditionally, accounts of general historiography have portrayed the emergence of the modern historical discipline as the product of a linear, progressive development of Western thought. They often begin with histories written in ancient Greece, move through the humanist musings of the Italian Renaissance, and culminate with the fruits of Enlightenment philosophy and the writings of the first professional historians in the nineteenth century. The reality, of course, is far more complex. First of all, historical writing was by no means confined to the Western intellectual tradition. Although the contemporary discipline developed largely within a European and North American historiographical milieu, historical writing was a feature of a number of non-Western civilizations going back to antiquity. Today, the enterprise of academic history is shaped by scholars from around the world influenced by a variety of cultural traditions.

Second, it is misleading to conceptualize past instances of historical writing as mere forerunners of today's scholarship. While recognizing the intellectual debts that today's discipline owes to past historians, we must also assess historiographical episodes within their own context in order to understand the ways in which scholarship both reflected and shaped the perceptions of contemporaries. This demands that we not fall into a linear view of historiography but that we instead adopt a more genealogical perspective. As you may know, **genealogy** refers to the study of family lineages, but scholars have also used the term to describe ideas or trends that unfold not as a direct succession of events but as a complex set of relationships spread unevenly across a period of time. This is how we might understand the course of historiography, not as an accumulating body of knowledge and methodological thought but as a periodically intense engagement with the past drawn from the needs of unique moments and shaping indirectly the later development of professional academic history.

In the section below, we will review some of the key moments from the traditional narrative of historiography, but we will approach each episode with an eye toward understanding how and why specific views about history appeared as they did. Think of this section not as a definitive account but as a highlight reel and focus on understanding how the study of historiography can help us understand the assumptions, beliefs, and perceptions of peoples in the past, along with the ways in which we think and write about history today.

Capturing the Greek Moment

Most accounts of the rise of the Western historical discipline look to the ancient Greeks as their point of departure. In part, this stems from long-standing perceived linkages between the Hellenic world and the modern "West," but it also speaks to the role that a handful of ancient Greek historians played in creating secular narratives of the past informed by defined methodology. The two most commonly cited figures are Herodotus

(c. 484–425 BCE) and Thucydides (c. 460–400 BCE), both of whom were active during the fifth century, **BCE** (**Before Common Era**). This was an era in which the Greek city-states were coming into closer interaction with each other and with the wider, so-called barbarian world around them. The ever-expanding horizons were evident in Herodotus' work, *The Histories*, which incorporated source material from across the Aegean Sea and Eastern Mediterranean. In his opening sentences, Herodotus claims that he writes "in the hope of thereby preserving from decay the remembrance of what men have done, and of preventing the great and wonderful actions of the Greeks and the Barbarians from losing their due meed of glory."[12] His book is part history and part ethnography and reflects the changing sense of the region's geography and politics. By identifying the Greeks as a common people and distinguishing them from the barbarians, Herodotus gives voice to an emerging collective Hellenic identity.[13]

At the heart of *The Histories* are the Persian Wars (499–449 BCE). Herodotus carefully explains their origins by combining semi-mythical tales and contemporary events to chart the rise and current state of the major polities in the Eastern Mediterranean. The stories that Herodotus tells of "great and wonderful actions" hearken back to the Homeric epic poems that had appeared centuries earlier, but *The Histories* breaks new ground not only through its broad scope but also through its concern for accurate accounts.[14] Herodotus often found himself contending with uncertain or differing perspectives on specific events. He recognized the need for assessment and interpretation in order to arrive at the truth, but he often lacked a means of corroborating or disproving specific narratives. His method was to strive for faithful renditions of conflicting accounts and to then leave it to the readers to make the final determination of what really happened.

A generation later, Thucydides was more explicit about the value of his historical subject, *The History of the Peloponnesian War*. As a former Athenian general, Thucydides had a unique perspective on the long-running conflict between Athens, Sparta, and their allies. In his opening lines, he alluded to its singular importance:

> Thucydides, an Athenian, wrote the history of the war between the Peloponnesians and the Athenians, beginning at the moment that it broke out, and believing that it would be a great war and more worthy of relation than any that had preceded it.[15]

As this quote attests, Thucydides felt the need to record the history of the Peloponnesian War not because of some lofty ideals about humanity or some sacred notion of the past, but because his own experience suggested that the event itself was especially momentous. And, as he explained, part of what made it so momentous was the scale of the conflict: "Indeed this was the greatest movement yet known in history, not only of the Hellenes, but of a large part of the barbarian world—I had almost said of mankind." He then makes proving this point a goal of his study: "An examination of the facts will show that it was much greater than the wars which preceded it."[16] As evidence, he reaches back, just as Herodotus had done before him, into the Archaic years of the Homeric epics to show how the relatively small size of the Greek city-states and the political disunity of the region precluded the kinds of mobilizations that characterized the Peloponnesian War. Like Herodotus, Thucydides uses a long narrative to support an overarching interpretation of contemporary events. But where Herodotus captured the first stirrings of Greek identity, Thucydides narrated the dramatic coalescence of the Hellenic world.

Thucydides believed that tracing the war between Athens and Sparta warranted great care and accuracy, and he thus consciously wrote in opposition to older means of recording the past:

> The conclusions I have drawn from the proofs quoted may, I believe, safely be relied on. Assuredly they will not be disturbed either by the lays of a poet displaying the exaggeration of his craft, or by the compositions of the chroniclers that are attractive at truth's expense; the subjects they treat of being out of the reach of evidence, and time having robbed most of them of historical value by enthroning them in the region of legend.[17]

Unlike Herodotus, Thucydides adopted a much more authoritative role, choosing the versions of events that seemed to him to be most accurate. In adopting this method, he implicitly criticized his forebears:

> I grant that there will be a difficulty in believing every particular detail. The way that most men deal with traditions, even traditions of their own country, is to receive them all alike as they are delivered, without applying any critical test whatever.[18]

In this way, Thucydides defined the role of the historical writer. The importance of certain periods demanded that a historian accept responsibility for delivering a competent and truthful rendition of the events that unfolded. Thucydides, of course, realized that he had only witnessed a fraction of what had transpired and that his account would lack an unassailable level of certainty. He asked readers to rely upon his methodology to support his interpretations. For instance, in an era that produced very few written documents, one of Thucydides' most important sources for understanding wartime policy were the speeches of Greek leaders. The problem was that no one, including Thucydides himself, had completely accurate recollections of what had been said. He explains his solution to the problem in Book I:

> With reference to the speeches in this history, some were delivered before the war began, others while it was going on; some I heard myself, others I

got from various quarters; it was in all cases difficult to carry them word for word in one's memory, so my habit has been to make the speakers say what was in my opinion demanded of them by the various occasions, of course adhering as closely as possible to the general sense of what they really said. And with reference to the narrative of events, far from permitting myself to derive it from the first source that came to hand, I did not even trust my own impressions, but it rests partly on what I saw myself, partly on what others saw for me, the accuracy of the report being always tried by the most severe and detailed tests possible.[19]

This description suggests that Thucydides did not have complete information about some of the speeches he reported. The fact that he chose to report the text of speeches based on "what was in my opinion demanded of them by the various occasions" is a poor use of evidence. Rather than using the speech to explain the origins of a political or military decision in the war, Thucydides was most likely deriving the intent of the speaker from the events that followed. In so doing, he undercut the value of the speech as a historical source, since he imposed a perspective upon the words rather than drawing conclusions from them. Nevertheless, the approach is significant in that it gave the historian the authority to assess and interpret sources. It suggested that only in this way could the powerful events of the present be properly historicized while ensuring that its significance would remain a part of the future. As he explained, "I have written my work, not as an essay which is to win the applause of the moment, but as a possession for all time."[20]

Reclaiming Tradition in the Renaissance

Historical writing did not cease with the waning of classical Athens. Roman historians such as Quintus Fabius Pictor (254–201 BCE) and Marcus Porcius Cato (234–149 BCE) wrote histories during the second and third centuries BCE that followed an **annalistic** style, which focused less on specific events and instead recorded a broad collection of facts and observations grouped by year. In this way, Roman annalists chronicled both foreign conflicts such as the Punic Wars with Carthage and domestic strife like the Struggle of the Orders between the plebeian lower classes and the noble patricians. Like the Greek historians before them, the Romans responded to the transformations wrought by the foreign and domestic crises by grounding them in a deep history stretching back into mythology.[21] If later historians such as Sallust (86–35 BCE) and Livy (59 BCE–17 CE) exhibited more narrativity and literary style, they showed no less concern for the dire challenges facing the final years of the Roman Republic.[22]

Nor were developments confined to the classical Mediterranean. During the same period, new strains of historical writing appeared independently in China during the Han Dynasty (206 BCE–220 CE). There, Sima Qian (147–87 BCE), who held a hereditary position as court astrologer and historian, attempted a grand synthesis of Chinese history in *The Records of the*

Grand Historian (Shiji). Georg Iggers and Q. Edward Wang have interpreted Qian's work as the first of a tradition of Confucian historical writing that became a hallmark of Chinese imperial bureaucracy and was "both historical and normative, motivated as much by the desire to build a repository of historical knowledge as by the pursuit of an ideal sociopolitical order."[23] Where Herodotus used history to make sense of new Greek encounters with "barbarian" outsiders, Sima sought to capture the essence of the world in a single text during a period of expansion in the Han Dynasty.[24] Centuries later, the rise of the monotheistic religions of Christianity and Islam informed historical writing in Europe and the Middle East, as medieval Christian and Muslim writers often focused on moralistic accounts that sought the working of God in the deeds and actions of people in the past.[25]

By the fourteenth and fifteenth centuries, **CE** (**Common Era**), European intellectuals began to sense a widening rupture between their own times and those of recent centuries. This was especially the case in the city-states of the Italian peninsula, where broadening engagement with the wider world and where great wealth produced by trade with the East informed a sense of a new age distinct from the period that contemporaries came to define as the *Middle Ages*. Many of the elites of this new era sought to emulate the style and spirit of the classical Mediterranean. Such was the intellectual foundation for an age that later scholars dubbed the Italian Renaissance, which witnessed a supposed "rebirth" of classical learning and attitudes. It had begun as a simple fascination with the Latin writing found in ancient Roman texts but quickly shifted from a focus on language to an engagement with content. What followed was an intense labor of love for Renaissance thinkers, who scoured churches and monasteries and pored over copies of ancient manuscripts preserved by medieval monks. With texts in hand, Renaissance writers inaugurated a flurry of fresh historical writing informed both by the traditions of the Greco-Roman world and by a new sense of the value of the past.

Among the more famous early progenitors of Renaissance ideals was the poet Francesco Petrarch (1304–1374), whose intellectual pursuits led to the discovery of the forgotten letters of Marcus Tullius Cicero (106–43 BCE) in a church library in Verona. In the first century BCE, Cicero had been a leading figure in the Roman Senate and an outspoken defender of the Republic in its waning days, and no doubt his political leanings appealed to the republican sentiments of Petrarch's Italy. But it was the quality of Cicero's rhetoric and his command of Latin that Petrarch found most inspiring, so much so that he wrote a heartfelt letter praising his ancient literary hero. "O great father of Roman eloquence!" he declared, "Not I alone but all who deck themselves with the flowers of Latin speech render thanks unto you."[26] Petrarch's flattery spoke to the ways in which early Renaissance writers saw value not simply in unique moments but in distinct eras, as they looked to the ancients with awe and longed to reclaim the spirit of classical Greece and Rome. Petrarch, although himself a gifted writer, considered Cicero's works to be far superior: "They are still in existence, glorious volumes, but we of today are too feeble a folk to read them, or even to be acquainted with their mere titles."[27] Petrarch's fawning letter was an early sign of the Renaissance penchant for studying history as a means of placing the Greco-Roman past into a direct relationship with the present.

Over a century later, such sentiments shaped one of the most well-known works of the Italian Renaissance, Niccolo Machiavelli's *The Prince* (1513). Scholars continue to debate whether Machiavelli's famous book was intended as serious advice for a new ruler or as an ironic critique of contemporary political leaders, but whatever its intentions, *The Prince* is emblematic of a Renaissance orientation to history. Here Machiavelli treated the reader to pithy bits of advice dealing with a wide range of potential military and political situations. He supported his views by drawing on ancient examples, exhibiting the same sort of admiration for the Romans seen in the work of Petrarch. But Machiavelli was equally interested in contemporary figures. For instance, he seems to have especially admired the exploits of Cesare Borgia, an illegitimate son of Pope Alexander VI who fought to control the Duchy of Romagna in the early sixteenth century. Although Borgia's short reign was a failure, Machiavelli nonetheless painted him as a skilled prince undone only by poor luck.

The sort of secular, political lessons contained within *The Prince* did not differentiate among historical periods. Ancient Romans and fifteenth-century Europeans served equally to illustrate Machiavelli's lessons. For instance, when discussing how to control a territory in a foreign land, Machiavelli suggested that a ruler "should make himself the leader and protector of neighboring powers who are weaker" and "set out to weaken his powerful neighbors."[28] He argued that the Romans used this strategy successfully, while King Louis of France had only recently ignored this advice when he invaded Italy in 1499, and the missed chances had cost him control of Lombardy.[29] In another section of the book, Machiavelli offered what is perhaps his most famous piece of advice on the question of whether a ruler should be loved or feared. He uses the example of Hannibal, whose armies allegedly remained intact while crossing the Alps and invading Italy in part because of Hannibal's reputation for cruelty. He contrasts Hannibal's unyielding style with that of his adversary, Scipio, whose troops mutinied in Spain. Such examples lead Machiavelli to conclude that one should seek to be "both loved and feared," but that "it is much safer to be feared than loved."[30] Such striking axioms have made Machiavelli a perennial favorite of humanities and social science courses, but they derive from a historical approach seemingly unconcerned with notions of change over time.

From the Enlightenment to Historicism

The modern historical discipline owes debts to a long tradition of historical writing, but its clearest roots reach back to the Enlightenment, a broad intellectual movement that first arose in Europe at the turn of the eighteenth century. While the focus and content of Enlightenment ideas varied from region to region and evolved over time, one of its founding assumptions was a belief in a rational, knowable universe. In fact, the historian Peter Gay has argued that the first moment of the Enlightenment began in 1687 with the publication of *Mathematical Principles of Natural Philosophy* by Isaac Newton (1642–1727).[31] Newton's work was critical because it suggested that the universe was governed by immutable laws. This breakthrough moment in science led philosophers to apply the same sort of thinking to humankind. They came to believe that if human beings existed within a rational universe, then they too must be rational creatures. The Enlightenment thus considered humanity within this context and wrestled with its implications for society and politics.

Along with the growing optimism about the perfectibility of human societies were new perspectives on history. Whereas Renaissance humanists like Petrarch had lavished praise on the achievements of the Greeks and Romans, Enlightenment thinkers began to emphasize the potential of their own age. Such a transformation became evident in the same year that Newton published his scientific masterpiece, when the French literary scholar Charles Perrault (1628–1703) inaugurated an episode that came to be known as the Quarrel of the Ancients and the Moderns. In an address at the Académie française in Paris, Perrault read aloud a narrative poem that argued for the distinction and superiority of the modern age over antiquity. His speech engendered an intense public debate about the relationship between past and present, the trajectory of human history, and the role of tradition and authority.[32] Ultimately, many eighteenth-century thinkers came to see things Perrault's way. Among them was the French philosopher Voltaire (1694–1778), who wrote several histories of the eighteenth century in which he distinguished between ancient history as a "curiosity" and modern history as "a matter of necessity."[33] For his *Essay on Universal History: The Manners and Spirit of Nations* (1756), Voltaire portrayed the years since the sixteenth century as an unprecedented era that transcended the legacies of the ancient and medieval worlds. Two decades later, the work of the English historian Edward Gibbon (1737–1794) showed reverence for the classical world, but his magisterial six-volume *Decline and Fall of the Roman Empire* placed its principal emphasis on the moral failings of Roman civilization. In his account, Gibbon portrayed "the greatness of Rome" as "founded on the rare, and almost incredible, alliance of virtue and fortune," but declared that it was precisely the abandonment of virtue and martial vigor that hastened its decline. "At length," he wrote, "verging towards old age, and sometimes conquering by the terror only of her name, [Rome] sought the blessings of ease and tranquility."[34]

The shift in attitudes toward the past had important political and social corollaries. They expressed themselves most notably in the tumultuous trans-Atlantic revolutions at the end of the eighteenth century, first in North America (1776) and then in France (1789), Haiti (1791), and ultimately in other parts of Europe and in South America. In these cases, the notion of a superlative present reinforced the tendency of these revolutions to reject past tradition and seek new patterns of governance, political participation, and social change. Yet, amid these transformations, history continued to serve as a valuable resource. For instance, new narratives of history proved invaluable for emerging nation-states. It was no coincidence that Voltaire's preference for modern history should accompany his role as historiographer to King Louis XV of France. Gibbon was even clearer about his loyalties, writing, "I shall ever glory in the name and character of an Englishman: I am proud of my birth in a free and enlightened country; and the approbation of that country is the best and most honorable reward of my labors."[35] Historical studies played an important role in shaping national consciousness, particularly among the emerging middle classes, and the cultivation of national identities often entailed the formation of historical or antiquarian societies promoting connections between locales, regions, and larger national communities. Eventually, nations themselves became principal units of analysis and areas of specialization for professional historians in the nineteenth and twentieth centuries.

The fresh turn to history during the Enlightenment also shaped a growing attachment to the notion of progress. The reversal in views on the ancient world was critical in shaping a philosophy of history that reflected the era's optimism about the prospects of improved social relations, a more just political system, and an enhanced standard of living.[36] For example, the French philosopher Nicolas de Condorcet (1743–1794) suggested the historical record itself was the best evidence for progress. In Condorcet's *Sketch for a Historical Picture of the Progress of the Human Spirit* (1795), he presented history as an accumulated series of developments and lessons that shaped the improvement of humankind:

> Everything tells us that we are now close upon one of the great revolutions of the human race. If we wish to learn what to expect from it and to procure a certain guide to lead us in the midst of its vicissitudes, what could be more suitable than to have some picture of the revolutions that have gone before it and prepared its way?[37]

Condorcet's central assumptions about history extended beyond the Enlightenment era. In the nineteenth century, philosophers such as Georg Wilhelm Friedrich Hegel (1770–1831) and Karl Marx (1818–1883) articulated ideas about the trajectory of their own times that were based on similar assumptions about a clear trajectory directing the course of history. And, as we have seen in the example of George Santayana, the idea of progress retained much of its appeal into the twentieth century.

In an emerging modern age that favored novelty and celebrated the present, history thus remained an indispensable element, but the result was a sense of separation between past and present that was palpable within European culture by the beginning of the nineteenth century. Indeed, feelings of alienation were crucial elements of the Romantic movement, which at times embraced and at others rejected the ethos of the foregoing century. The Romantics drew upon a different emotional palette to carry forward the rational emphases of the Enlightenment while contending with the uncertainties that accompanied the spread of French revolutionary ideas and the tumult of the Napoleonic Wars. Among the most visible hallmarks of these years were representations of nostalgia, a feeling of longing for a lost past. Poets and novelists pushed back against Enlightenment optimism with reflections on themes of impermanence and decay, while artists found solemn beauty in old ruins slowly surrendering themselves to the forces of nature. The nostalgic impulses of European Romanticism never denied the march of progress but found inspiration in lamenting the seemingly inevitable passage of time. They empathized with ancestors at risk of being forgotten and saw in the rapid changes of the modern era the signs of their own ephemerality. From these sentiments emerged a new historical consciousness viewing the past as distinct but worthy of remembrance.[38] It was from this constellation of changes, including the rationalism of the Enlightenment and the emotionalism of the Romantic era, that the study of history evolved from an eclectic interest of learned humanists into an organized academic pursuit.

Key to the emergence of a new discipline of history was an expanding institutional landscape and a shared methodology for approaching historical sources. Developments were perhaps most pronounced in Germany, where the dramatic expansion of universities in the early nineteenth century accompanied a shift from theological to secular learning and the appearance of a new school of thought known as **historicism**.[39] In some ways, the historicists were heirs to the Enlightenment principles, maintaining on the one hand that the past was knowable and subject to rational scrutiny and seeing on the other a clear link between the study of history and the search for universal truths about humanity. In 1821, Wilhelm von Humboldt, the founder of the University of Berlin and an early progenitor of historicism, stated that the historian must present the past as accurately as possible in order to capture the larger truth embedded within the whole. For Humboldt, the value of historical study lay with the reality unveiled by the totality of the past. He declared, "The historian has all the strands of temporal activity and all the expressions of eternal ideas as his province."[40]

In practice, however, the historicists who followed Humboldt built their discipline less around the ways that history could reveal universal truth and more around a focused study of the particulars of the past. At the forefront of historicism, and perhaps most emblematic of the emerging field as a whole, was Leopold von Ranke (1795–1886), a historian at the University of Berlin. Ranke's career spanned six decades and included sweeping works on the German states, the French monarchy, and the Roman Papacy. He went to great pains to articulate the uniqueness of historical scholarship in part by redefining its objectives and outcomes. As he explained, the historian should start with "a feeling for and a joy in the particular in and of itself."[41] Only then should the historian note the connection between the historical moment and a larger underlying truth. From Ranke's perspective, a greater concern for concrete events separated the historian from the philosopher. "He will not have preconceived ideas as does the philosopher," he wrote, "but rather while he observes the particular, the course which the development of the world takes will be clear to him."[42] At the same time, Ranke maintained that even the realization of the general was not essential to good historical scholarship. He wrote, "The investigation of the particular, even of a single point, is of value if it is done well. If devoted to things human, it will always reveal something worth knowing in itself."[43]

At the heart of Ranke's historicism was his belief that the historian's task was to reconstruct the past as faithfully as possible. This was central to the development of the discipline, since it demanded that historians move away from superficial reflections and adopt instead a rigid **empiricism** aiming to recover the past accurately and authentically. The historian required methods that could facilitate systematic analyses. Ranke called for historians to become masters of archives, and his contemporaries sought to distinguish their discipline through proper identification and verification of sources, through close scrutiny and comparison of texts, and through assessments of shared results. As Frederick Beiser has explained, historicism thus sought "to legitimate history as a science."[44] But Ranke argued that historians also wanted their discipline to take care to capture the proper depiction of the past. He wrote, "History is distinguished from all other sciences in that it is also an art. History is a science in collecting, finding, penetrating; it is an art because it recreates and portrays that which it has found and recognized."[45] This was an important distinction, because it spoke to the challenge of overcoming the chasm between past and present, of recognizing the uniqueness of yesterday while still allowing it to speak to today, and, as Ranke famously believed, of representing the past *wie es eigentlich gewesen*, or "as it actually was."

Historiography and the Modern Practice of History

In these vignettes, we can see that there has been no single, fixed motivation for studying history. The writers discussed here seem to have agreed that history could illuminate the human condition, but the specific "whys" of history were far-ranging and subject to change over time. Moreover, the cases show that engagement with the past was by no means the preserve of the West or of any individual country or tradition. As is true for so many other aspects of the past, its attraction to scholars, writers, and statesmen was **historically contingent**, which meant that it depended on the specific context—in terms of both time and place—in which it was studied. The impulse to investigate and draw upon the reservoir of history stemmed from very different circumstances facing disparate societies. In turn, these conditions produced perspectives on the past that on the one hand reflected the **zeitgeist**, or the "spirit of the times" in which they appeared, and on the other hand played a role in a process of cultural, intellectual, political, and social change.

The modern discipline of history emerged at least partly from its own context, developing from the unique set of conditions prevailing at the end of the eighteenth and the beginning of the nineteenth centuries in Europe and North America. Ranke's notion of history shared common features with Machiavelli, Thucydides, and Sima Qian, including a sense of history's power to inform the present, a common concern for reliable sources, and attention to authentic accounts. But that does not mean that these writers formed a chain leading to the scholarship of today. It is misleading to see historiography as a linear tale of steadily increasing methodological competence and theoretical sophistication, of primitive attempts to grapple with the past yielding to the "right way" to study history today. Just as we express skepticism of progress as a dynamic of historical change, so too do we reject a progress narrative when discussing the origins of the modern discipline.

DISCOVERY EXERCISE

Earlier we said that one of the values of history lay with its role in helping us "understand ourselves." Discuss what the historical writers mentioned above wanted to know about themselves and their world and explain why this led them to the study of history.

Change, Continuity, and the Contemporary Discipline of History

We have observed how the historical discipline emerged within a specific nineteenth-century context. Perhaps, then, it is not surprising to discover that the rapid transformations of the twentieth and early twenty-first centuries shaped both the practice and landscape of the profession. Indeed, important changes were already under way at the end of the nineteenth century, as scholars began to critique the limits of contemporary historical writing, resulting in what Georg G. Iggers has called a "crisis of classical historicism."[46] During these years, attempts to emulate the natural sciences came under scrutiny as scientific practice veered more firmly toward rational deduction and demanded a firmer empirical basis for scientific discovery. This placed a burden on historians, who faced gaps in their sources and lacked the ability to reproduce their results (since, as we have said, history does not precisely repeat itself). In the mid-twentieth century, the philosopher Karl Popper (1902–1994) expressed doubts about the historical discipline's power to yield grand truths, particularly its ability to identify "patterns" or "laws" that "underlie the evolution of history."[47] Finally, the historicist emphasis on political history drew criticism that the field had grown to become a "handmaiden of the nation-state" to the exclusion of other avenues of historical study. By the 1890s, historians in both Europe and the United States had begun calling for social histories informed by Marxist theories or by the approaches of other emerging social sciences.[48] In the ensuing decades, the cultural and social transformations of the twentieth century led to the long-term expansion and diversification of the field. Taken together, these developments wrought a series of key changes in the discipline.

New Subjects of Historical Inquiry

As the historical discipline established itself more firmly within the university landscape, its growth facilitated a tremendous expansion of the types of subjects under study and of the range of historical questions. Even as politics, diplomatic relations, and national or regional specialties remained important topics during most of the twentieth century, new possibilities appeared for studying the history of culture, economics, and thought, among many others. In many cases, these subfields grew from linkages with other disciplines, as in the case of the histories of science and medicine, or from broader social concerns, as with environmental history, which was connected to late twentieth-century anxieties about resource scarcity and the effects of human activity on the natural world. Perhaps most significantly, the broadening of the discipline facilitated histories of marginalized groups seeking a voice in contemporary society. Labor historians, for example, turned attention away from elites in an attempt to capture the experiences of the working classes. In the United States, social historians brought to the fore the stories of African-Americans as an important corollary to the Civil Rights Movement. Such histories quickly came to include other minority groups, such as Latino-Americans, Native Americans, and Asian Americans. Similar sentiments informed a postcolonial mood in other parts of the world that included new histories of peoples subjected to Western imperialism. And the emergence of second-wave feminism in the 1960s led a number of scholars to develop a robust field of women's history, which itself broadened during the 1980s through studies of gender and sexuality. In each instance, historians applied their methods to questions that had direct relevance to critical social, cultural, and political issues of their own day. Judith Bennett, a historian of medieval women's history, has argued that even scholarship on more remote periods carries meaning for today's problems and can even shape the motivations of the scholar. She recalls, "In the 1970s, when I was a young feminist, the distant past was integral to the ways in which we critiqued the present day and envisioned a better future."[49]

Transformations of Time and Space

The widening array of research questions also entailed a different view of temporality within historical study. For instance, a shift away from narratives exclusively centered on the exploits of political or military figures facilitated the work of historians like Fernand Braudel (1902–1985), who was a founding member of a multi-generational group of historians known as the **Annales School**. Braudel's 1966 work, *The Mediterranean and the Mediterranean World in the Age of Philip II*, captured a key part of the Annales approach to history, which was to shift the focus away from single events and trace instead cumulative changes over a much longer period of time that Braudel referred to as the *longue durée*.[50] With this perspective, Braudel and his colleagues were able to ask questions beyond the deeds of visible historical figures and inquire into the lives of ordinary people. On the other end of the time spectrum, Carlo Ginzburg was among those pioneering the exploration of the overlooked and the marginalized by examining individual lives through a technique called **microhistory**. Ginzburg framed this approach most famously in his 1976 work *The Cheese and the Worms*, which focused on the life of Domenico Scandella, a miller in northern Italy who was executed for heresy by an ecclesiastical court in the sixteenth century. By examining the records of Scandella's trial, Ginzburg was able to draw upon the court's inventory of the miller's books to reconstruct his mental world and thus open a larger window into the scope of thought that was becoming possible during the era of the Reformation and at the dawn of the print age.[51]

Other scholars sought to widen the spatial boundaries of the discipline. After the Second World War, the changing relationship between Western nations and the rest of the world began to lead historians away from a central focus on nation-states to a consideration of historical writing on a larger regional or worldwide scale. William H. McNeill's *The Rise of the West*, published in 1963, was an early example of studies that began to look at encounters between civilizations or cultures as key drivers of historical change. In the ensuing decades, scholars found different approaches for capturing world history. Immanuel Wallerstein used his world systems approach to understand the development of the world through the emergence of capitalist economic networks, while Philip Curtin and Alfred Crosby were among those focusing on specific themes, including the transformative impact of trade and biological exchange on the participants of growing global networks.[52] The contemporary study of global history has since grown tremendously alongside rising awareness of the impact of globalization, but its reach now extends beyond recent history to encompass the modern and premodern eras with approaches that include sweeping histories of worldwide networks and more intimate studies of how global forces impacted individual communities. As Sebastian Conrad has explained, recent global histories have coalesced around a set of approaches that include comparisons among cultures, examinations of connections among groups over time, studies of the processes of integration that result from intercultural encounters (such as the creation of hybrid or creole cultures), and assessments of the ways in which intercultural or transnational trends engendered historical change.[53]

These same inclusive trends have also opened space for historians working in non-Western traditions. In the post–Second World War era, as nations in Africa and Asia gained independence from European empires and as others began asserting themselves in an increasingly globalizing world, scholars sought to frame the growing autonomy of these regions not as new innovations but as the culmination of long histories of indigenous agency. Following the example of Western historiography and building upon older traditions in historical writing, scholars in China, Japan, India, Turkey, and Egypt had already by this time developed robust modern national historiographies.[54] As Manuel Perez Garcia has observed in the case of East Asian historiography, the challenge has since been to integrate these national trends with new thinking about global history. Indeed, a number of non-Western scholars have been suspicious of the kind of global historiography defined by Sebastian Conrad, seeing it as a new hegemonic narrative emphasizing the growth and spread of Western capitalism as the hallmark of a globalizing world. Critics argue that such accounts present a one-dimensional view of globalization that diminishes the role of non-Western cultures. This does not mean that historians in these countries have rejected global approaches, but they have tended to define them within the contours of their own historiographical traditions. In China and Japan, for example, many historians have preferred to approach global history not as a story of deepening connections but as universal histories linked to but in some ways distinct from national or civilizational narratives. Garcia has emphasized that the dialogue among scholars writing in different geographical and cultural contexts has nonetheless been fruitful not simply in promoting one historiographical perspective over another but in moving together toward a more inclusive and "polycentric" history.[55]

New Methods and Sources

During the second half of the twentieth century, the perception of firm boundaries between scholarly disciplines came into question. Scholars in a variety of fields found themselves asking overlapping research questions and recognized the value of borrowing from the techniques and approaches of other fields. Today, the practice of history has a strong **interdisciplinary** quality built upon a range of partnerships with other fields. For instance, the interest in studying broader temporal and spatial scales led to a close relationship between history and the social sciences. Beginning in the 1960s and 1970s, historians turned to statistical approaches commonly found in such fields as economics and demography. These quantitative methods, which in history became commonly known as **cliometrics**, sought to understand the lives of broad social groups through an analysis of patterns yielded by large quantities of data. By contrast, the 1980s and 1990s saw the emergence of a so-called **cultural turn**, in which historians sought to understand processes by which cultures created shared meanings. The cultural turn entailed a much stronger set of connections between anthropology, history, and humanities fields such as literary studies and philosophy.[56]

As you will see in the chapters that follow, history remains a field utilizing multiple methodologies for research and operating within both the humanities and social science spheres of scholarship. Indeed, this makes history an especially unique field of study, because it utilizes empirical methods but often frames its investigations using narrative techniques. And in between lies a great deal of space for innovation. Text-based, qualitative approaches are still central for many scholars, while others work with more quantitative methods, and both increasingly make use of computing technology to derive new insights from their sources.

Taken together, these changes underscore the ways in which the practice of history has expanded and diversified over the last two centuries. Not only does the profession today invite a much more open view of the subjects, scales, and approaches that generate scholarship, but it has also welcomed a more diverse body of scholars hailing from a variety of backgrounds. While most historians would agree that the discipline has a long way to go to be able to study the past free from gendered, elitist, and Eurocentric biases, its members nevertheless seem to emphasize as never before the importance of historical study for all human beings.

Continuities

At its core, the study of history is about continuity and change, and the same may said about the development of the discipline. Despite the breadth of the foregoing changes, a number of practices, norms, and assumptions of the discipline remain closely connected to their roots in the nineteenth century. Such continuities are key to defining history as an organized body of knowledge whose professional standards and practices are meant to ensure the reliability of its investigations and interpretations. For these reasons, the discipline remains connected to its traditions in several fundamental ways.

Institutional Frameworks

Before its integration into universities in the nineteenth century, history was an armchair pursuit practiced by nonspecialists with overlapping and often dilettante interests in fields such as antiquities, numismatics, and theology. Today, the university is the principal location for practicing historical scholarship. In the United States, historians tend to belong to dedicated departments that include their own administrative structure, professional resources, and protocols for maintaining academic quality. There are currently over 1,200 such departments and programs granting baccalaureate degrees in history in universities and colleges across the United States; more than 350 of these also award graduate degrees.[57] Other scholars may similarly work in research centers, such as the Institute of Contemporary History (Institut für Zeitgeschichte) in Munich, Germany, or in museums like the Smithsonian Institution in Washington, D.C. Many such institutions provide access to archaeological, archival, and library resources, and many also foster an interdisciplinary environment for collaborative research on questions that stretch beyond the boundaries of the historical discipline.

Of course, not all professional historians need to practice their scholarship within a university setting. Professional historians may work as independent scholars apart from the university and still participate as members of the disciplinary community by publishing with recognized academic journals, book publishers, or digital media and by taking part in the scholarly activities of a number of professional organizations. The largest organizations in the United States include the American Historical Association and the Organization of American Historians, and there are a number of affiliated specialist organizations, such as the American Philological Association and the Society of Historians of American Foreign Relations, among others. The main historical organization in the United Kingdom is the Royal Historical Society, and there are also a number of groups for particular fields and specialties, such as the British Association of American Nineteenth Century Historians.

Yet universities remain central to the discipline. They provide the financial and logistical resources necessary for conducting research. This includes awarding salaries that permit historians to devote their time to research and maintaining libraries, archives, and publishing houses. They also take responsibility for training and credentialing new historians. Within the select history programs that offer graduate degrees, the faculty articulate standards for proper training based on an understanding of common practices in the discipline. The Master of Arts (M.A.) and Doctor of Philosophy (Ph.D.) degrees awarded by these institutions are important hallmarks of mastery of scholarly skills and of admission into the profession. They are usually required for those who wish to assume positions in universities and teach undergraduate or graduate students. Finally, universities traditionally supervise a system of ranks for practitioners in the profession. Through regular assessments of scholarship and teaching effectiveness, university faculties assure the quality of the historian's work, and they mark the historian's scholarly development by awarding tenure, promotions, and recognitions. In this way, universities provide the crucial framework that facilitates historical research, bring scholars together in common pursuit of the past, and create a venue for historians to pass their knowledge to students and to the broader public.

Methodological Foundations

Although the range of sources and techniques has expanded greatly since the days of Ranke, historians are still committed to answering historical questions by a process of rigorous examination of verified sources. Despite their interest in a wide variety of sources, historians continue to stress the overarching value of texts, and they continue to view the library and the archive as primary (though by no means exclusive) sites of their investigations. In reporting the results of their studies, historians also adhere to shared guidelines. They seek to preserve their sources and document their process so that other scholars can follow their line of research and verify their conclusions. They are thus expected to cite their research in their publications, and their work must undergo a process of **peer review** before publication, in which fellow specialists review findings and affirm whether the research appears accurate, methodologically sound, and ethically produced.

Ethical Standards

The acceptance of scholarship within the discipline is contingent on adherence to ethical norms. We will discuss these in greater depth in Chapter 8, but they include accurate reporting of sources for research, faithful representation of material derived from sources, proper respect for the preservation, and care of historical resources. They also include a commitment to, as the American Historical Association stresses, a "critical dialogue" among historians that entails "mutual respect," "constructive criticism," and professional behavior toward peers, colleagues, students, and members of the public.[58]

History in Practice: Personal Experiences and Pathways to Research

The structure and habits of the discipline of history are intended to render the past as plausibly and comprehensively as possible while answering the overarching "why" question we identified at the beginning of the chapter. But the individual "why" questions that lead professional historians to the study of the past vary widely and depend on their unique experiences. In the examples that follow, you will see how the broad questions of history and personal motivations come together to shape the goals of professional historians and help lead them to their research projects.

Jack Wells

My own pathway into the field of history began late in my undergraduate career. I became an historian because I met two professors who loved their disciplines and brought their passion for them into the classroom. I was a science major, but when my roommate told me about a history professor who gave spellbinding lectures, I decided to take his class, and after that I was hooked. I began reading history, particularly the history of ancient Greece and Rome, for fun. In my junior year I met an ancient studies professor who discovered my interests and encouraged me to pursue them as a career. So, I added history as a major, began taking Greek and Latin courses, and have never looked back.

Why the ancient past? There are a number of disadvantages and advantages to studying the history of the Ancient Mediterranean. The chief scholarly disadvantage is the number of languages required for research. Patience and a lot of time must be put into language study before one can even begin to write about the history of the ancient past. In addition to ancient Greek and Latin, a competent scholar must be able to read material in German, French, Italian, and often Modern Greek and Spanish. The other disadvantage is professional: there are homes outside academia for many students of history, particularly modern history. Governments, private research institutes, and businesses need experts to help them make policy or conduct economic transactions. The US Congress, however, has no committee on relations with Pericles' Athens, and no major business is being carried out with an ancient Roman multinational.

But to me, the advantages of studying the ancient past greatly outweigh the disadvantages. It is, for instance, easier to move beyond issues of personal bias when looking at the source material. Though all historical research is to some extent subjective, I do not have as much cultural baggage weighing me down when I study the ancient world as I might if I studied, say, the US Civil War, graves of soldiers that I can see from my office window, or the Reagan administration, which I remember from my youth. The primary source material is also much easier to locate and study. This is, of course, because there is so much less of it, which presents its own set of challenges. But the world of ancient history is a fascinating one where the small number of sources paradoxically leads to a large number of ways of interpreting them. Though the field presents challenges, I have never lost my amazement at being able to study events that occurred in a remote time, even if the reconstructions of those events can be problematic.

My decision to study the religion and politics of ancient Rome is also a personal one. Being raised in the American South, in the "Bible Belt," as it is popularly known, I live in a world in which religion affects everything. There is a church on almost every street corner, and the police cars that patrol the streets of my hometown prominently display the words, "In God We Trust." Thomas Jefferson's supposed "wall of separation" between church and state is particularly porous here. The religious environment of ancient Rome was very different from the one I experience today.[59] A polytheistic system emphasizing ritual communication with the gods through animal sacrifice little resembles the staid but sincere pronunciations of Christian faith that I hear today. Yet religion was thoroughly woven into the fabric of the lives of ancient Greeks and Romans in ways not completely unfamiliar to those of my own community. Furthermore, the Christianity practiced by many of my neighbors had its origins in the Roman Empire and probably owes its importance to the fact that it became the empire's dominant religion in the fourth century CE.

Bruce E. Baker

The main reason I became a historian was because I grew up in an extended family in the American South with a strong sense of its own history, going back to the Civil War and even the Revolutionary War before that. As a child, I spent hours listening to my grandparents talk about our ancestors and came to know people who had died decades before I was born. I felt like I could find my way in the dark around the places in Kentucky and Missouri they described, though I had not yet been there. These stories kindled a strong interest in the past and the forces that had shaped the fortunes (mostly lack of fortune) of my family. I studied folklore for my M.A. degree and became interested in how stories and oral traditions like the ones I had grown up with reflected the ideas and culture of the groups of people who told them. This led me to my earliest historical work, which was about how lynchings were recorded and remembered in various forms of vernacular culture in the South, in ballads and local stories.[60] Later, I brought these questions about memory and history to understand how the Reconstruction period was remembered in the twentieth century.[61]

More recently, I have become increasingly interested in how different aspects of the economy worked, starting with how poor people in the South made a living in the years after the Civil War, but more recently encompassing the cotton trade. Again, the first part of this is based on my own family background and the place where I grew up. I have puzzled over how freedpeople in South Carolina earned a living and found ways of working for themselves instead of for a boss, and I have also given serious consideration to how foraging for blackberries supplemented the incomes and diets of southerners in that time period (as, indeed, they did for me in later decades).[62] The work on the cotton trade came from a more classic historical approach: finding something that no one had explained before. I ran across a reference to a cotton broker named William P. Brown in New Orleans who cornered the world's supply of cotton in 1903. When I went looking for a book or article to explain more about this, I found that no one had written much about it. So, I did it (with help from a colleague,

Barbara Hahn). Over the course of the next three years or so, this led to a book explaining the history of cotton futures trading at the turn of the twentieth century.[63] At present, I am working to understand more about the role of crime and corruption in shaping the cotton trade and, by extension, capitalism in general in the South. All of this work builds, in part, on an idea derived from my early folklore studies in the work of occupational folklorists such as Archie Green and Robert McCarl: "The core of any occupational culture lies in the work techniques needed to succeed on the job."[64] Similarly, I think, to understand people's economic lives, you must begin not with broad statistical measures of economic activity but with the immediate material realities of that economy, such as actual bales of cotton.[65]

APPLICATION EXERCISE

Describe your own "pathway" to history and discuss how it connects to a potential historical topic that interests you.

Notes

1   Vincent Tinto, *Leaving College: Rethinking the Causes and Cures of Student Attrition* (Chicago: University of Chicago Press, 1993); Alexander W. Astin, "Student Involvement: A Developmental Theory for Higher Education," *Journal of College Student Development* 40, no. 5 (September/October 1999): 518–29; Matthew J. Mayhew et al., *How College Affects Students: 21st Century Evidence that Higher Education Works* (New York: Wiley, 2016).

2   George Santayana, *The Life of Reason: Volume 1: Reason in Common Sense* (New York: Scribner's, 1905), 184.

3   Walter Benjamin, "Theses on the Philosophy of History," in Benjamin, *Illuminations*, edited by Hannah Arendt, translated by Harry Zohn (New York: Schocken, 1968), 257–8.

4   John McCole, *Walter Benjamin and the Antinomies of Tradition* (Ithaca, NY: Cornell University Press, 1993).

5   Norman F. Cantor and Richard I. Schneider, *How to Study History* (New York: Crowell, 1967), 3.

6   L.P. Hartley, *The Go-Between* (London: Hamish Hamilton, 1953), 1.

7   R.G. Collinwood, *The Idea of History* (Oxford: Oxford University Press, 1946), 7.

8   Geoffrey Cubitt, *History and Memory* (Manchester: Manchester University Press, 2007), 30.

9   Hartley, *The Go-Between*, 1.

10 Herbert Butterfield, "Historiography," in *The Dictionary of the History of Ideas*, edited by Philip P. Wiener, vol. 2 (New York: Scribner's, 1973), 464–98, 464.

11 Jeremy D. Popkin, *From Herodotus to H-Net: The Story of Historiography* (Oxford: Oxford University Press, 2016), 3–4.

12 Herodotus, *The Histories*, translated by George Rawlinson (New York: Knopf, 1910), 5.

13 Philip A. Starter, "Historical Thought in Ancient Greece," in *A Companion to Western Historical Thought*, edited by Lloyd Kramer and Sarah Maza (Malden, MA: Blackwell, 2002), 35–59, 37.

14 Popkin, *Herodotus to H-Net*, 27–9.

15 Thucydides, *History of the Peloponnesian War*, translated by Richard Crawley (Oxford: Oxford University Press, 1943), 3.

16 Ibid.

17 Ibid., 14.

18 Ibid., 13.

19 Ibid., 14.

20 Ibid., 15.

21 Hans Beck, "The Early Republican Tradition," in *A Companion to Greek and Roman Historiography*, edited by John Marincola, vol. 1 (Malden, MA: Blackwell, 2007), 259–65.

22 Michael Grant, *Greek and Roman Historians: Information and Misinformation* (London: Routledge, 1995), 14–17; Stephen Usher, *The Historians of Greece and Rome* (Norman: University of Oklahoma Press, 1985), 125–98.

23 George G. Iggers and Q. Edward Wang, *A Global History of Modern Historiography* (Harlow, England: Pearson, 2008), 47–8.

24 Grant Hardy, *Worlds of Bronze and Bamboo: Sima Qian's Conquest of History* (New York: Columbia University Press, 1999); Siep Stuurman, "Herodotus and Sima Qian: History and the Anthropological Turn in Ancient Greece and Han China," *Journal of World History*, 19, no. 1 (2008): 1–40.

25 Gabrielle M. Spiegel, "Historical Thought in Medieval Europe," in *Companion to Western Historical Thought*, 78–98; Iggers and Wang, *Global History of Modern Historiography*, 33–8.

26 Francesco Petrarca, *Petrarch: The First Modern Scholar and Man of Letters*, edited and translated by James Harvey Robinson (New York: G.P. Putnam, 1898), 249.

27 Ibid., 250.

28 Niccoló Machiavelli, *The Prince*, edited and translated by David Wootton (Indianapolis: Hackett, 1995), 10.

29 Ibid., 11.

30 Ibid., 51–3.

31 Peter Gay, *Age of Enlightenment* (New York: Time, 1966), 12.

32 Joan DeJean, *Ancients against Moderns: Culture Wars and the Making of a fin de Siècle* (Chicago: University of Chicago Press, 1996), 42–51.

33 Quoted in Pierre Force, "Voltaire and the Necessity of Modern History," *Modern Intellectual History* 6, no. 3 (2009): 457–84, 467.

34 Edward Gibbon, *The Decline and Fall of the Roman Empire*, vol. 2 (New York: Harper, 1849), 245.

35 Gibbon, "Preface to the Fourth Volume of the Original Quarto Edition," in Ibid., *xxxii*.

36 George H. Nadel, "Philosophy of History before Historicism," *History and Theory* 3, no. 3 (1964): 291–315.

37 Condorcet, Jean-Antoine-Nicolas de Caritat, Marquis de, *Sketch for a Historical Picture of the Progress of the Human Mind*, translated by June Barraclough (New York: Noonday, 1955), 12.

38 John Lukacs, *Historical Consciousness: The Remembered Past* (New York: Harper & Row, 1968), 17–18; Susan A. Crane, *Collecting and Historical Consciousness in Early Nineteenth-Century Germany* (Ithaca: Cornell University Press, 2000).

39 Peter Watson, *The German Genius: Europe's Third Renaissance, The Second Scientific Revolution, and the Twentieth Century* (New York: Harper, 2010), 49–53, 69–73.

40 Wilhelm von Humboldt, "On the Historian's Task," translated by Louis O. Mink, *History and Theory*, vol. 6, no. 1 (1967): 57–72, 59.

41 Leopold von Ranke, "On the Relations of History and Philosophy," in *The Theory and Practice of History*, edited by Georg G. Iggers and Konrad von Moltke, translated by Wilma A. Iggers (Indianapolis: Bobbs-Merrill, 1973), 29–32, 30.

42 Ibid., 31.

43 Ranke, "The Role of the Particular and the Universal in History," in ibid., 57–9, 58.

44 Frederick Beiser, *The German Historicist Tradition* (Oxford: Oxford University Press, 2011), 6.

45 Ranke, "On the Character of Historical Science," in *Theory and Practice of History*, 33–46, 34.

46 Georg G. Iggers, *Historiography in the Twentieth Century: From Scientific Objectivity to the Postmodern Challenge* (Hanover: Wesleyan University Press, 1997), 31–5.

47 Karl Popper, *The Poverty of Historicism* (New York: Harper & Row, 1957), 3.

48 Iggers, *Historiography*, 31–3; Gary J. Kornbluth and Carol Lassiter, "More than Great White Men: A Century of Scholarship on American Social History," in *A Century of American Historiography*, edited by James M. Banner, Jr. (Boston: Bedford/St. Martin's, 2010), 11–20.

49 Judith M. Bennett, *History Matters: Patriarchy and the Challenge of Feminism* (Philadelphia: University of Pennsylvania Press, 2006), 31.

50 Fernand Braudel, *On History*, translated by Sarah Matthews (Chicago: University of Chicago Press, 1980), 27.

51 Carlo Ginzburg, *The Cheese and the Worms: The Cosmos of a Sixteenth-Century Miller*, translated by John and Anne Tedeschi (Baltimore: Johns Hopkins University Press, 1992).

52 Patrick Manning, *Navigating World History: Historians Create a Global Past* (New York: Palgrave, 2003), 55–67; Immanuel Wallerstein, *The Modern World System: Capitalist Agriculture and the Origins of the European World-Economy in the Sixteenth Century* (New York: Academic Press, 1974); Philip D. Curtin, *The Atlantic Slave Trade: A Census* (Madison: University of Wisconsin Press, 1969); Alfred Crosby, *The Columbian Exchange: Biological and Cultural Consequences of 1492* (Westport, CT: Greenwood, 1972).

53 Sebastian Conrad, *What Is Global History?* (Princeton: Princeton University Press, 2016).

54 Iggers and Wang, *Global History of Modern Historiography*, 194–243.

55 Manuel Perez Garcia, "Introduction: Current Challenges of Global History in East Asian Historiographies," in *Global History and New Polycentric Approaches: Europe, Asia, and the Americas in a World Network System*, edited by Manuel Perez Garcia and Lucio De Sousa (London: Palgrave Macmillan, 2018), 1–17.

56 See Lynn Hunt, ed., *The New Cultural History* (Berkeley: University of California Press, 1989).

57 American Historical Association, "Data on the History Profession," accessed May 7, 2018, https://www.historians.org/jobs-and-professional-development/career-resources/data-on-the-history-profession.

58 American Historical Association, "Statement on Standards of Conduct," updated 2018, accessed May 7, 2018, https://www.historians.org/jobs-and-professional-development/statements-standards-and-guidelines-of-the-discipline/statement-on-standards-of-professional-conduct.

59 An example of my study on the connections between religion and politics can be found in "Impiety in the Middle Republic: The Roman Response to Temple Plundering in Southern Italy," *Classical Journal* 105 (2010): 229–43.

60 Bruce E. Baker, "Under the Rope: Lynching and Memory in Laurens County, South Carolina," in *Where These Memories Grow: History, Memory, and Southern Identity*, edited by W. Fitzhugh Brundage (Chapel Hill: University of North Carolina Press, 2000), 319–46; Bruce E. Baker, "North Carolina Lynching Ballads," in *Under Sentence of Death: Lynching in the South*, edited by W. Fitzhugh Brundage (Chapel Hill: University of North Carolina Press, 1997), 219–46.

61 Bruce E. Baker, *What Reconstruction Meant: Historical Memory in the American South* (Charlottesville: University of Virginia Press, 2007); Carole Emberton and Bruce E. Baker, eds., *Remembering Reconstruction: Struggles over the Meaning of America's Most Tumultuous Era* (Baton Rouge: Louisiana State University Press, 2017).

62 Bruce E. Baker, "The Growth of Towns after the Civil War and the Casualization of Black Labor, 1865–1880," *Tennessee Historical Quarterly* 72, no. 4 (Winter 2013): 289–300; Bruce E. Baker, "'A recourse that could

be depended upon': Picking Blackberries and Getting by after the Civil War," *Southern Cultures* 16, no. 4 (Winter 2010): 21–40.

63 Bruce E. Baker and Barbara Hahn, *The Cotton Kings: Capitalism and Corruption in Turn-of-the-Century New York and New Orleans* (New York: Oxford University Press, 2015).

64 Archie Green, *Wobblies, Pile Butts, and Other Heroes: Laborlore Explorations* (Urbana: University of Illinois Press, 1993); Robert McCarl, *The District of Columbia Fire Fighters' Project: A Case Study in Occupational Folklife* (Washington, D.C.: Smithsonian Institution Press, 1985), 14.

65 Bruce E. Baker, "The Loose Cotton Economy of the New Orleans Waterfront in the Late Nineteenth Century," in *Hidden Capitalism: Beyond, Below and Outside the Visible Market*, edited by Kenneth Lipartito and Lisa Jacobson (Philadelphia: University of Pennsylvania Press, 2019) 67–80.

Suggested Reading

Breisach, Ernst. *Historiography: Ancient, Medieval, and Modern*. Chicago: University of Chicago Press, 2007.

Feldner, Heiko, Kevin Passmore, and Stefan Berger, eds., *Writing History: Theory and Practice*. 2nd ed. London: Bloomsbury, 2010.

Gaddis, John Lewis. *The Landscape of History: How Historians Map the Past*. New York: Oxford University Press, 2002.

Iggers, Georg G., Q. Edward Wang, and Supriya Mukherjee. *A Global History of Modern Historiography*. 2nd ed. New York: Routledge, 2016.

Maza, Sarah. *Thinking about History*. Chicago: University of Chicago Press, 2017.

Tosh, John. *The Pursuit of History: Aims, Methods and New Directions in the Study of History*. 6th ed. New York: Routledge, 2015.

Wineburg, Sam. *Why Learn History (When It's Already on Your Phone)*. Chicago: University of Chicago Press, 2018.

2

From Critical Thinking to Historical Thinking

What we will do in this chapter:

➢ **REFLECT** on truth, objectivity, and critical thinking in historical scholarship.
➢ **DISCOVER** the processes of critical thinking and the unique attributes of "historical thinking."
➢ **APPLY** the principles of critical and historical thinking to understanding history lectures.

Before learning how to work like a historian, we must first understand how to think like one. That requires an appreciation for **critical thinking,** which counts among the most important skills for both scholars and students in every field of study. Cultivating critical thinking is a foundational goal of university curricula, and it is what gives students an edge not only for success in their university learning but also for their careers after graduation. Research has shown that a majority of employers favor job candidates who demonstrably possess the ability to use so-called soft skills related to critical thinking, including the capacity to innovate, solve problems, exercise sound judgment, and communicate ideas effectively.[1] Unfortunately, many of these same employers report that candidates with university degrees tend to be poorly prepared to utilize their skills.[2] As a result, a number of universities have recently considered ways to boost critical thinking training.

History offers a great way to train students to understand and use this important skill. Recent measures of student performance suggest that critical thinking outcomes in history and related humanities fields at times surpass those of neighboring disciplines.[3] Part of the reason for this success may have to do with the ways in which history uses examples of how past societies tackled concrete human problems. It thus allows students to learn critical thinking with a hands-on approach. In fact, these principles have long guided the practice of teaching history.[4] Moreover, historians use critical thinking skills as tools for research, employing them in unique ways that we might broadly refer to as "historical thinking." In this chapter, we will discuss what critical thinking is and what it entails in order to explain the more specific operations of historical thinking and understand why they are essential to engaging the past.

The Problem of Truth in History

Crucial to the enterprise of critical thinking is the pursuit of truth. Historians work as critical thinkers precisely because they want to interpret the past authentically. For this reason, we might say that the truth is a historian's first commitment. This seems like a straightforward assertion, but it is not so simple. Since the founding of their discipline in the nineteenth century, historians have stressed the importance of representing and interpreting the past as accurately and truthfully as possible. Yet even if the fundamental orientation remains the same, attitudes about the pursuit of truth have changed quite a bit over time. In the first chapter of this textbook, we learned that the establishment of modern disciplines in the nineteenth century entailed a powerful optimism about the power of scholarship to discover and uphold knowledge deemed to be objectively true. As the intellectual historian Peter Novick has rightly observed, contemporaries saw objectivity as a prerequisite for studying history. Novick explains that the notion of objectivity subsequently remained an important source of cohesion for the historical discipline.[5] As it turned out, however, such confidence was misplaced, and many of the "truths" discovered in the scholarship of the era exhibited the biases of the researchers and reflected the contexts in which they worked.

In the second half of the twentieth century, three key trends forced historians to confront long-standing assumptions about truth and objectivity. The first was *postcolonialism*, which was a set of theories that appeared after the Second World War in response to the decline of European empires. For historians, an interest in the emerging subfield of global history accompanied the process of decolonization. The changing geopolitical landscape informed new perspectives on relationships among world regions, but for the first few decades, the narratives remained largely fixed on the West, placing Europe and America at the center of the story. This was partly because the experience of the leading researchers was limited to the records of European and American archives. William H. McNeill, whose 1963 work, *The Rise of the West*, is often cited as a foundational book in global historiography, acknowledged decades later that his account of the precursors of Western power in the later Middle Ages "gave undue attention to Latin Christendom" and missed the seminal importance of developments in China that spurred changes in European culture. "My excuse," he explained, "is that the historiography available a generation ago still reflected the traditional valuations of China's past."[6]

At the same time, the predilection for Western histories often led to what Gareth Austin has called "conceptual Eurocentrism," which referred to the tendency to treat Western norms and ideas, such as the nation-state or citizenship, as universal ideas (often unconsciously) and hold them up as templates for assessing developments in non-Western regions.[7] Dipesh Chakrabarty went a step further in his 2000 work, *Provincializing Europe*, arguing that the very notion of modernity was based entirely on a Western standard, and its relative absence in the rest of the world placed non-Western cultures on a lower rung on the ladder of progress in the minds of many scholars. Chakrabarty maintained that historians, in embracing such a conflated conception, played a key role in this particular form of Western cultural power by crafting a narrative of the West as the first to arrive at the threshold of modernity. He wrote, "Historicism is what made modernity or capitalism look, not simply global, but rather as something that became global *over time*, by originating in one place (Europe) and then spreading outside it. This 'first Europe, then elsewhere' structure of global historical time was historicist."[8]

Chakrabarty's innovative perspective owed a debt to a second broad intellectual trend known as *postmodernism*, which came to represent a salient intellectual challenge to historical writing. Postmodernism essentially refers to a collection of intellectual and artistic currents that responded to the successes of Western modernity, including the spread of capitalism and material abundance, the increasing efficiency of economic production and distribution, and the cultural and artistic breaks with tradition that had been a hallmark of modernist thought. As the philosopher Jean-François Lyotard (1924–1998) observed in *The Postmodern Condition*, the movement's proponents turned the modernist penchant for novelty and iconoclasm into a radical critique of the consequences of modernity's signature developments.[9]

Among the fundamental ideas that came under postmodern attack was the notion of linear historical development. Lyotard maintained that the entire project of modernity has been constructed by a unique historical perspective. Specifically, history has made possible our shared idea of "modernity," that is, as a condition categorically different from those of past centuries, by framing it as the endpoint of what we now refer to as a **metanarrative**. Metanarratives are grand overarching stories that set the stage for smaller accounts (i.e., of countries, peoples, etc.). Among the most significant metanarratives in historical thought has been a classical liberal notion of progress. As we saw in the first chapter, an underlying belief in progress emerging from Enlightenment thought informed the work of the nineteenth-century German historicists. Indeed, historians such as J.G. Droysen (1808–1884) and Heinrich von Sybel (1817–1895) wrote histories that portrayed the unification of the German nation-state in the 1870s as the logical outcome of historical progress.[10] In other words, they posited German history as the story of German unification. Such ideas then remained entrenched within the German academy until they came under intense scrutiny in the wake of the Second World War.

One of the central accomplishments of postmodernism has been to expose all metanarratives as fictions. Indeed, Jean-François Lyotard summed up postmodernism by calling it a "crisis of narratives,"[11] which entailed, on the one hand, an emphasis on the power of language and, on the other, a skepticism about the ability to represent truth. By the 1970s, these critiques emerged as a third intellectual trend known as *poststructuralism*. In previous decades, many linguists, psychologists, and anthropologists had explored the relationships among seemingly disparate linguistic and symbolic expressions in order to uncover deeper "structures" at work in the human mind that operated as a natural organizing principle across cultures. Poststructuralists attacked such ideas by denying that language, symbols, and cultural practices reflected an underlying mental reality; instead, they argued that the expressions themselves created the appearance of reality. Poststructuralist scholars like the philosopher Jacques Derrida (1930–2004) revealed the flaws in structural assumptions by "deconstructing" assumed relationships between language and meaning in academic texts and by thus showing how language and text were the vehicles with which subjects created their own truth.

The implications for history have been profound.[12] If texts cannot adequately reflect an underlying reality, then how can historians represent the past objectively? In practice, historians have responded to the postmodern and poststructuralist challenges in a number of ways. Some have simply ignored them to greater or lesser degrees. As Kevin Passmore has explained, "Many historians continue to write as if poststructuralism–indeed, theory of any kind–did not exist."[13] But others have used them to reflect on the ways in which historians work. As early as 1973, the intellectual historian Hayden White (1928–2018) compared many of the historical narratives written in the historicist heyday of the nineteenth century and revealed how they were unconsciously shaped by a small set of classic literary tropes such as tragedy or comedy.[14] How, White implicitly asked in his principal work, *Metahistory*, could historians tell the truth about the past when they were obliged to render it not "as it actually happened," but according to the schemas of fiction? In more recent years, a number of historians have launched more focused critiques on metanarratives, as in Konrad H. Jarausch and Michael Geyer's survey of predominant metanarratives at work in German historiography. In their view, these "master narratives" not only stand as flawed representations of the country's history but have also limited other potential avenues of research.[15]

Other ambitious historians have harnessed the critical edge of postmodern thought, particularly its emphasis on the unstable relationship between language and meaning, to ask new historical questions and to interrogate the assumptions of past societies. Among the most notable is the French historian Michel Foucault (1926–1984), who traced the histories of such big themes as knowledge, madness, punishment, and sexuality in Europe. Rather than attempt to describe how they developed over time, Foucault focused on the transformation of the language used to describe them. He concluded that the contemporary understanding of these themes was created and shaped by bodies of language that he referred to as "discourses," which included all the ways that contemporaries talked about the theme. Studying the evolution of discourses, Foucault claimed, exposed how relationships of power functioned in society, since the discourses featured language that designated what was normal and deviant, or acceptable and unacceptable within society. Foucault similarly scrutinized the human sciences, writing in his 1971 work, *The Order of Things*, that certain discourses had become associated with specific disciplines of knowledge and had thereby come to set limits on what could be said and thus what could be known.[16]

In the following decade, Joan Scott revolutionized the study of women's and gender history with her 1986 article, "Gender: A Useful Category of Analysis." Scott argued that historians should think of gender not as a fixed category but as a fluid way of assigning identity and meaning to oneself or to aspects of politics, society, and culture. She invited historians to consider how past peoples determined what made something "feminine" or "masculine" or what it meant to see oneself as gendered. She explained, "Historians need ... to examine the ways in which gendered identities are substantively constructed and relate their findings to a range of activities, social organizations, and historically specific cultural representations."[17]

Many other historians, even when not engaging directly in poststructuralist theory, have nonetheless paused to consider the limits of objectivity in their research.[18] This is in line with a similar reevaluation that has taken place in many disciplines. Even within the natural sciences, often seen as the model of disinterested research, there has been a sustained discussion about the ways in which cultural biases shape scientific processes and conclusions.[19] Historians have played a key role in this discussion, using the records of past scientists to reveal the human dimension of scientific research.[20] Within their own field, historians are more circumspect in claiming strict objectivity in their research, and they seldom claim to seek a deeper metaphysical truth.[21] Yet truth remains the top commitment in the sense that historians strive to create interpretations that are consistent with and faithful to a critical reading of the evidence and are able to stand up to external scrutiny. Broadly speaking, historical research seeks to establish an accurate account while recognizing that perceptions are shaped by context, both past and present. In other words, the study of history recognizes the significance of both objective and subjective views shaped by the limits of available evidence, the vagaries of language, and the perspective of the researcher. It is by raising awareness of these limitations that historians hope to achieve the greatest possible fidelity to the subject matter.

To overcome the field's inherent constraints and negotiate a more nuanced pursuit of truth, the practice of good critical thinking is key. It provides a shared set of principles that guide the structure of claims to historical knowledge. It allows historians to share their interpretations and thus to seek greater accuracy through a process of consensus and disagreement with peers. And, as we shall see, it assists historians in addressing the limitations of their sources and in mitigating their own limitations by helping them reflect on their views and maintain internal consistency in their conclusions. And, consequently, it facilitates the creation of scholarship that historians can present, as far as it goes, as true.

REFLECTION EXERCISE

On your own, identify what you see as the three most important events within the last fifty years that have shaped today's world, and describe why they have proved significant. Compare your results with those of a partner. To what extent do your choices and reasons overlap? What similar or different assumptions lie at the roots of your respective choices? Next, discuss ways to convince your partner that your choices are correct. What evidence would you need to establish the facts of the events you selected? What sources would be required to persuade your partner that your events were the most significant? Finally, summarize your discussion to the class and discuss what this exercise suggests about the challenges of establishing the truth in historical analysis and in creating historical narratives.

The Fundamentals of Critical Thinking

Critical thinking has both a long and a short history. It connects, on the one hand, to centuries of innovation in logical thought stretching back to the ancient Greeks. On the other hand, critical thinking did not emerge as a pedagogical priority for general education in the United States until the mid-twentieth century.[22] In the ensuing decades, scholars debated the proper definition of the term, and in the late 1980s and early 1990s, they formed a consensus on what critical thinking is and what it entails. In 1987, Michael Scriven and Richard Paul of the National Council for Excellence in Critical Thinking defined it as "the intellectually disciplined process of actively and skillfully conceptualizing, applying, synthesizing, and/or evaluating information gathered from, or generated by, observation, experience, reasoning, or communication, as a guide to belief and action."[23] Three years later, the American Philosophical Association formed a committee to develop a more formal definition. In their report, the committee defined critical thinking as "purposeful, self-regulatory judgment which results in interpretation, analysis, evaluation, and inference, as well as explanation of the evidential, conceptual, methodological, criteriological, or contextual considerations upon which that judgment is based."[24]

The definitions offered by experts represent an earnest attempt to encapsulate a broad concept. They are admittedly a lot to unpack, so it is helpful to begin with a more fundamental approach. Essentially, critical thinking concerns claims to truth responding to a particular question or issue. This includes moments in which one is making claims or when one is assessing the claims of others. For our purposes, we can focus on three attributes embedded within the definitions above:

- *Critical thinking is active.* This type of thinking requires both planning and reflection. When we think actively, we are aware of the problem that we face, and we consciously follow the evidence to a conclusion. And then we think back on what we have done to ensure that we are right in our judgment.

- *Critical thinking is rational.* This means that critical thinkers adhere to a logical process that in its most basic form starts with a question or issue; weighs a set of reasons or evidence related to that issue; and uses them to arrive at a decision, conclusion, or "judgment."

- *Critical thinking is defensible.* When we follow a critical thinking process and form a "judgment," we should be able to share our reasoning with others and explain why we think as we do. Presumably, others would assess our reasoning and come to share our view, or they would convince us why our reasoning was flawed.

With these three criteria in mind, we might offer a simpler definition of critical thinking that we can use as we practice the fundamentals. In 1985, Robert H. Ennis, a philosopher of education, defined critical thinking this way: "*Critical thinking is reflective and reasonable thinking that is focused on what to believe or what to do.*"[25] Ennis does not give us the precision found in more technical definitions, but his version encapsulates nicely the fundamental elements that constitute critical thought.

Just as academics have struggled to explain precisely what critical thinking means, so too have they faced challenges in incorporating it into the curriculum. Despite the significance of critical thinking to the work of scholars and students, this essential skill often resides in the background of a university education.[26] One 2013 study suggested that many faculty members do not specifically address or assess critical thinking skills in their courses, but instead teach it "as implicit and integrated with disciplinary content."[27] Part of the reason for this benign neglect is that the need for critical thinking lacks a certain visibility. On the one hand, it is inseparable from the practice of any discipline, but it operates at such a fundamental level that many professors assume students will come to university already equipped as critical thinkers and thus in no further need of dedicated training. Students, too, often treat critical thinking as a given and do not value it as a skill that they must learn at university. Instead, they tend to lay more stress on more specialized skills such as software design or economic forecasting, which they identify with certain professional careers. For students, it is easy to see why a biochemist would need to know how to synthesize proteins in a laboratory but harder to value the underlying thought process that framed the experiment.

In some ways, these perspectives are not wrong. They are right to believe that critical thinking is a fundamental skill that every person performs practically every day. It is not a skill that one must necessarily attend university to learn. As we go about our daily routine, we face problems or questions and have to make decisions about them that require critical thought. For example, when making simple decisions about what to wear in the morning, we have to weigh the weather forecast, our destinations, and the things that we will be doing. If it is the middle of winter and we have to shovel snow off the walk, then we might reasonably conclude that warm clothing is in order, and as our coat slides over our shoulders, we have completed a minor critical thinking task. One hardly needs a bachelor's degree to know when to bundle up for the day. Yet critical thinking is not always so simple. It rests upon a spectrum running from the most mundane uses of reason to the most complex. Learning how to operate on the more complex end of the spectrum requires the far more intricate applications found in the academic pursuits of a university.

A similarly correct assumption that many students and faculty make is that critical thinking requires cultivation. If students enter the classroom already possessing some skills, then they will improve by performing the normal tasks of the discipline and gaining experience. Unfortunately, this does not mean that universities can expect students simply to pick up critical thinking as a healthy by-product of their normal studies. Coursework may have some effect on skill levels, but it omits the degree to which cultivation also requires self-awareness. In the 1970s, the psychologist John H. Flavell stressed the importance of what he called **metacognition**, which describes the self-reflective component of problem-solving. Flavell defined metacognition as "one's knowledge concerning one's own cognitive processes,"[28] and he noted that it was essential to identifying problems, following the rules of critical thinking, and assessing the validity of solutions. For this reason, students and instructors cannot hope for strong thinking skills as a natural outcome; rather, they must work together to raise self-awareness and improve through both training and self-conscious practice.

The Elements of Analysis

Properly cultivating strong critical thinking skills demands an understanding of its fundamental contours. As a point of departure, we can focus on three principle operations that take place when applying critical thinking skills to historical scholarship. The first is *analysis*, which occurs when we break down the critical thinking process of others. The second is *evaluation*, or the determining of the strength or accuracy of the outcome of a critical thinking process. The third is *construction*, or the creation of our own claims based on an investigation of evidence.

Sometimes the best way to learn critical thinking is by watching others. For starters, we can begin with a very simple exercise to learn the components that comprise the critical thought process. In this scenario, imagine a mother is attempting to tell her seven-year-old son that it is time for bed:

Mother:	Okay, son, it's time for bed.
Son:	(with a tone of mournful despair) Nooo!
Mother:	Honey, it's almost 9:30, and you still need to brush your teeth.
Son:	Do I have to go to bed now?
Mother:	Yes, of course. It's a school night, and your brothers are in bed. They know it's bedtime.
Son:	But I'm not tired.
Mother:	Well, you look sleepy, and you need plenty of rest so that you can do your best in class …

Embedded within this all-too-familiar example are many of the most common elements of the critical thinking process. In this exchange, the mother has already taken a position on the issue of whether the child should go to bed. For her, the answer to the question of whether it is bedtime is most decidedly "yes." Because she accepts the answer as a claim to truth, her position represents an **opinion**. For his part, the seven-year-old clearly does not share the mother's opinion, and he pointedly asks her to defend her pronouncement. As with many parents in these situations, it is likely tempting for the mother to explain herself by simply appealing to her authority as a parent: "It's bedtime because I said so!" This might suffice in practice, but the rules of critical thinking demand a clear explanation of the reasons behind her opinion. This is what separates an opinion from an **argument**. The philosopher T. Edward Damer describes an argument as a "claim supported by other claims," and it is the central outcome of the critical thinking process.[29] Critical thinkers must always be willing and able to support their arguments. In turn, our task in analyzing the argument is to discern the conclusion and the supporting claims.

Supporting claims go by different names. They are often referred to as **premises**, which designate them as claims in themselves that together form a broader conclusion. Premises include reasons or points that can be derived from conventional logic or past experience and **evidence**, which comes from empirical observations. In many cases, the premises are clearly stated in the argument. We refer to these as **explicit premises**. In our example, the mother's argument is supported by at least five explicit premises, which we can place in a diagram:

Premise 1:	It is approximately 9:30 p.m.;
Premise 2:	It is a school night;
Premise 3:	The child's brothers know that it is bedtime;
Premise 4:	The child looks sleepy;
Premise 5:	The child needs adequate rest for class;
Therefore,	
Conclusion:	The child should go to bed.

This seems straightforward. There is, however, a bit more going on under the surface. Though there are some clear bits of empirical evidence, such as the time and day of the week, and some conventional knowledge, such as that children need rest to do well in school, other parts of this argument are not immediately visible. Sometimes premises may not be clear to outsiders but are supposedly understood by the participants in the critical thinking exercise. The child probably knows, for example, that he has a 9:30 p.m. bedtime on school nights and does not need to be reminded of this point. This would thus serve as an **implicit premise**. Upon closer inspection, we can identify a number of implicit premises at work in this exchange. Most are fairly obvious because we likely share the same base of conventional knowledge and experience, but since we do not share the precise context, we would list them conditionally:

Explicit premise:	It is approximately 9:30 p.m.;
Implicit premise:	9:30 p.m. is the agreed-upon bedtime;
Explicit premise:	It is a school night;
Implicit premise:	Bedtime is strictly observed on school nights;
Explicit premise:	The child's brothers understand that it is bedtime;
Implicit premise:	The children all have roughly the same bedtime;
Explicit premise:	The child looks sleepy;

Implicit premise:	You should go to bed when you are sleepy;

Explicit premise:	The child needs adequate rest for class;
Implicit premise:	If the child does not go to bed now, then he will not get enough rest.

It is important to be as certain as possible about what the supporting claims mean. Our analysis must be faithful to the intentions of the person making the argument. Anytime we misconstrue the claims or conclusions of another, we have violated the rules of critical thinking. Sometimes this happens intentionally, as when parties to a discussion "twist the words" of another to gain an advantage in a dispute. But just as often it is inadvertent, as when people misunderstand a conclusion or when they make unwarranted assumptions. Therefore, in listing the presumed implicit premises of the argument in this case, we would be obliged to ensure that our analysis is indeed correct by raising questions or otherwise verifying our assumptions. In response, we would expect the person making the argument to clarify either by making implicit premises explicit or by adding subpremises, or additional reasons and evidence, to support the main premises.

Evaluating Arguments

Assessing the strength of an argument often takes place alongside the task of discerning its components and structure. As the components emerge and the connections among them become clear, it becomes possible to determine how well and how completely they are shaping and supporting the conclusion. In particular, an evaluation should begin with the premises and consider the following criteria:

- *Are the premises and conclusions clear?* Evaluators should consider each supporting claim and determine if they make sense or if more information is needed. Are the premises buried in the text or speech? Are they implicit when they should be explicit? In our bedtime example, we noted that the child likely knew the implied premises but that outside observers might need them to be directly stated.

- *Are the supporting claims convincing?* In order for the premises to support the conclusion adequately, there must be no lingering doubts about their validity. In the case of empirical evidence, observers must possess the experience or conventional knowledge required to agree with the premises, and they must be able to verify any empirical evidence. If that is not the case, then the supporting claims must be strengthened with more evidence or with a more thorough explanation of why they are true. In our example, the child could in principle verify the time and date by checking a clock and calendar, and he may well know that not sleeping long enough leaves him feeling sleepy in class. But he might disagree with his mother's assessment that he "looks sleepy." Here the mother has offered a subjective observation as a reason. The child may or may not see the same signs, and whether he will accept it as a valid claim will depend on the degree to which he trusts his mother's judgment.

- *Are the premises clearly relevant to the conclusions?* All components of a successful argument should work together to explain and ultimately support the conclusion. Extraneous elements can distract or even mislead from the critical thinking process. Moreover, the elements of the argument should be relevant for all involved. With this in mind, everything in the bedtime argument seems to be in order except for the mother's claim about the brothers agreeing that it is bedtime. This is a clear point, and there is no immediate reason to doubt that it is true. But the fact that the brothers believe it to be bedtime does not necessarily mean that it is.

- *Do the premises warrant the conclusions?* This criterion asks us to decide whether there is enough support to agree with the conclusion proffered in the argument. We must consider whether there are questions that remain unanswered or other overlooked factors to weigh. It may be the case that either more support is needed or the conclusions should be modified or qualified to correspond more closely with the available evidence or reasoning. Based on our analysis and evaluation of the bedtime argument, the discussion could conceivably go further, but the child might reasonably agree that he should go to bed.

The example we used for this section was a relatively easy one, but it seems clear that even simple arguments can exhibit errors in critical thinking. These errors, which violate the rules of good critical thinking, are called **fallacies**. There are dozens of common fallacies, and we will see some examples as we move through the sample research projects in this textbook. Even in our evaluation of the bedtime discussion, we can observe a possible error known as the **bandwagon fallacy**. This fallacy occurs when an arguer attempts to suggest that the strength of others' opinions affirms the strength of a conclusion. When the mother says, "Your brothers know that it is bedtime," she might be implying that the brothers agreed that all children should go to bed. But that does not necessarily make the claim true. To correct the error, the mother would have to explain her point more clearly, perhaps by arguing that what she meant was that all children should go to bed at the same time.

Constructing Arguments

Once we have gained experience with analyzing and evaluating the arguments of others, we are ready to apply that experience to building our own arguments. As we will see in the third chapter of this textbook, the process of launching and completing a research process follows the rules of effective constructive critical thinking. For now, we can introduce the process with another simple example:

> You and your roommate are first-year university students who share a history class early in the morning on Mondays, Wednesdays, and Fridays. It is Monday morning, and the alarm clock is blaring. You shut off the alarm and see that your roommate is similarly reluctant to get up and face the day. Your roommate groggily asks, "Should we bother going to class this morning?"

This is a familiar dilemma that we have all faced from time to time. In reality, it is likely difficult to think this through carefully early in the morning, but this is a good issue to consider beforehand. To resolve it with good critical thinking, you might observe the following five-step process:

Step 1. Identify the issue: The goal here is to state the issue at hand as precisely as possible, whether it is a question to be answered or a problem to be solved. Doing so affords a firmer sense of the critical thinking task and sustains a consistent argument. In the scenario, the immediate question, "Should we go to class this morning?" is connected to some broader questions, most notably, "Do we want to succeed in the class?" Let's assume in this case that both of you do indeed wish to succeed, so your inner debate might focus on a modified question, "Do we need to go to class this morning in order to succeed?"

Step 2. Determine the premises and procedures needed to resolve the problem: Here you must consider what you need to know in order to answer your question and how you will obtain the information required. In this case, linking attendance to success will depend on knowing whether students generally perform better when they attend class and how attendance is treated in the specific class you are taking. For the former point, some conventional knowledge might do, but knowing a little about the research on the topic would be better, because a first-year student likely lacks the experience to make an informed decision. Meanwhile, reading the course syllabus would help answer the latter point, so overall it appears that answering the question demands some textual evidence.

Step 3. Assess the evidence: This crucial step entails gathering and weighing the supporting evidence. That might include fumbling around your dorm room looking for your course syllabus. For this scenario, imagine that you also locate an article about absenteeism from your first-year transitions course. On the syllabus, you observe that attendance is counted as 10 percent of the course grade. Since this is your first absence, you may not incur a penalty, but it means that you will lose points if you need to miss class for some reason later in the term. Meanwhile, you note that the author of the article posits a strong correlation between attendance and performance and states that the evidence suggests that even missing one time tends to have a negative impact.[30] The available evidence thus makes it clear that course attendance is important for success as a rule, so you might conclude that the answer to your question, "Do I need to go to class this morning in order to succeed?" might be answered by stating that one should attend every morning.

Good critical thinking involves faithful consideration of all sides of a debate. In order to be thorough, you might consider why you do not wish to attend. You talk it over with your roommate:

Are you ill?: No.
Are you tired?: Yes.
Are you able to function?: ... Yes.
Are you feeling lazy?: Definitely.
Is laziness a reason to miss class?: I guess not.
Is there any compelling immediate reason why you cannot attend?: No.

Finally, you might acknowledge that attendance is important generally, but perhaps this particular morning is not so critical. A glance at the syllabus reveals that no assignments are due (hopefully you knew this already), but the class is meeting this morning, and the plan indicates a lecture on the Progressive Era in the United States. The syllabus also indicates that the midterm exam is a week away and that this topic will likely appear on the examination. Based on this evidence, one could argue that attendance matters, but that a student could miss today because there is no graded assignment and you may be able to get the notes from another student. Now your task is to weigh evidence, leading you to one conclusion or another Whatever you decide, you should provide reasons why you have chosen the stronger argument. In other words, you must offer a **rebuttal** for any likely counter-arguments.

Step 4. Structure the argument: Once you have made your determination, it is time to frame your argument so that it is clear and convincing to others, faithful to the supporting evidence, and free of errors. In this case, you (rightly) decide that attending is key to success and that to argue the alternative would be an example of a **rationalization fallacy**, which involves representing weak or false reasons as strong reasons to support an argument. With your conclusion in mind, you begin by listing your reasons and then your rebuttals to your roommate:

In my transitions class, we learned that attendance is one of the most important things to doing well in class. In our history class, we are graded on attendance. If we miss today, it might not hurt our grade right away, but we will make it harder on ourselves if we have to miss class later in the term. We might be tired, and today may seem less important than other days, but the material will be on the exam, and we will likely do better if we take notes ourselves. So, I say we go.

Step 5. Evaluate the results: As a final step, reflect on the criteria for good arguments. Are the premises convincing and relevant to the argument, and do they warrant the conclusion? Are the premises and conclusions clear, and do they satisfactorily answer the question that you posed? Presumably your roommate would help with the assessment process and might even add something to the argument. For instance, a wise roommate might add that a good history student should attend to learn about the topics rather than merely to do well on an exam. With the evaluation completed and any fallacies addressed, the critical thinking process is complete, and all that is left is to get up and go to class.

Critical Thinking and Active Learning

As these exercises show, even very commonplace arguments can involve a fairly complex critical thinking process. We simply do not notice it because we seldom take the time to analyze our daily decisions so thoroughly. For history students, however, becoming more aware of how argumentation works can be very useful for succeeding in a history course. As the attendance discussion shows, cultivating critical thinking and metacognitive perception can play an important role in strategies for student success, even simple ones like showing up for class. It is sometimes not enough for a professor or academic adviser to tell a student that it is important to take notes or to study; it is also important for the student to understand the logic behind such habits lest it become too easy to fall into a rationalization fallacy or simply not bring them to mind during the day. Indeed, the principle of metacognition, of being aware of our thinking, correlates nicely to self-awareness of healthy student practices.

Critical thinking and metacognition are also essential for **active learning**, in which the learner shifts from being a mere receiver of knowledge to being an engaged participant. Rather than going to class expecting to hear a lecture and write down the information as it is presented, active learners share control of the learning process by preparing for lessons in advance to know better what to expect, by asking questions and joining in discussions during class, and by reflecting on what they have learned after class and addressing any deficiencies. And, as we shall see in the next section, one way students can employ their critical thinking skills in the classroom and become active learners is by analyzing and evaluating the structure of academic lectures. Better understanding the perspective of the history professor can mark a key distinction between listening and learning in a classroom.

DISCOVERY EXERCISE

Working with a group of three to four peers, find an editorial in your university's newspaper taking a position on a campus policy. On your own, independently analyze and evaluate the argument. Diagram the editorial's premises and main conclusion and then assess the strength of each premise and the degree to which they support the conclusion. Compare your diagram with your group and work together to create a new argument either supporting or rejecting the position in the editorial.

From Critical Thinking to Historical Thinking

The same rules and principles that help us make the simplest decisions also apply to the most advanced historical scholarship. Historians, after all, are always making arguments. Through their engagement with a variety of sources, historians form judgments about what happened in the past, why it happened, and what it means, both over time and in the present. In fact, this is what makes history such a dynamic field of study. If it were simply a matter of blindly reporting the past "as it was" without the need for interpretation, then the field would be a stultifying exercise in rote memorization and repetition. But for better or worse history is full of uncertainties and questions. Sources are often incomplete or unclear and are usually subject to varying interpretations. Historical events, meanwhile, have complex origins and implications, and historical figures, like all human beings, carry deep-seated motives, unique perspectives, and internal contradictions. Our own perspectives, meanwhile, tend to be skewed by the strangeness of the past to our own times. We struggle to understand the past on its own terms and to refrain from imposing our own views and norms. And as we move forward in time, our views on the past can change along with the questions that we pose.

For these reasons, historical research always involves both *exposition*, in which the historian relays information about the subject under study, and *persuasion*, in which the historian attempts to make an interpretive claim and convince readers to accept the interpretations as valid. Accomplishing these twin tasks demands that historians draw from the fundamental processes of critical thinking to construct their arguments, utilizing texts, artifacts, oral accounts, and other sources as evidence to support their claims. And they build upon those principles to address the specific problems related to historical interpretation in a process that we can refer to as **historical thinking**.

As in the case of critical thinking, pinning down a definition of historical thinking can be tricky. In the United States, the *National Standards for History* for primary and secondary pupils includes a set of overarching goals for historical thinking compiled by a panel of professional historians:

- *Chronological Thinking* is designed to help students understand the sequence of past events and to understand narrativity and change over time.

- *Historical Comprehension* aims to convey the complexity of the past and of historical causality. Students are expected to learn to avoid applying their own standards to past events (**presentism**) and to gain a sense of how to understand the structure and meanings of historical narratives.

- *Historical Analysis and Interpretation* calls for students to break down historical narratives, to learn how historians use evidence to interpret the past, and to comprehend the basics of historiography.

- *Historical Research Capabilities* asks students to make their own interpretations using the techniques of historical research.

- *Historical Issues-Analysis and Decision-Making* engages specific historical problems or present-day issues with historical relevance. The goal is to teach pupils how to apply their historical thinking skills to specific challenges.[31]

The American model clearly groups a very broad set of skills under the rubric of historical thinking, thereby effecting a tidy separation between historical thinking and content, or, more simply, between skills and knowledge. More recently, education professionals in the United Kingdom have created a more nuanced framework that hinges on a distinction between **substantive knowledge**, which refers to the concrete names, dates, and events of history, the related **substantive concepts** such as political regimes, ideas, and movements whose meanings and forms can change over time, and the **second-order knowledge**, or processes, problems, and protocols, that historians observe to interpret the substantive components of the past. Assessing historical thinking in this British model entails a focus on developing and applying this second-order knowledge.[32]

Finally, *The Historical Thinking Project* has become an important guide for Canadian schools. Peter Seixas, a historical education researcher and one of the project's founders, has explained, "The model of historical thinking was developed—pragmatically, like the American and the British—in order to be communicable and intelligible to teachers and their students, and yet rich enough … to lead them into explorations of fundamental epistemological and ontological problems of history."[33] The Canadian model preserves an interest in second-order concepts, but frames them specifically as "problems, tensions, or difficulties that demand comprehension, negotiation, and, ultimately, an accommodation that is never a complete solution."[34] The result is a model resting on six core concepts:

- *Establish historical significance:* this skill requires pupils to articulate the reasons why a specific historical event, figure, or trend is "worth remembering." Seixas asks, "How does a meaningless jumble of particulars become meaningful?"
- *Use primary source evidence:* pupils are asked to understand the challenges of reading a historical source to answer questions about the past.
- *Identify continuity and change:* pupils are asked to understand the dynamic quality of history.
- *Analyze cause and consequence:* pupils must reflect on the complexities that attach to the origins and outcomes of events.
- *Take historical perspectives:* this concept leads pupils to appreciate the differences between how people thought and lived in the past and how they do so today. It calls for "understanding the foreignness of the past."
- *Understand the ethical dimensions of historical interpretations:* pupils consider both ethical dilemmas in past situations and the burdens of the past for living generations.[35]

The Canadian Historical Thinking Project team further complicates the skills designation by drawing a line between historical thinking and historical literacy, which they define as a "deep understanding of historical events and processes through active engagement with historical texts."[36] The concepts in the Canadian model are expected to link the cognitive process that characterizes historical thinking with the reading knowledge and skill that constitute historical literacy.

Although there are some clear areas of overlap in the American, British, and Canadian models, many of the differences among them are quite significant, making it difficult to draw from them an overarching definition of historical thinking. As in the case of critical thinking, what is needed is a broad and inclusive definition. Based upon the criteria presented here, we might suggest that, at its core, *historical thinking is a process in which we think about or with history in order to make sense of the past, present, or future.* This means that we make an active attempt to understand what happened in the past but also try to use events and trends in the past to illuminate questions or issues we face today or expect to face in the future. The definition offered here is meant to demonstrate that historical thinking is something that we all do quite frequently. Just as we showed in the first chapter of this textbook that everyone encounters the past, so too does everyone engage it intellectually at some level. Such an inclusive conception also allows for different levels of historical thinking. As the psychologist Sam Wineburg has shown, successful historical thinking demands cultivation. "Historical thinking," he concluded, "in its deepest forms, is neither a natural process nor something that springs automatically from psychological development. Its achievement, I argue, goes against the grain of how we ordinarily think."[37]

Decoding Historical Lectures

Students of history need not wait until they are neck-deep in an archive to begin employing their critical and historical thinking skills. Rather, these are already implicated in our first encounters with history in the classroom. Historians make arguments in lectures just as they do in books and articles. In fact, working to analyze and evaluate lectures can be a fantastic way to hone a student's critical thinking skills and to understand how historical thinking works in practice. Approaching a lecture as a set of arguments to be analyzed can also help make the content of lectures clearer and improve performance in a history course.

The purpose of class lectures is to convey information about a particular historical period, but within this exposition of facts is a set of interpretations sometimes stated explicitly and other times implicated within the structure of a narrative. If, for instance, a professor is lecturing on the French Revolution but mainly talks about how the price of bread informed popular resentment, then the professor is implicitly arguing that economic factors were the most significant in explaining the origins of the upheaval. Taking notes is essential in any lecture, but rather than simply writing down in sequence everything you hear, it might be more profitable to identify the overarching argument or arguments as you listen, and then try to understand how the "facts" embedded within the lecture support the arguments. In other words, instead of focusing on rote memorization of names or dates, try to think of them as evidence supporting a point and find ways to articulate that connection. It may be necessary for you to go back over your notes later in order to understand the links, but doing so will give you a more structured way to study and will likely help you retain the information more effectively by placing dates, events, ideas, and names in context.

Once you have organized the lecture material as well as possible, you will be able to evaluate the argument and create questions that may help you further enrich your understanding. What connections are not completely clear to you? Which ideas or points need more support for you to understand them or accept them as supporting the overarching interpretations? What alternative explanations for historical events might be possible? After reviewing your notes and formulating questions, you can bring them to the next lecture and seek clarification, and this may help you connect the previous session's lecture to future lectures and gain a clearer sense of the material as a whole.

History in Practice: Critical and Historical Thinking in the Classroom

Before choosing a research topic, many students discover their interests in a simple classroom lecture. In the sample below, Jack Wells provides a portion of a lecture surveying historical explanations for the collapse of the western Roman Empire in the fifth century CE. Later, Wells will construct a sample research project based on this historical problem.

Jack Wells on the "Fall of the Western Roman Empire"

Scholarly explanations for the "decline and fall" of the western empire are too numerous to detail fully, and, of course, many scholars would prefer we view the transition from Late Antiquity to the Middle Ages through the perspective of transformation rather than decline. One popular view has argued that the Roman state helped contribute to its own weakness by imposing a crushing bureaucracy and high taxes on the people of the empire. The argument basically runs that after the military anarchy of the third century, the restoration of the Empire under a series of generals culminated in the reign of the emperor Diocletian (r. 284–305), who radically reformed the Roman military. In particular, he—or his successors, especially Constantine (r. 306–337)—increased the size of the army and emphasized the development of large but expensive cavalry units. This increase, from around 250,000–400,000 or more, and the additional expense, required the imposition of an enormous tax burden, weakening an economy already suffering from years of civil war and rampant inflation. Furthermore, Diocletian also changed the Roman provincial structure, creating numerous new provinces that were smaller and had separate military and civilian officials. The apparent goal was to make it more difficult for Roman governors to rebel against the emperor, because no military official had an army large enough to be threatening. It might also have been envisioned as a way to limit corruption, since now each province had two administrations. However, the additional bureaucratic apparatus only added to the tax burden, since many new offices had to be staffed and the officials paid.

There is some evidence that might support this interpretation. The heavy-handedness of Diocletian's administration and its potential for economic disruption can be most effectively seen in the Edict of Maximum Prices of 301 BCE. In an attempt to combat the inflation that was troubling the empire, Diocletian attempted to use imperial administration to organize economic life, including establishing maximum prices for important goods and regulating the exact payment for different occupations. Those who violated the law could be punished with death in some cases. The edict seems to have been a total failure that was quickly abandoned, but it does give us an insight into the policy of the emperors of the fourth century, in particular their determination to subordinate many aspects of Roman life to their own view of what was good for the state.

The state in the fourth century also responded harshly to those who tried to avoid traditional civic responsibilities. The towns of the empire had been managed by an upper class known as the decurial class, after the common name for a town councilor—decurion. This group of men represented a local elite who ran for office, contributed money to public building programs, and paid some of the expenses for festivals. It seems that in times of economic instability, carrying out the obligations of the decurial class was no longer attractive, and the struggling elite were no longer willing to serve in public office and undertake the requisite expenses. Therefore, imperial edicts tried to force obligations on the town councilors. They made membership on the councils hereditary and mandatory and tried to limit the ability of councilors to escape their obligations. The Theodosian Code, for instance, records an edict of Constantine in CE 326 that is aimed to prevent decurions from escaping their burdens by becoming members of the clergy, who were exempted from many imperial taxes. Although Constantine wanted to support the church, he also wanted his cities properly maintained, stating that "it is proper that the rich should bear the burdens of the world and that the poor should be supported by the wealth of the Church."[38]

We find an interesting piece of evidence suggesting the burden that the tax system had on the Roman people in the writings of the fifth-century author Salvian. Writing in the 440s, Salvian argued that the Roman officials and the wealthy were so oppressive to the poor that many found refuge fleeing to the barbarians, smelly and uncivilized though they may have been.

The primary sources therefore suggest that high taxes and bureaucratic mismanagement were having a negative effect on the Roman economic base. Modern scholars have carried things further though, and it is illustrative of the complexity of the problem that the same evidence can be interpreted in a number of ways. Peter Brown, for instance, noted that the result of all this was corruption, concentration of wealth in the hands of a very few, and occasionally even peasant revolts.[39] But to Brown, the military weakness was not the whole and perhaps not even the most important story; instead it was the social and cultural transformations that happened after, but not entirely as a result of, the Germanic conquests, which were more important. G.E.M. de St. Croix prefers to focus on the rapacity of the tax collectors as part of a larger problem: the rich exploiting the poor so successfully that the poor were apathetic or even willing to live under invaders, in hopes that the old imperial system would be removed.[40]

APPLICATION EXERCISE

Practice your analytical and note-taking skills. Read the transcript and take notes, identifying the main argument in the lecture and listing the premises that support the argument. Then connect the facts and dates listed in the argument to the supporting premises. See if you can use your notes to answer the following critical and historical thinking questions:

1   On what central cause for the collapse of the western Roman Empire do the historians mentioned in the lecture seem to agree? On what details do the historians seem to disagree?

2   Many historians date the final collapse of the western Roman Empire in 476 CE, when the Germanic chieftain Odoacer deposed the last western Roman emperor. Why, then, do you think Wells focuses his lecture on the fourth century CE?

3   In thinking with the sources mentioned in the lecture, you might notice that they allude to the Christian church but do not directly discuss its role. What do you think the sources suggest about the role of Christianity in the collapse of the western Roman Empire?

Notes

1   Hart Research Associates, "It Takes More than a Major: Employer Priorities for College Learning," *Liberal Education* 99, no. 2 (2013): 22–9, 24.

2   Hart Research Associates, "Falling Short?: College Learning and Career Success," *NACTA Journal* 60, no. 1 (2016): 1–6, 4–5.

3   Jeffrey T. Steele and Michael Bradley, "Majors Matter: Differential Performance on a Test of General Education Outcomes," Paper presented at the Annual Meeting of the American Educational Research Association, Vancouver, Canada, 2012.

4   Malcolm Provus, "Teaching Critical Thinking through History," *The School Review* 63, no. 7 (1955): 393–6.

5   Peter Novick, *That Noble Dream: The "Objectivity Question" and the American Historical Profession* (Cambridge: Cambridge University Press, 1988).

6   William H. McNeill, "*The Rise of the West* after Twenty-Five Years," *Journal of World History* 1, no. 1 (1990): 1–21, 5–6.

7   Gareth Austin, "Reciprocal Comparison and African History: Tackling Conceptual Eurocentrism in the Study of Africa's Economic Past," *African Studies Review* 50, no. 3 (2007): 1–28.

8   Dipesh Chakrabarty, *Provincializing Europe: Postcolonial Thought and Historical Difference* (Princeton: Princeton University Press, 2000), 5.

9   Jean-François Lyotard, *The Postmodern Condition: A Report on Knowledge*, translated by Geoff Bennington and Brian Massumi (Minneapolis: University of Minnesota Press, 1984).

10 See Robert Southard, *Droysen and the Prussian School of History* (Lexington: University Press of Kentucky, 1994).

11 Lyotard, *Postmodern Condition*, 3.

12 See Keith Jenkins, *The Postmodern History Reader* (New York: Routledge, 1997).

13 Kevin Passmore, "Poststructuralism and History," in *Writing History: Theory and Practice*, edited by Stefan Berger, Heiko Feldner, and Kevin Passmore, 3rd ed. (London: Bloomsbury, 2013), 123–46, 143.

14 Hayden White, *Metahistory: The Historical Imagination in Nineteenth-Century Europe* (Baltimore: Johns Hopkins University Press, 1973).

15 Konrad Jarausch and Michael Geyer, *Shattered Past: Reconstructing German Histories* (Princeton: Princeton University Press, 2003).

16 Michel Foucault, *The Order of Things: An Archaeology of the Human Sciences* (New York: Pantheon, 1971).

17 Joan Scott, "Gender: A Useful Category of Analysis," *The American Historical Review* 91, no. 5 (1986): 1053–75, 1068.

18 Novick, *That Noble Dream*, 625.

19 Helen Longino, *Science as Social Knowledge: Values and Objectivity in Social Inquiry* (Princeton: Princeton University Press, 1990).

20 One particularly critical example of this literature is Thomas Kuhn, *The Structure of Scientific Revolutions* (Chicago: University of Chicago Press, 1962); for a more recent example, see Steven Shapin, *Never Pure: Historical Studies of Science as if It Was Produced by People with Bodies, Situated in Time, Space, Culture, and Society, and Struggling for Credibility and Authority*, 2nd ed. (Baltimore: Johns Hopkins University Press, 2010).

21 John Tosh, *The Pursuit of History: Aims, Methods, and New Directions in the Study of History*, 6th ed. (New York: Routledge, 2015), 148–75.

22 Educational Policies Commission, *The Purposes of Education in American Democracy* (Washington, D.C.: National Education Association, 1938), 157; Harvard Committee, *General Education in a Free Society: Report of the Harvard Committee* (Cambridge: Harvard University Press, 1955), 65.

23 Michael Scriven and Richard Paul, Statement at the 8th Annual International Conference on Critical Thinking and Education Reform (1987), quoted in The Foundation for Critical Thinking, "Defining Critical Thinking," accessed July 18, 2018, https://www.criticalthinking.org/pages/defining-critical-thinking/766.

24 Peter Facione, *Critical Thinking: A Statement of Expert Consensus for Purposes of Educational Assessment and Instruction. Research Findings*

and Recommendations (Millbrae, CA: The California Academic Press, 1990), 3.

25   Robert H. Ennis, "A Logical Basis for Measuring Critical Thinking Skills," *Education Leadership* 43, no. 2 (1985): 44–8, 45. Emphasis added.

26   Ballou Skinner, "The Myth of Teaching for Critical Thinking," *The Clearing House* 45, no. 6 (1971): 372–6; James H. McMillan, "Enhancing College Students' Critical Thinking: A Review of Studies," *Journal of Research in Higher Education* 26, no. 1 (1987): 3–29.

27   Marck C. Nicholas and Chalmer E. Labig, Jr., "Faculty Approaches to Assessing Critical Thinking in the Humanities and the Natural and Social Sciences: Implications for General Education," *The Journal of General Education* 62, no. 4 (2013): 297–319, 304.

28   John H. Flavell, "Metacognitive Aspects of Problem Solving," in *The Nature of Intelligence*, edited by Lauren B. Resnick (Hillsdale: Erlbaum, 1976), 231–6, 232.

29   T. Edward Damer, *Attacking Faulty Reasoning: A Practical Guide to Fallacy-Free Arguments*, 7th ed. (Belmont, CA: Wadsworth, 2013), 14.

30   These are genuine conclusions. See Steven E. Gump, "The Cost of Cutting Class: Attendance as a Predictor of Student Success," *College Teaching* 53, no. 1 (2005): 21–6.

31   National Center for History in the Schools, *National Standards for History* (Los Angeles: National Center for History in the Schools, 1996).

32   "ASCL Guidance: Progression and Assessment in History," Association of School and College Leaders, accessed July 26, 2018, https://www.ascl.org. uk/help-and-advice/guidance-papers/ascl-guidance-paper-progression-and-assessment-in-history.html.

33   Peter Seixas, "A Model of Historical Thinking," *Educational Philosophy and Theory* 49, no. 6 (2015): 593–605, 596.

34   Ibid.

35   The Historical Thinking Project, "Historical Thinking Concepts," http:// historicalthinking.ca, accessed July 26, 2018.

36   Ibid.

37   Sam Wineburg, "Historical Thinking and Other Unnatural Acts," *Phi Delta Kappan* 92, no. 4 (2010): 81–94, 91.

38   James Harvey Robinson, *Readings in European History, Vol. 1* (Boston: Ginn and Company, 1904), 24.

39   Peter Brown, *The World of Late Antiquity: AD 150–750* (New York: Norton, 1971), 43–4, 118–19.

40   G. E. M. de Ste. Croix, "The 'Decline and Fall': An Explanation," in Donald Kagan, *The End of the Roman Empire: Decline or Transformation?* 3rd ed. (Lexington, MA: D. C. Heath and Company, 1992), 58–9, 64–5.

Suggested Reading

Breisach, Ernst. *On the Future of History: The Postmodernist Challenge and Its Aftermath*. Chicago: University of Chicago Press, 2007.

Brown, Callum G. *Postmodernism for Historians*. New York: Routledge, 2016.

Damer, Edward T. *Attacking Faulty Reasoning*. 7th ed. Boston: Wadsworth, 2012.

Novick, Peter. *That Noble Dream: The "Objectivity Question" and the American Historical Profession*. Cambridge: Cambridge University Press, 1988.

Wineburg, Sam. *Historical Thinking*. Philadelphia: Temple University Press, 2001.

3

Goal Planning and Research Design

What we will do in this chapter:

➢ **REFLECT** on the importance of planning for adjusting to university work and for managing large research projects.

➢ **DISCOVER** strategies for layered goal planning.

➢ **APPLY** planning techniques to the development of research projects.

From an outside perspective, university life looks terrific. The image of a student or scholar walking on a beautifully landscaped campus or working amid the solemn silence of a library or the purposeful chatter of a classroom certainly lends itself to the impression of a quiet "life of the mind" in the "ivory tower." In reality, the serenity and beauty of a university campus belies the stresses that attach to the rhythm of the university. Immense deadline pressures and a dizzying variety of tasks can be frazzling both for students and seasoned scholars. For undergraduates, being away from home, navigating the social environment of the university, and taking responsibility for their own finances can compound the academic challenges.[1]

In order to ensure healthy and productive work, it is important to take care of yourself physically as well as psychologically. Such self-care includes taking active steps to manage stress both with the social aspects of living on campus and with the rigors of a university curriculum. This is where successful planning enters the picture. Making planning a central part of your work can let you maximize your activities while helping you avoid overcommitting. At the same time, planning ahead allows you to take the best advantage of available opportunities and thereby make the most of your university education. Of course, careful planning is a prerequisite for practically any profession, but it demands somewhat unique approaches for students and faculty. Students and faculty must not only juggle numerous responsibilities at once and maintain an erratic work schedule but must also balance long-term and short-term tasks and maintain perspective in performing daily activities that may not bear fruit for months or years into the future.

The rigors of university work apply equally to completing a course, fulfilling an academic degree, and pursuing a research project. All three represent significant investments of time and energy and require sustained motivation. Fortunately, the same principles of planning that work for one apply to all three. In this chapter, we will learn how to take a "layered" approach to goal planning and discover how to apply it to the process of developing and writing a research essay. Some of the suggestions may diverge from the system that you currently use to keep track of your work, but you may find that it is easy to integrate the principles you will learn here into your own preferred approaches.

REFLECTION EXERCISE

Describe your current planning strategies.

1   What strategies help you identify and stay focused on your goals?

2   What tools do you use to keep track of upcoming tasks and events and maintain your daily schedule?

3   How often do you make, update, or change your plans or schedules?

4   What experience do you have managing a long-term project?

5   In what ways would you improve your planning habits?

Layered Goal Planning

Careful goal planning can mean the difference between surviving and thriving in a university setting. No one enrolls in a course of study without at least an implicit set of goals, but sometimes, the motives that bring a student into the classroom either are not their own or are not framed in the most positive way. Maybe a student is seeking to meet a parent's set of expectations or to uphold a family tradition. Or perhaps the student simply wishes to buy time with a course of study and avoid making hard decisions about a choice of careers. Even when a student holds a set of goals in mind (e.g., to become a lawyer or to earn a high salary), he or she may not have a strong conception of the connections between the end goals and the daily tasks required to reach them. In each of these cases, the result can be low levels of engagement with coursework. Recall in Chapter 2 the example of the two students discussing whether to skip their US history course. They ultimately decided to attend class based on an evaluation of its impact on their performance, but with greater awareness, they might also have connected the lessons in the course to their overarching academic goals. Similar dilemmas appear in the course of a long research project, in which it can be difficult to stay focused on the end goal while working on the minute details.

The key to maintaining perspective and orienting your work toward your objectives is to be intentional about what you want to accomplish. This means more than simply identifying objectives and putting them to paper. It also entails careful assessment of your own values and motives and using them as a foundation upon which to base your goals and plans. At the same time, it means that you should be aware of the expectations of others and consider how to negotiate your own desired outcomes with any external constraints.

The best way to begin is to determine the roots of your ambitions. As a point of departure, you should work to create a *value inventory*. This may at first seem an odd place to begin to think about your goals for a spring semester or a research essay, but keeping your values in mind can shape the way you set goals for yourself and later will help you stay motivated to meet them. It can also help you negotiate your ambitions with the expectations of others. To start a value inventory, first make a random list of the things that are most important to you. These can be tangible items like a place or certain possessions, or even passions like music or art, but should also include qualities by which you would like to define yourself, a lifestyle that you might endeavor to follow, or ideals such as social justice or the pursuit of knowledge.

To explain this further, let's consider an example from history. In 1923, the British mountaineer George Mallory (1886–1924) was planning a new expedition to the Himalayas with the goal of being the first human to reach the summit of Mount Everest. Asked by the *New York Times* why he wanted to make the dangerous ascent, Mallory was famously quoted as saying, "Because it's there." What does this tell us about Mallory's motives? Certainly, he had already achieved a measure of fame for his attempts, and the reporter helpfully pointed out that the expeditions might yield tremendous scientific benefits. Yet Mallory held firm to his response, explaining, "The answer is instinctive, a part, I suppose, of man's desire to conquer the universe."[2] By pushing at the limits of human experience, Mallory saw himself doing something preeminently human. Yet he was but one of a few humans who have ever scaled Everest, so we must surmise that he was also motivated by more personal values. One could argue that he possessed a strong spirit of adventure and cherished achievement for its own sake. Ultimately, these values led him to the foot of Mount Everest to undertake three dangerous expeditions up its slopes, including the one in June 1924, which claimed his life.

Unlike Mallory, your own goals certainly need not be so death-defying, but your commitment to them may be similarly strengthened if they are rooted in your values. It is thus important to create a list that reflects who you are and who you want to become. Perhaps like Mallory you are motivated by achievement, but you may just as likely value other things, like the prestige of a particular career, or wealth and a comfortable lifestyle, or even the prospect of having fun in life. Maybe your personal qualities are key. You may be moved with deep compassion for others and seek a life oriented toward service, or you may feel the desire to place a particular faith tradition at the center of your life. Or you might value your home and wish to make an impact on your community.

In all likelihood, you will identify several values in your list. So, the next step is to prioritize their place in your inventory. Use your critical thinking skills wherever possible to articulate why some values are more significant than others, but also trust your instincts. It might be the case that you prize both financial success and a commitment to service, but you decide that the latter is more important because it gives you a greater sense of satisfaction. Thus, you decide that if possible, you would like to achieve both, but if necessary, you would be willing to sacrifice wealth for an opportunity to serve others. In reconciling seemingly incompatible values, you might also think historically, recognizing that your priorities will probably change over time and weighing which values are most important to you at different stages of your life. If you value both exotic travel and your home community, you could elect to prioritize travel now while you are young and lay stress in the future on remaining closer to home. Finally, you should understand why your values are indeed your own. It is almost inevitable that some of your motives will be shaped by others in your life, whether it be a family member or a teacher or a friend. It is perfectly fine to listen closely to what others advise and hope for you, and to incorporate them into your own values, but ultimately you have to decide whether you share their views in the same way. As an example, imagine the following scenario:

> Colette is a first-year student in an American university with an interest in history and political science. In her value inventory, she decides that she prizes among other things a commitment to service and social justice. Her family back home in a small rural town have always expressed hopes that Colette will be the first in the family to earn a university degree and perhaps go on to become a doctor or lawyer. Colette takes pride in the prestige that comes with professional success, and she is grateful for the support she received growing up to be able to earn a place in the university. At the same time, she is energized by the opportunities that come with a university education, and particularly with the idea of foreign travel. In the end, Colette decides that in the short term she is most interested in learning as much as she can and in seeing the world, but later hopes to fulfill her passion for seeing justice done and for helping others. So, she prioritizes education, international experience, service, justice, and professional success in her values inventory.

Once you have an inventory to serve as a working foundation, you can establish meaningful goals. The next steps in a layered plan include establishing *long-term goals* rooted in your values that you wish to achieve years or even decades into the future and then forming intermediate and short-term goals that make it possible to reach the loftier objectives. In other words, you should work from the end goal back to the beginning, creating layers along the way that ultimately link aspirant accomplishments in the future with objectives for this week or this month. In such a layered goal plan, of course, the time scales may differ from person to person, and a proper set of long-term goals will vary across time. Some have a sense of what they want to achieve over the course of their entire lives, while others may be unsure what lies over the horizon beyond a few years. In the very least, you should develop an idea of what you would like to achieve after university study and then take some time to consider goals for the next ten years or so. Your long-term goals might include among others a specific career choice, a particular achievement, or the acquisition of a tangible good. At this point, you should feel free to be vague if you do not have a precise sense of the goal in mind. Moreover, your long-term goals need not conform to the same schedule; some may be realized earlier or later than others. In all instances, you should be able to articulate the link between your goals and your values and, in this way, distinguish goals that are especially meaningful to you from those that may be abstractly noble or worthwhile but that engender less personal motivation. Returning to the example of Colette:

> Colette sets her long-term sights on making a meaningful impact on human rights policy, which conforms to her interests in social justice and service. Her mentors advise her that there are a number of ways to go about accomplishing this broad goal. After some consideration, Colette elects to pursue a course of study leading to expertise in human rights law, which will in turn form the basis of a future career in law, politics, or in foreign service. This pathway, she determines, allows her to work toward a high-profile professional career while holding possibilities for living abroad or otherwise working regularly with people from other cultures.

Colette expresses an interest in some broad ambitions but matches them with concrete long-term objectives that conform to her values. Nothing is set in stone at this point in her university career, but she has nonetheless built a framework for shaping the other layers of her goal plan. Like Colette, you can utilize your slate of long-term goals by considering the sorts of tasks you must complete in order to realize them:

- Do you need to complete an undergraduate degree, and will you also require a graduate or professional degree?
- Do you require special skills and/or particular certifications?
- Are there certain kinds of experience needed for your goals?

- Are there known challenges that you must overcome in order to succeed?
- What sorts of individuals might serve as good mentors?

Answering questions like these will enable you to form the *intermediate goals* that comprise the next layer of your plan. Intermediate goals can include completing a university degree, mastering a foreign language, studying abroad in a foreign country, completing an internship, writing a thesis or dissertation, or earning a leadership position in a student organization.

> Colette knows that in order to pursue a career in law, she will need a law degree, so her intermediate goals include finishing her BA degree and preparing for admission to a strong law program. At the undergraduate level, this will include writing an honors thesis to hone and showcase her writing and research skills. Her interests in foreign travel tell her that she will need foreign language training and experience with intercultural environments. Studying at least one foreign language and participating in a study abroad program will thus be important goals. Finally, in order to explore her interests in law, policy, and human rights further, Colette will need to become involved in student government and with volunteer or advocacy opportunities.

The final layer of the goal planning process entails *short-term goals*, including those that you wish to accomplish within the next term or the next academic year. As before, setting short-term goals entails consideration for meeting the requirements of your intermediate goals. These can include decisions about courses and extracurricular activities. The advantage to thinking about your immediate goals in this way is that it can provide an important perspective on what you are doing right now. It can, for instance, help you bear in mind how a specific course fits into your overall curriculum. That way, you can see the course as important to your long-term goals instead of viewing it as something that you have to "get through" and that can help raise your level of engagement and performance in the course.

In the process of articulating your goals, it is usually wise to consult with university counselors, advisers, or faculty mentors. In fact, identifying and working with mentors should be one of your short-term objectives. Mentors, especially those who understand how universities work or who have achieved some of the goals to which you aspire, can help you understand your options, articulate your goals more clearly, and make the right connections among the layers of your plan.

In our example, imagine that first-year student Colette visits her faculty mentor in her university's history program:

> After consulting with her mentor, Colette understands that preparing for law school will entail cultivating strong research and writing skills,

and that she should participate in her university's pre-law program. She chooses to accomplish this by exploring a double major in two subjects that she enjoys: history and political science. Her mentor also advises on some opportunities for campus involvement. She ultimately volunteers with a local nonprofit that provides legal aid to migrants and begins attending meetings of her student government organization and a campus interest club in foreign relations. Finally, she decides to begin a course of study in Spanish and gathers information on a scholarship program for a potential study-abroad trip to South America in the next two years.

Notice that each layer of Colette's goal plan includes objectives that are more specific than the last. It is perfectly acceptable to have long-term goals that are somewhat vague, but in order to achieve them, you need to be able to articulate clearly the steps that you will need to take to reach them. This is a process that management specialists refer to as **operationalization.** When your goals are operationalized, they are reframed using sets of concrete actions that can be achieved in specific periods of time. In this case, Colette seeks to promote human rights, but in order to do this, she needs to understand human rights policy and the mechanisms of change, and she needs to find venues in which she can make an impact. Her intermediate and short-term planning thus entail operationalized goals by specifying activities that as a whole put her on a path to making the meaningful contribution she ultimately seeks. In these two layers, each of Colette's choices gives her valuable training and experience on the way to her long-term plans, and they also allow her to explore her options and make sure that she is on the track that is right for her. Moreover, since many of the opportunities that Colette is interested in pursuing require some planning (such as running for an office in the student government or applying for a study abroad program), she is taking important steps to being ready to seize on these opportunities when the time is right.

DISCOVERY EXERCISE

Create your own layered goal plan by following these steps:

1   Develop your own values inventory by making a ranked list of a minimum of three to five values that are important to you. Explain your reasons for your choices and why you rank them as you do.

2   Write down a list of long-term goals and write a brief statement about how they stem from your values and when you would like to achieve them. If possible, focus on long-term aspirations for the next five to ten years.

3   Choose up to three of your long-term goals and state the
    intermediate goals that will help you realize these deeper
    ambitions. Choose intermediate goals that you can meet within
    five years. For each intermediate goal, explain how it helps you
    meet one or more long-term goals.

4   Create a list of short-term goals for the next six to twelve months
    and explain how they support your intermediate goals.

Designing a Research Project

Historical research may be defined as *a process of identifying, analyzing, evaluating, and synthesizing information from and about the past in order to answer historical questions and resolve historiographical problems.* Research lies at the heart of what historians do. As we have discussed, everyone is connected in some way to the knowledge of the past. We all "swim" in the "seas" of history. Professional historians are unique in that they seek to work within a disciplinary framework committed to the systematic interpretation of history. In other words, historians are not simply about promoting preservation of the past; they are tasked with producing new knowledge about history. And their principal method is through the practice of ethical and methodologically sound research.

As it happens, research is also a very useful way for students to learn about history, in part because proper research requires the very skills that we have learned thus far. Research generates interpretations about history that depend upon critical and historical thinking skills, while the process of making those interpretations—identifying a research question, finding and utilizing information, and writing results—is built on the sort of task-oriented goal planning that students should practice every day. As in the case of our layered goal planning examples, the research process entails long-term, intermediate, and short-term objectives that must be balanced and managed within a finite amount of time. The choice of research topic and approach, meanwhile, often entails consideration of the researcher's motives and values. In short, you must practice focused thinking and careful planning if you want to become a strong researcher.

The process that we will describe in this volume strives toward an important long-term goal: *to express an original discovery or interpretation about a historical topic that is broadly acceptable as both valid and meaningful among the members of the historical discipline.* By achieving this goal, a research project aims to participate in the work of the discipline to advance our understanding of the past. In this section, we will briefly describe the steps that lead to a successful outcome, and then in later chapters, we will explain the components of the process in greater depth.

In general, the steps in the process unfold in a way that mirrors the process of constructing critical arguments that we discussed in Chapter 2. This is because completing a project represents a complex act of constructive critical thinking. Just as building an argument requires critical thinkers to identify an issue, the research process begins by articulating a question about a specific topic and then formulating a related research problem based on previous scholarship. Where constructive critical thinkers determine the sources and procedures needed to resolve an issue, so researchers locate sources and express methodological approaches. They then "assess the evidence" by reviewing the relevant primary literature. When reporting their results, they are inevitably attempting to persuade readers to accept their interpretations, so they are obliged to "structure an argument." Finally, they "evaluate" their arguments by presenting their work for peer review and soliciting feedback on how effectively their project has provided a resolution to the problem and an answer to the research question.

There are caveats to this sequence. Sometimes, the practical steps can be highly variable and depend on a number of factors, including the researcher's prior knowledge, the amount of preexisting scholarship on the topic, and access to primary sources. In other instances, certain steps may overlap or repeat themselves. But it is usually the case that the process occurs within three distinct phases, which we refer to as the *query, discovery*, and *presentation* phases:

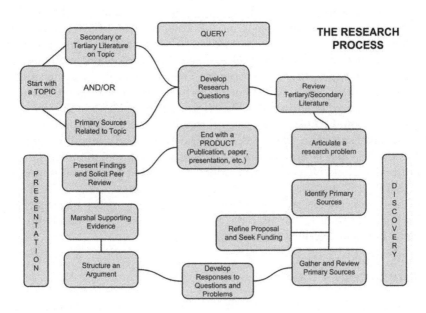

FIGURE 3.1 *Diagram of the research process.*

Selecting a Topic

The place to begin, of course, is with the selection of a topic. Topics in history typically include a place to be studied, such as a town or country; a period of time, which can stretch from a single day to a span of centuries; and something that takes place within that time and space. This may involve a single event, such as a conflict or an election; a longer term development, such as the transformation of a political system; a cultural or intellectual innovation, such as an idea or an artistic work; or a more general theme, such as the economy or social relations. For undergraduate students, the choice of topic often relates directly to a particular course or program. If you are writing a term paper for a class on China during the Qing dynasty, then your topic will likely fall within the geographical boundaries of the empire sometime after the mid-seventeenth century. When embarking upon a major thesis or graduate-level dissertation, however, you will likely have a great deal more freedom to determine the parameters of your own study. Indeed, graduate students tend to define their own aspirant research specialties as part of their application to graduate school, and they choose mentors whose work overlaps with their desired research area. Advanced undergraduates sometimes have the same option; indeed, it is usually compulsory for undergraduates studying history in the UK, provided they can locate a mentor in their institution capable of supervising the research in which they are interested.

The choice of topic should be one that you are willing to work with for several months or in some cases several years, so choose carefully. This means that your approach to a specific area of research, particularly when settling in for more than a year, might include consideration of your underlying values and motives for studying history. Curiosity about personal identity or family heritage may draw you to a specific place or time or theme. Or a particular experience—an encounter in a museum or in a meaningful book—can also lead students to rich historical topics. Sometimes the pathways can seem unorthodox. The historian Geoff Eley found his way to his field of modern German history through his daily experiences growing up in postwar Britain. He recalled, "World War II had been all around me as a child: British culture–political and intellectual, popular and polite–was suffused with its effects." But he added, "I couldn't help being impressed with the spectacular qualities of the recent German past, its lurid and violent momentousness," and when the time came to select a specialty for his graduate studies, "German history was easy. Big things had happened there. It was an excellent laboratory."[3]

The Query Phase

With a topic in mind, the next step is to determine what you wish to know about it. This will launch you on the process toward defining one or more **research questions** that will guide the rest of your work. Before you can say something new about a topic, you need to have a sense of what previous scholars have said about it. This is precisely what happens in the **query phase**, when researchers examine the preexisting body of scholarship in order to understand past and current interpretations; analyze the framing of past research questions; and assess previous approaches, methods, and sources used to answer them. The intermediate goal for the query phase is to create a synthesis of the historiographical literature, frame viable research questions, and articulate a clear research problem.

Remember that research is about gathering information to answer a question, so it is critical to state it clearly and to keep it firmly in mind throughout the process. It often takes time to refine and articulate a suitable question. You must first consider its scope, which refers to the size and complexity of the argument required to answer it satisfactorily. Questions that require highly complex answers can be too much to accomplish in a single project, while overly narrow questions may not make a significant contribution. It is, however, acceptable to begin the process with larger questions, particularly if you are new to the topic. A student of the First World War, for example, might simply begin by asking, "What were the causes of the conflict?" This, as the researcher quickly discovers, is an enormously complex question, but it makes a reasonable place to begin on the pathway to developing a more manageable research project. Attempting to find the answer to a larger question can be a good way to delve into the existing scholarship.

Entering into the scholarship can take one of two pathways. Sometimes, it makes sense to launch directly into an analysis of the **primary sources** related to the topic, which are those directly connected to the era, event, person, or place under study. For instance, an art history project investigating a particular artistic style might begin with an examination of representative works, or a music historian studying Mozart may want to become familiar with his symphonies and operas. Some graduate advisers even send their students into archives to get a feel for the sources before engaging the scholarship.

More commonly, however, researchers begin by studying the **secondary sources**, which are the accounts or representations of a subject by those who did not live during the time period or directly experience the events related to the topic. Secondary sources are indispensable to any type of scholarship, because they provide a wealth of information beyond what is possible for a single historian and because they help guide the creation of new historical questions. Defining a research question through engagement with the secondary literature is the only way to ensure the originality of your research. You certainly do not want to reinvent the proverbial wheel and simply repeat what other historians have said. Moreover, it is the only way to be sure that your work relates to the discussion among other scholars about a topic and thus has meaning in the field. The idea is to be a part of the conversation about a historical topic or research question.

You want to contribute to the historiography by correcting the errors of past scholars, adding to their scholarship, or presenting a new perspective or new questions. To do this, you can take your broad initial questions and determine how well the literature answers them. In Chapters 4 and 5, we will show you how to find and assess historiographical sources on a given topic. For now, it will suffice to say that your mission is to review the literature in search of unanswered or inadequately explored questions, errors in the historiographical record, or alternative interpretations to existing discussions. In other words, you are looking for a place where the disciplinary community's knowledge about a topic is incomplete.

A review of the scholarship should help you focus and sometimes narrow your research questions, and it should always lead to one or more **research problems**. As you progress through the literature, you can expect to find answers to your initial questions, but you may see places where you are not wholly satisfied. There may be gaps in the available information, uncertain or incorrect conclusions, new sources available or new methods of approaching older questions. These instances in which the secondary literature is incomplete constitute a problem that your project may aim to solve. In other words, your work will contribute by changing or adding to existing writing on a topic and thereby building our collective understanding of the topic. In this way, your research questions will become more focused and will better guide your project, while the research problem you address will lend value to your finished project.

The Discovery Phase

The **discovery phase** is so-named because it entails the portion of your project in which you are doing something new. Either you are looking at new sources or you are looking at known sources in a new way or with fresh questions in mind. In any case, you will craft an interpretation that involves "discovering" something previously unknown. Normally, historians enter this phase by determining the feasibility of their approach to the research questions. Here they must determine how to answer the questions they have framed. What primary sources will they use? How well will they be able to access the sources? Are there special skills required, such as foreign language fluency or digital training? How much time is available to complete the project?

If you can answer these sorts of questions satisfactorily, then you are ready to draft a research proposal, in which you detail your topic, questions, and research problem, and then explain your prospective approach and sources. You will learn more about writing a proposal in Chapter 8. One of the most important reasons for preparing a research proposal is to solicit support for the project. Historians typically spend at least a portion of the discovery phase working in an archive finding and analyzing primary sources, and that often requires financial support and time to work. Proposals help explain your project to others, such as institutions and grant agencies that can provide that support.

During the discovery phase, it is critical to keep your principal research questions in mind to guide your analysis, but also to be open to letting the evidence lead you to your conclusions. Remember that your ultimate goal is to create scholarship that adheres to the truth, so it is perfectly appropriate to change your research questions and objectives in response to what you find. You should use your best critical and historical thinking skills along the way and be willing to stay engaged with the secondary sources as needed to help contextualize your work. Careful note-taking is also a must during this phase to ensure that you correctly and ethically use and acknowledge the sources in your work. We will discuss that further in Chapter 7.

The Presentation Phase

Once your primary, secondary, and tertiary sources have yielded answers to your research questions, your obligation as a historian is to share the results with your peers. This entails formulating your response to the research questions as a sound set of arguments, selecting a means of presentation, and finding a venue to present. Many undergraduates end their projects with a polished term paper, but it is also possible to find a place to present your findings by delivering a paper to a live audience or by designing a poster, slide show, or website. Traditionally, professional historians aim to publish their work as an article, a book chapter, or a **monograph**, which is a book dealing solely with the topic of their research. Government agencies also have a long tradition of commissioning historical work on their areas in the form of published reports.

In recent years, more historians have begun to disseminate their work through scholarly online publications in the form of websites and other digital content. New technologies and a concern about excessive commercialization of publicly funded research have led to the growth in the open access movement, the idea that the results of research should be available free of charge. This can be problematic in a discipline like history, where most research is published in the form of monographs and journal articles and publishers rely on revenue from books and journals to stay in business. An alternative some historians have explored is "open notebook" history, making research notes and drafts freely available online in real time as the research is being conducted. This is the equivalent of a scientist making her experiment results available, and it has the added benefit of soliciting feedback and ideas from those interested in the topic while the work is still taking shape.[4]

Publications and presentations are not meant to be ends in themselves. Rather, the objective is to share the work with interested peers in order to receive feedback and thereby bring your findings into the larger academic discussion. Indeed, historians usually present their work in multiple formats, first offering short presentations at specialized conferences or workshops where like-minded scholars gather. The audience can then listen to the argument and offer comments and questions that sharpen the project. Then the historian can look to publishing the project in a journal or through a book press aimed toward a selected audience of specialists. Depending on the complexity and level of interest of the project, the scholar may also wish to share the results with the broader public by publishing in mainstream journals or through larger trade presses. Usually, publishers send the submitted manuscripts through a peer-review process to assure its significance, validity, and originality. Publishers may reject manuscripts based on a review, or they may request specific revisions based on reviewer comments. Even after publication, works come under academic scrutiny, as academic journals often invite other scholars to review the finished work. This final review process, which usually appears as published book reviews, helps promote awareness of new titles and shape their reception within the disciplinary community. As a result of these processes, the work becomes available to assist other students and scholars who may wish to work on a similar topic.

As we explore these phases of research in greater depth in the next chapters, it is important to note that while they often unfold sequentially, there is often a great deal of back-and-forth and overlap among them. Researchers frequently find themselves reading secondary literature during the entire process, particularly as new scholarship appears. Feedback during a presentation or in a peer review may lead a historian back to the archives for fresh discovery. Every project unfolds differently, but knowing the differences between the distinctive phases can be useful in creating a goal plan and schedule for completing a project. It makes it easier to predict how long a project may take by breaking it down into its constituent tasks and by establishing deadlines as a way to stay focused and budget the available time. Moreover, knowing the steps can help you schedule research trips or apply for grants, which sometimes include a specified time frame for financial support.

History in Practice: Identifying a Research Topic

Below are descriptions of two sample topics that will serve as models of the research process described above. The first topic, drawn from the history of ancient Rome, is intended as a short example for undergraduate researchers. The second, from a more advanced book project relating to US history in the nineteenth century, is meant to showcase a complex project fitting for a graduate student or professional historian. Here the researchers describe why they chose their topics and how they articulated their initial research questions. As we enter into a more detailed discussion of the techniques associated with each step of the process, these sample projects will provide more concrete guidance illustrating the methods taught in this book.

Jack Wells, "Christianity and the Fall of Rome"

The inspiration for this sample project came to me when I realized how frequently undergraduate history students want to tackle big questions in their first research project, questions such as "Why did the North win the US Civil War?", "Why did Britain become the first nation to industrialize?", and "How did Hitler take power in Germany?" Questions like these tend to be massive in scope with enormous bibliographies. Although important and exciting, they are far too broad to be managed in a single semester. When I first started teaching, I tried to steer students to away from these topics, fearing the results would be frustrating for both me and the students. Yet I decided that it really was not my job to take the joy out of history. (My students might be surprised that I say that.) Instead, I try to help them turn the big questions into manageable projects. This can be done by getting them to focus on small topics related to the bigger issues. In particular, I put them to work evaluating small amounts of primary and secondary source evidence and synthesizing a reasonable conclusion from those small pieces of evidence. Projects like this may not contribute much new information to the discipline. But they will help the students grow as historians, because they will get experience in library research, source criticism, and interpretation of articles and monographs.

The big sample question I want to tackle is, "Why did the western Roman Empire collapse in the fifth century CE?" Wow. For historians of late antique and early medieval Europe, this might be the biggest question of all. In modern times, the debate got started in 1776 when Edward Gibbon published the first volume of *The Decline and Fall of the Roman Empire*. Nearly 250 years later, the discussion continues. And it sure is a great story. It has everything: war, love, betrayal, triumph, tragedy, God, and Attila the Hun.

How might we make this manageable? We might start by picking one and only one of the hundreds of suggested explanations for the western empire's collapse, doing a primary source review, and asking ourselves whether the explanation makes sense, that is, supported by the evidence. This is manageable, because it requires a review of neither all of the primary source evidence nor all of the modern bibliography, but it does give students an opportunity for them to get their eyes on the problems and exercise that critical and historical thinking that we discuss at such great length in this volume.

Since I like looking at the history of religion, let's start with secondary sources and go all the way back to Edward Gibbon. One of the suggestions that Gibbon made was that Christianity bore some responsibility for the empire's fall, and the suggestion has been surprisingly resilient, though few today give it the weight that Gibbon did. There's a lot that can be done with this topic. We could look at why Gibbon might be inclined to see Christianity as responsible for the end of the empire and put him into the intellectual context of the eighteenth century. We could take a single text, say Augustine's *City of God* (a very large single text, in this case), and decide whether Augustine's attitude toward the empire supports Gibbon's thesis. We could look at whether the Christian emphasis on the hereafter rather than the here and now undermined the Roman defense of the border or made the Romans more willing to accommodate their conquerors. But by approaching the subject in this way, we can tackle one small part of a much larger issue and learn a lot about how history is written and about how historians think.

Bruce Baker, "The Cotton Kings"

The Cotton Kings: Capitalism and Corruption in Turn-of-the-Century New York and New Orleans (2015) was meant to be a footnote: the story of the research project that resulted—several years later—in a book can be considered a cautionary tale to show the benefits of following the methodical approach to research outlined in this chapter. And yet, halting and shambolic as it was, the research process for *The Cotton Kings* does illustrate many of the key processes and also demonstrates that the final product is seldom final. It is often also the preparation for other research projects. *The Cotton Kings* is unusual, though hardly unique, within historical scholarship for another reason: it had more than one author, a practice that is common in most disciplines but not in history.

In autumn 2010, I was annotating a series of letters by a journalist that were later published as *The South at Work: Observations from 1904*. The writer, William Garrott Brown, spent two paragraphs describing the New Orleans Cotton Exchange and commented on a man named Brown, who had cornered the market for the first time in the history of cotton trading the year before, controlling the world's cotton supply for several weeks and doubling the price. I went looking for an article or book that identified "Brown" and discussed the details and significance of this event, but I could find nothing. In other words, the beginning of my query phase was an encounter with a primary source that led me to search for secondary sources. Finding no secondary sources, I began to seek out more primary sources in the form of contemporary newspaper articles, using online databases. Each scrap of information I found gave me new clues to guide my search, and before long, not only did I have more information about William Perry Brown (a topic for another time is the challenge of researching historical figures with very common names like "William Brown") and how he cornered the market in 1903, but I realized, hazily, that this was part of a larger process that unfolded over twenty-five years and involved the increasing dysfunction of cotton futures markets, competition between the cotton exchanges of New York and New Orleans, and eventually the first federal law regulating a financial derivative.

At this point, I realized that I had a potentially interesting topic that no one else had written about, but I also realized that I had little background in business history or the history of agricultural commodities. Fortunately, I had a friend who knew about both of those things, so I asked Barbara Hahn if she would like to collaborate on the project. This combining of skills and expertise is still not very common within history, partly because of the way we have to immerse ourselves so deeply in the primary and secondary sources around a particular topic, but when it works out, it can be a very rewarding way of doing history. Over the next couple of years, Barbara and I tracked down many additional sources, mostly by considering what individuals and groups would have been involved in the cotton futures trading we were interested in. A bit of looking around showed that William Perry Brown's papers were held by the Historic New Orleans Collection and were unprocessed, meaning no other historians had even looked at them since they had been donated to the archive decades earlier. Congress and various branches of the federal government, especially the Bureau of Corporations, did investigations and heard testimony about the problems with how cotton exchanges worked. And we read acres of newspaper articles, some of them detailed portraits of the individuals involved, but more of them dry accounts of the daily transactions of the cotton market. The writing process involved one of us doing an initial draft of a chapter or part of a chapter and then e-mailing it to the other (using the "track changes" feature); we bounced each chapter back and forth about twenty times. What finally came out was a book so thoroughly coauthored that there are few sentences either of us can claim was entirely our own work and untouched by the other.

APPLICATION EXERCISE

It is time to come up with a topic of your own. Think about the historical periods, places, events, and people that interest you and make a ranked list of the top 3–5 that you might wish to investigate further. Depending on the class, you may need to confine your topics to things that are related to the focus of the course. For each topic choice, use the sample above as a model to write a brief statement explaining why it interests you and how it relates to your broader interest in history as well as your personal values or academic goals. Then, discuss the projects with a faculty mentor and select the one that works best for you.

Notes

1   R. Dyson and K. Renk, "Freshman Adaptation to University Life: Depressive Symptoms, Stress, and Coping," *Journal of Clinical Psychology* 62, no. 10 (2006): 1231–44.

2   Ibid.

3   Geoff Eley, *A Crooked Line: From Cultural History to the History of Society* (Ann Arbor: The University of Michigan Press, 2005), 61.

4   The leading practitioner of "open notebook" history is Caleb W. McDaniel of Rice University, and a full discussion of the idea may be found on his website: https://wcm1.web.rice.edu/open-notebook-history.html.

Suggested Reading

Booth, Wayne C. et al., *The Craft of Research*. 4th ed. Chicago: University of Chicago Press, 2016.

4

Information Literacy and Research Strategies

What we will do in this chapter:

➢ **REFLECT** on the transformation of the information landscape in the twenty-first century.
➢ **DISCOVER** the information literacy skills that help you find sources in libraries and archives and define a research question.
➢ **APPLY** research query strategies to building an annotated bibliography.

Historical research happens in the library and the archive. It is in these spaces that historians pose questions and make discoveries. Together, libraries and archives comprise enormous storehouses of information, and navigating them successfully requires competency in **information literacy**. According to the American Library Association, information literacy encompasses the ability "to recognize when information is needed and have the ability to locate, evaluate, and use effectively the needed information."[1] Much like critical thinking, information literacy is a general skill often taught indirectly in a university curriculum but which is nonetheless indispensable to conducting research and studying history. Moreover, information literacy is critical beyond the classroom for navigating the dramatically increasing amounts of information that are shaping the contemporary labor force and global economy. Fortunately, even if few university courses set themselves exclusively to the task of teaching information literacy, the practice of research offers excellent training for mastering this essential skill. As we will learn in this chapter, however, the challenge lies with approaching information literacy as a lifelong learner and with adapting to the rapid changes underway within libraries and archives.

Libraries and Archives between Evolution and Revolution

Libraries are cornerstones of modernity, even if they are not uniquely modern. Certainly, the library as a storehouse of information has existed far longer than the modern era. Ancient Greece and Rome saw the Western world's first public libraries. The most famous was the Great Library in the city of Alexandria, capital of Ptolemaic Egypt. Founded in the fourth century BCE, the complex was part royally funded research institution and part library, but it was in every way intended for a political purpose: to magnify the royal dynasty by making the Ptolemies the supreme patrons of Greek culture. The Ptolemies gave famous Greek writers and scholars a handsome salary and lodging, along with access to the greatest collection of written works the world had ever seen, almost 500,000 scrolls, organized—for the first known time—alphabetically.[2] The imperial libraries of the Sui dynasty in China, meanwhile, preserved hundreds of thousands of volumes in the sixth and seventh centuries CE.[3] In medieval Europe, the growth of trade and the gradual consolidation of monarchical and Church power in Western Europe led rulers and bishops to maintain a variety of documents, including foreign correspondence, royal decrees, and taxation records. As Markus Friedrich has explained, in this period, "The act of archiving often anticipated actual archives."[4] Thus, long before archives and libraries served as vital resources for historians, they served to legitimize secular and ecclesiastical authority by preserving records of their legal frameworks, court decisions, official actions, and the ways in which they intervened in the lives of their subjects, whether through census information or certifications of births, marriages, and deaths.[5]

It was in the sixteenth century that libraries and archives began to proliferate as a network of permanent institutions. In these years, the technological breakthroughs in printing joined other hallmarks of Western modernity, including the emergence of capitalism as a prevailing economic ideology, the political consolidation and cultural integration of large nation-states, and the growing bureaucratic complexity of government ministries, in both producing and demanding unprecedented amounts of data. Such developments informed a turn toward rationalism in Western thought and facilitated the broadening of European power. Economic and political policies at home came to inform the lives of millions, while widening trade networks and imperialist ventures opened previously unknown parts of world and raised awareness of new peoples, cultures, and natural phenomena.

Even as they served to measure and inventory the expanding domains of European states, libraries and archives also played important roles as cultural institutions. They supported an emerging print culture that in turn fueled the humanistic pursuits of the European Renaissance. A number of educated Europeans began to accumulate books as part of broader collections of artifacts, natural specimens, and other curiosities. Together, the elements of these collections made a statement about the wealth and worldly status of the collector. While the books spoke to the status of individuals, libraries often became visible expressions of royal power.

Over the course of the eighteenth century, the growth of private and state collections provided a valuable resource for the scientific and philosophical inquiries of Enlightenment thinkers. In turn, Enlightenment thought transformed attitudes about libraries. Central to this change was the notion that it was possible to understand the world systematically, which led eighteenth-century intellectuals to impose a sense of order on their erstwhile loose collections of artifacts and books. At the same time, the changing geopolitical landscape demanded more functional libraries and archives. The massive scale of maintaining modern political states and cultural institutions demanded the systemization of memory. Standardization was a key principle of modern rationalization, and continuity was the bedrock of order for advanced polities. Knowledge regimes, meanwhile, were cumulative, and the success of scientific endeavors depended on preserving and organizing past discoveries. Organized library and archival collections consequently became instrumental in the creation of new disciplines in the natural sciences, social sciences, and humanities and formed the research "conversations" that offered platforms upon which scholars contributed new knowledge.

The systemization of knowledge in this period gave rise to modern classification schemes for library holdings. In older institutions like the Austrian National Library, books had been organized by their physical size rather than their content, and locating particular volumes depended on the knowledge of the librarian. By the nineteenth century, however, increasing literacy rates democratized reading, which in turn demanded more standardized classification schemes that could apply across institutions. In the United States, a number of potential classification schemes were set up in the last decades of the nineteenth century. The two most successful were the Dewey Decimal System, established in 1876, and the Library of Congress system, created in 1897. Such systems helped a growing network of public libraries to expand education and promote civic life across the United States even as research libraries continued to advance the interests of knowledge production in universities. In the United Kingdom, a mixed system prevails. Because they are often very old and have no equivalent institution to the Library of Congress, many British research libraries use a variety of idiosyncratic classification schemes, meaning that researchers must simply familiarize themselves with the system in place at any given library.

In recent decades, libraries on both sides of the Atlantic have undergone a new metamorphosis. Perhaps the most visible sign of these changes has been the decline of open stacks offering unfettered access to print holdings. In the summer of 2018, for example, visitors to the David W. Mullins

Library at the University of Arkansas were shocked to see that books had suddenly vanished. Patrons were greeted with row after row of empty shelves stretching across the upper flows, the skeletal remains of a once vast collection of books and journals.

But this was no mystery. In the foregoing months, the library team had warned of the impending changes and assured faculty and students that the books were safe and sound and on their way to a new annex off-campus, where they would be available for off-site retrieval. As for the Mullins library building, the removal of the collection coincided with remodeling plans that would soon offer new technologies and information resources to serve researchers as never before. In this way, the library was merely the latest to join a worldwide series of innovations, paving the way for the research of the twenty-first century.[6] The library was dead. Long live the library.

The scope of such changes places libraries and archives once again at the forefront of a modern revolution. It is incredibly far-reaching and informs not only the ways in which we learn but also how we work, form relationships, govern ourselves, and carry out our daily lives. Yet it is also surprisingly subtle. This is no political revolution or military coup. There are no street protests or barricades, and no anthems herald the dawning of a new era. Like the halls of an empty library, it is a silent transformation unfolding in virtual space. It is first and foremost a revolution of technology, communication, and information.

FIGURE 4.1 *Off-site storage site for print materials at the University of Arkansas. Courtesy of the University of Arkansas Libraries.*

Historians, of course, know better than to try and make sweeping pronouncements about trends unfolding in the present. Our "owl of Minerva" is best set to the skies at dusk, and we tend see anything less than the 20/20 clarity of hindsight as myopic. Yet it is hard to deny that the technological advancements of the last few decades have brought about dramatic changes. Although we may need a few more decades before we can hazard interpretations about the causes, scope, and direction of these developments, they are already palpable enough for some contemporary commentators to begin applying labels. The economist Erik Brynjolfsson and engineer Andrew McAfee have declared that we are living in the "Second Machine Age" ushered in by the advent of new information technologies. As they explain, "Computers and other digital advances are doing for mental power–the ability to use our brains to understand and shape our environments–what the steam engine and its descendants did for muscle power."[7] Klaus Schwab, the founder of the World Economic Forum, has gone a step further and announced the arrival of the "Fourth Industrial Revolution." According to Schwab, steam engines and assembly lines shaped the first two revolutions, while computer technology, robotics, and the internet had already brought about a third revolution in the late twentieth century. Now, he argues, advances in artificial intelligence, the "Internet of things," and biotechnology have enabled a new realm of manufacturing innovations and global connectivity.[8]

At the heart of these developments are innovations in information processing. Computers have become faster, smaller, cheaper, and more versatile. Improvements in connectivity infrastructure now allow computers all over the world to share information. Taken together, these advances have made information available more quickly, more widely, and in much greater volume than has ever before been possible. As early as the 1970s, the sociologist Daniel Bell and the economist Fritz Machlup independently identified the ways in which the data processed and transmitted by a new computing infrastructure were fashioning a "postindustrial" economy that hinged on an "information labor" sector.[9] Years before the widespread adoption of personal computing, and a full decade before the public availability of the commercial internet, a number of observers were already assessing the economic, social, and cultural impacts of computer technology as the event horizon of a new "Information Age" that they predicted would offer both unprecedented opportunities and daunting new challenges.[10] Interest in the concept of the Information Age and its corollary, the information society, has since grown, with new advances in computing leading to synonymous notions of a "Digital Age" in the twenty-first century.[11]

Not everyone agrees on either the description or the promise of the Information Age. One early critic, the historian Theodore Roszak, argued that the prophets of information were peddling a dangerous conflation of information and thought.[12] More recently, skeptics like Frank Webster have questioned the ways in which we assess the trappings of the Information

Age and whether such an idea represents a true historical rupture or if its technological novelties obscure long-standing continuities.[13] They have also raised doubts about its outcomes, expressing concerns that an emphasis on the virtues of a so-called information society may unduly stress the quantity of data at the expense of quality. Roszak, in particular, lamented the collapsing boundaries among "data" and "information" on the one hand, and "knowledge," "experience," and "wisdom," on the other.[14]

These fears of a paradoxical decline of knowledge in a purported Information Age have informed responses to the empty shelves of the modern library. For some scholars, the trends toward a more virtual library experience threaten to exacerbate the eroding distinctions among different types of information. Years ago, information theorists predicted that increasing shares of available knowledge would be stored and made available on the internet over time.[15] Not only has this theory largely proved true in the twenty-first century but it has also given rise to a sort of **digital positivism**, which refers to the belief that digital information is superior to information delivered through other means. For many scholars, the shift leads to anxieties about print books locked away unread, library terminals gushing undifferentiated flows of information, and students left to discern good scholarship from a morass of unchecked facts, ranting blogs, and cat videos. As the historian Antony Grafton explained in response to the transformation of the New York Public Library in 2012, "My stomach hurts when I think about NYPL, the first great library I ever worked in, turned into a vast Internet cafe where people can read the same Google Books, body parts and all, that they could access at home or Starbucks."[16]

Librarians often respond to faculty worries with assurances that they have not ceded their role in preserving meaningful knowledge. Indeed, libraries have the potential to become critical institutions in a recent turn toward a "knowledge society," which scholars have posited as both a logical outcome of the Information Age and an alternative to its worst excesses. Although it currently exists as an aspirational concept, the knowledge society is generally one that favors a particular type of information with a shared sense of meaning among the members of society. Knowledge in this sense is distinct in part because it derives from a specific intellectual or cultural milieu and carries the possibility of action within that milieu. It stands apart both from disaggregated data flowing freely through cyberspace and from information that serves in economic terms purely as a commodity. As one group of scholars explains, "In general terms, knowledge is different from information in that it requires frameworks and commonplaces or resources to create it as well as the cultural and intellectual interpretation to analyze it and put the data to use."[17]

From this perspective, librarians and archivists play central roles in preserving the boundaries between information and meaningful knowledge. They curate and promote existing bodies of knowledge while also providing the resources and the institutional frameworks required for producing new knowledge. In this way, their work is indispensable to the historians who sort through the mountains of available information to create new knowledge as original and meaningful answers to important questions about the past. Yet, at the same time, the critics who raise objections to the direction of library practices are right to suggest that the changes underway pose serious challenges for students and researchers. The dynamism of the modern library, with its closer integration with technology and its growing capacity to handle a larger volume and greater diversity of sources, is a boon to historians, who may now ask a wider range of questions and enjoy fresh sources and perspectives with which to investigate them. But adapting to the new possibilities and new techniques requires a firm grounding in information literacy and a willingness to become lifelong students of information practices. The key is not to learn to work in libraries and archives as they are, but to develop strategies for adapting to what they are becoming.

REFLECTION EXERCISE

Schedule a tour or talk with a librarian in order to learn about the resources in your university library. What print and electronic resources are available? What primary source collections does your library possess? What services are available to acquire materials outside the library's collections? Following your visit, write a description of the ways that the new information landscape has affected your campus. In what ways do you believe that your specific research project will be impacted by the changing information landscape?

Information Literacy and the Query Phase of Research

The point of departure for the Query Phase of research is the search for information. With a topic in mind and research questions at the ready, a researcher now engages the existing body of knowledge in order to find pathways for new discoveries within the chosen topic area. The focus now shifts to the task of navigating the information landscape and acquiring the sources that are most relevant for the project. This is easier said than done. Most libraries in research universities have millions of volumes housed in several library facilities on a campus, on multiple floors in most library buildings, and in row after row of packed shelving. Much of the information may be available online, but even then, the researcher is confronted with millions of websites of varying quality buried within the expansive but hidden terrain of the internet. The key to navigating this maze is to go in with strong research questions, a general foreknowledge of the terrain, both virtual and physical, and a familiarity with fundamental search techniques.

Developing Research Questions

The good news is that libraries, for all of their vastness, are actually designed to make this process easier. But in order to avail themselves of the available services, researchers absolutely must first articulate a clear and viable research question in order to frame the search. Indeed, research questions are prerequisites for working on library or archival research, and they should mature over the course of the query. So before setting foot in the library, researchers must have firmly in mind at least one good question. But what constitutes a "good" research question for history?

As a general principle, historical research questions must facilitate critical thinking. In other words, a researcher seeking answers to a question must be able to answer the question by employing collected information into the critical thinking process that we discussed in Chapter 2. For this reason, David Hackett Fischer has explained that the act of posing historical questions can fall prey to logical fallacies. "Without questions of the right sort," he writes, "[historians'] empirical projects are consigned to failure before they are fairly begun."[18] Drawing upon a number of examples of historical scholarship, Fischer delineates a number of criteria that define logically sound research questions. Four of those are of particular interest for the work of student research.

First, historical research questions must be operational. This means that researchers should be able to answer the questions through empirical means. They cannot, among other things, expect to answer metaphysical questions, such as "what does it mean to be human?" or "Is war a permanent feature of world societies?" within the parameters of an empirical research project. This was a principle stressed by the early historicists, who argued that one must focus on particularities of history in order to muse on the grander lessons. It is worthwhile, of course, to reflect or even speculate on more abstract questions using historical evidence, but researchers must maintain a central focus on questions with answers deriving from tangible, observable sources from and about the past: texts, oral accounts, photographs, and so on.

Second, historical research questions must be feasible. They should, in other words, enable answers from sources that are **extant** (which means they are still around today), accessible, and comprehensible. If there are no sources available on a particular topic, then historians must suspend judgment until a researcher turns up evidence. Or if the available sources are not legible, then the inability to read or translate the text stymies the research. This was the case for ancient Egyptian hieroglyphics, for which there was no means of translation until the discovery of the Rosetta Stone in 1799 provided a text written in both hieroglyphics and the known language of ancient Greek. For students doing projects, questions that require texts in a foreign language can be prohibitive if the student does not have reading knowledge of the language. In a similar way, projects that require sources in overseas archives may be beyond a student's reach if no travel funding is available, and questions requiring a lengthy period of research may be difficult for students working on tight time schedules, as in the case of a term paper or undergraduate thesis.

Third, historical questions must be open-ended. This means that the conclusions are not predetermined but emerge through engagement with the evidence. Fischer suggests that some of the more unrecognized fallacies violating this principle are **semantic fallacies**, in which the goals of research are overly constrained by labels or categories. Fischer includes in this category the **fallacy of the dichotomous question**, in which questions are directed toward two outcomes that are "mutually exclusive and collectively exhausting." As an example, he provides a sample question: "Plato: Totalitarian or Democrat?"[19] To ask whether Plato is a "totalitarian" is to employ an **anachronism**, which is anything invoked out of its historical temporal context. Plato could never have been totalitarian, because the concept refers to dictatorships in the twentieth century. The question is also flawed because it creates a strict opposition between two terms (and thus is mutually exclusive) while leaving no room for nuance or alternatives, and thus it is "collectively exhausting."

Fourth, good questions must be explicit and precise. When completing a project, the conclusion, argument, or thesis that rests at the center is nothing more than the answer to the research question that you ultimately pose. Thus, the question should never be implied or forced to reside in the background. As you go through the research process, it is important to keep your questions firmly in mind so that they guide your journey into the sources and focus the argument that you build. For the same reason, the questions must be as clearly stated as possible. The caveat to this principle is that questions need not be inflexible. Indeed, as the process winds forward, it is highly likely that the question will evolve in accordance with the state of the secondary literature and later in response to the primary sources. They may in some cases become more focused, their parameters narrower, and their wording more precise.

Sample Projects: Points of Departure

Below are the preliminary questions for our two sample projects. In the first case, Jack Wells approached a very large topic and refined it into a more manageable and focused question. In the second project, Bruce Baker began with a small question and worked outward, connecting it with larger issues.

Jack Wells, "Christianity and the Fall of Rome"

I am starting my project with a big question, "What was the role of Christianity in the decline and collapse of the western Roman Empire?" Obviously, the larger is too large, so I have focused on Gibbon's interpretation and specifically want to examine it through a focused study of one Christian author from the fifth century CE. To that end, I have chosen to study Augustine's work, *The City of God*. Thus, my more operational question becomes, "What do Augustine's views on the Roman Empire as expressed in *The City of God* tell us about Sir Edward Gibbon's thesis on the role of Christianity in the decline of the western Roman Empire?" This question, I think, is sufficiently open-ended to allow more than a simple confirmation or rejection of the thesis, and it is narrow enough for me to complete a study within the space of one semester.

Bruce "Baker, The Cotton Kings"

During the initial primary research Barbara Hahn and I did into the history of the cotton trade in New York and New Orleans, we became interested in the activities of William P. Brown. Thus, our preliminary question would simply be, "How did William P. Brown corner the cotton futures market in 1903?" This was a focused question that we could answer by examining sources specifically related to Brown's dealings on the market. In this case, we started from a narrow perspective, and through the course of our research, we were able to broaden our study. As our research grew into a book project, our question became more sophisticated. At the end, we asked, "Why did the cotton futures market become dysfunctional by the 1890s, and how did various actors (cotton brokers, farmers, politicians), seek to address its problems in the context of Progressive Era reform?"

DISCOVERY EXERCISE

Describe your principal research questions and explain how they are (1) operational, (2) feasible, (3) open-ended, and (4) precise. At this point, your question need not be fully refined. What you want for now is a viable starting point.

Building a Bibliography

With research questions and priorities in mind, you are ready to search the library to find historical scholarship on your topic that addresses your questions. Your objective in this part of the Query Phase is to create a

bibliography, which is a formatted list of sources that you will consult for your project. This will include the secondary, tertiary, and primary sources that you directly cite in your research project and those that you read as part of the project. As your project progresses, your bibliography will likely grow as you encounter new sources and engage ongoing scholarship. For your initial bibliography, you want your library search to yield the most comprehensive and relevant scholarship possible. In other words, you want to find all of the most important sources that address your research question.

Bibliographies are formatted according to a specific citation style, and particular styles vary from discipline to discipline. For historians, the most common style is the so-called Chicago Style (also called *CMS*), which is prescribed in *The Chicago Manual of Style*, now in its seventeenth edition.[20] Students not wishing to heft a ponderous *CMS* volume around campus may also find the guidelines of the Chicago Style in the much more accessible volume, *A Manual for Writers of Research Papers, Theses, and Dissertations*, first written by Kate L. Turabian (1893–1987) and now in its ninth edition.[21] The *Turabian Guide* is a good investment for any history undergraduate student, since it contains detailed guidelines for the most common citations and bibliographies and also contains helpful research and writing tips. Advanced graduate students and professional historians tend to decorate their offices with the larger *Chicago* manual, which details *Chicago* citation style and contains guidelines for publishing. For those just passing through, libraries also often provide brief online guides for many *CMS* citations, along with other common citation styles such as those of the *MLA* (*Modern Language Association*) and *APA* (*American Psychological Association*).

Assembling the bibliography means a trip to the library, whether going into the physical building or merely beginning on the library webpage. Indeed, this is the first challenge, since there is no universal pathway for searching for materials. With a wide diversity of information resources, a dizzying number of volumes, and overlapping holdings of print and electronic media, libraries offer multiple points of entry and require library science specialists to help guide even seasoned researchers through the holdings.[22] At the same time, the researcher's level of readiness can be highly variable. At the outset of a new project, scholars may know relatively little about a topic and need a wide-ranging search; at other times, they know precisely what they need and require little assistance finding it. For these different research needs, libraries provide an array of tools to facilitate the process of identifying and locating sources.

Collections and Databases

The aggregate body of books, journals, media holdings, and other information items contained within a library it is known as its **collection**. Librarians work to preserve and enhance collections by curating existing items, seeking opportunities to add new resources, managing the use and circulation of the collection, and by facilitating patron searches. In at least one crucial respect, the mechanism libraries use to make the collection available has not fundamentally changed. Both the card catalogs of yesterday, which allowed patrons to flip through printed cards in stacks of drawers, and the search tools of today, which use computers and internet connectivity, rely upon **databases**. Databases are collections of data, usually called "records," that are organized to allow searchers to use multiple "identifiers" to locate a given record. The main differences between the catalogs of the past and the computerized systems of today are the extent of their search parameters and their relative speed and convenience. Older databases typically had very limited parameters, with card catalog searches often limited to such identifiers as the title of a work, the author's name, and the subject headings. Today, however, libraries and archives offer electronic databases that allow researchers to narrow results by title, name, and subject, but also, among many others, by language, genre, type of source (e.g., books, articles, etc.), date, and keyword. Moreover, the search can in many cases extend beyond the title page to include **in-text searching**, which converts every word in the text into an identifier. And while older searches required a human being to flip through the available records, modern search engines are able to return long lists of focused results within mere fractions of a second. With an internet connection, a researcher can locate information in a library across town or across the world.

Modern research libraries maintain a variety of different types of databases. This includes the catalog database listing their own institutional holdings under such common identifiers as the title, author, subject heading, and the **call number** designating the item's location in the classification scheme (such as the Library of Congress System). Academic libraries also typically subscribe to a number of external databases provided by either outside vendors or nonprofit library cooperatives. These provide targeted searches across institutions for specific types of sources. They include sources that are in the researcher's institutions, but also sources found in libraries around the world. For example, the WorldCat database, offered by the Online Computer Library Center (OCLC), offers a large database of print and electronic media housed in over 70,000 libraries and archives around the world. Another popular database is JSTOR, which allows searches primarily of articles and reviews from thousands of academic journals in a number of disciplines. A number of for-profit companies offer similar access to a wide range of journals, newspapers, and periodicals, including *NewsBank*, and Ebsco information services, whose databases include Historical Abstracts, with search results that include brief abstracts available with many of the articles they index, including English-language summaries of articles in other languages. Others include databases from specific publishers, such as Cambridge Books Online and Oxford Online Resources. Finally, some databases provide access to primary sources, such as Adam Matthew Digital Services, which publish digital compilations of archival material for a variety of thematic areas such as war and conflict, politics, and globalization.

The resources available to a given academic library, along with its institutional research needs, will often dictate the size and scope of the collection and even the range of databases available to patrons, since no library can conceivably carry every information item. Instead, libraries cooperate to maximize their available resources. For instance, most academic libraries provide **interlibrary loan** services that allow patrons to request items from other libraries through their home institutions. Students and faculty can usually make interlibrary loan requests through their home institution's library webpage. Some items, such as journal articles, can be shared electronically, while some books can be delivered and used within a few days.

Library Searches

Faced with a bevy of databases providing access to a diverse and growing collection, researchers must be savvy about the techniques of a good search. Specifically, they must be able to make informed decisions about the scope of their search and the databases that are likely to return the best results. They must also define the proper parameters of a search using search terms, keywords, and delimiting techniques. Finally, searchers must manage the information they receive by searching within results and following up on their initial findings.

Libraries strive to make the process easier by offering different levels of searching. On their homepage, patrons often find a range of portals offering wide and narrow search possibilities. On most library pages, the broadest search is usually presented first. In Figure 4.2, drawn from the University of Arkansas' library homepage (https://libraries.uark.edu/), the first available portal is the "Quicksearch" tab.

This portal allows for so-called **federated searching** or meta-searching, which pools all the available databases to return a single set of results. In many ways, federated search options were a response to the user preferences for "Google-style," one-stop search options. They are especially useful for researchers who may not have much prior knowledge about their topic, but they can also be useful as shortcuts for very specific searches, allowing the patron to input the precise name of a source and thereby avoid several clicks into another database.[23]

The obvious drawback to a federated search is that it can return an enormous number of "hits," or records related to the search terms. The feature does include filters that allow users to narrow down the number of hits. In Figure 4.2, searches can be limited by type of sources, and searches can also be tied to specific publication dates, disciplines, language, or subject terms. Even so, the number of hits is likely to be quite large. If one is willing to accept the most relevant or the most recent results, federated searching can be a helpful

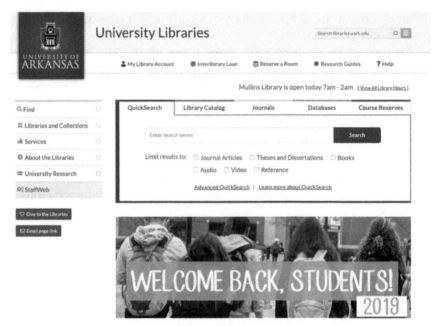

FIGURE 4.2 *The Library Homepage at the University of Arkansas. https://librar-ies.uark.edu/. Courtesy of the University of Arkansas Libraries.*

way of cutting through several databases quickly. In most other cases, however, a federated search will simply be too broad. Suppose, for instance, that you wished to launch a project on the history of climate change debates. If you attempted the "quick search" option on your library's website and simply typed in the words "climate change," you would in a matter of seconds be confronted with over six million "hits," or records of available sources, and even limiting the search to books in history published in English yields over 100,000 hits. For a topic of this size, a more nuanced approach may be in order.

Attempting a search for "climate change" as a **keyword** phrase in the adjacent library catalog portal produces around 3,500 hits that include a precise match for the keyword. This is far fewer than the federated search, but still daunting. Moreover, the results may not be immediately relevant, nor may they be comprehensive, since there are other keyword options and the search only includes materials in the library's collection. One alternative is to switch the search to **subject headings,** which are designated words that define a group of works. The Library of Congress Subject Headings is a common system that libraries use to classify their collection. Typing in the word "climate" as a subject heading returns over 500 matching subject headings, including "Climate and civilization—History," which yields three records. The subject heading search also suggests others, such as "Climatics," "Climate Changes," and "Global Warming."

Another technique is to use more focused types of search inputs. For example, when working in the databases, a researcher can use a **Boolean search**, which allows the searcher to narrow down a broad range of hits by including multiple search terms linked by "operators" such as "and," "or," and "not." A climate change search in this instance might be made more specific by searching for things like "climate change" and "history" and "policy," and finally a location, "United States." Boolean searches can help researchers wade through large sets of returns, but the more specific they are, the more they can lead the researcher to miss some important records. Another approach is to use a **truncated search**, also known as a stemmed search, which incorporates the root of a word with an asterisk "*" to allow a search algorithm to return hits for related terms. While this can naturally expand the number of hits, it can also provide new avenues of searching. In this case, instead of entering "climate" into a search portal, a search with "climat*" would return hits for related terms like "climatics," and "climatology."

Extrapolating from Initial Results

The best search features always omit something. The brave new world of digital information may be at hand, but for right now, no algorithm can precisely predict your research needs. Thus, there remains a need for some traditional gumshoe library work, and the best place to start is with your initial findings. As you work to collect the sources that you have painstakingly created for your bibliography, you should be on the lookout for new leads. As you acquire each book, make a note of the official Library of Congress Search Headings located both on the library catalog webpage and on the copyright page of the book. Many articles include keywords selected by the author or the editor. These search terms and keywords can, in turn, generate new lists of sources.

Another time-honored way of making your library research more comprehensive is simple browsing. Researchers seeking specific books in the stacks will often look at neighboring titles. Librarians point to evidence that questions the effectiveness of browsing the stacks, but many historians tell tales of unexpected finds.[24] For example, a scholar working on the history of human responses to climate change in the University of Arkansas library might use "climate" as an initial search term and easily find Wolfgang Behringer's *Culture and History* by doing a subject heading search and using the related subject heading "Climate–Civilization." However, a quick perusal of the books nearby reveals another interesting title, *The Cultural Landscape: Past, Present, and Future*, edited by Hilary H. Burks. Although this work is older, it nonetheless offers some new subject headings, including "Nature–Effect of Human Beings On," which leads to several dozen more historical works.

The removal of print books from many libraries does threaten some browsing activities, but many libraries have responded by making browsing available online. The University of Arkansas libraries use a "browse" button on each of their catalog entries. Each time you search for a specific work, you can use this feature to generate a "virtual shelf:" a list of icons showing adjacent works listed by call number. The advantage to this type of browsing is that the list includes both physical books available for circulation and electronic books that would otherwise not be visible to the searcher. In a similar way, browsing features on electronic academic journals allow readers to sift through the available articles in a given journal. And, finally, most libraries offer research guides for specific disciplines that allow researchers to browse the various journals, principal reference works, and most useful databases identified for a particular field of study.

The Reference Librarian and Other Human Resources

When is a good time to consult with a reference librarian during your research? The answer is simple: anytime! At any point during the process you have questions about library services, how to locate specific items, or how to use equipment in the library, you can either visit the staff on site or consult with them by phone or over the Web. Librarians likely do not know your specific subject area as well as a researcher, but they have a great deal of training with building and navigating a collection. Moreover, research libraries typically have subject specialists who may be able to offer general advice on ways to search for materials on a given subject. And, finally, libraries routinely offer training sessions on their services, from using online bibliographic managers to using databases to researching in their special collections. Even the most seasoned historian could not do his or her work without the assistance of a well-trained librarian.

Professional historians are also great resources. It is very likely that your professor, research supervisor, or another member of your university history faculty has some background knowledge related to your subject. Often they can assist you with identifying key works related to your topic as a starting point, and they can help you understand the main historiographical currents in your field. For long-term research projects, it may be wise to consult with an academic historian to get feedback on your initial research question, your first bibliography, and then later the way that you have articulated your research problem. Historical research, as you will recall, is a collaborative process, and this is a good opportunity to involve scholars in your research and along the way to find mentors who can help you not only with the project but with other aspects of your historical studies.

Finding Primary Sources in Libraries and Archives

Just as your initial research questions guide the development of a tertiary- and secondary-source bibliography, so too should they lead you to primary sources. Indeed, your bibliography is not complete until it includes primary and secondary material. As you may recall, primary sources are those that stem from and relate directly to the events, trends, or time periods under study. Diplomatic cables, court decisions, personal correspondence, or a private diary can all be primary sources, as can later accounts such as memoirs or oral interviews with participants in historical events. There is an incredibly wide variety of possible primary source information, and these sources are absolutely indispensable to original and empirically sound historical research.

A number of primary sources are available in libraries. Most are publications shelved in the regular stacks and can include correspondence, diaries, government records, published fiction, memoirs, map collections, and media resources, among many others. In some cases, historians may find all of their sources in the library. This is particularly the case for premodern specialists. As Marcus Bull has explained for medieval history, only a small percentage of all sources produced in the European Middle Ages is extant today, and "the written sources that have survived are by no means a random or fully representative sample of what once existed."[25] Over the years, historians have thoroughly researched and translated the extant texts and made them available in new print editions. This does not mean that there is no space for new research questions; it merely makes them more accessible for students and professionals. At the same time, many US research libraries serve as depositories for government records, and these are often available in noncirculating form. In these instances, the same techniques we learned for finding secondary sources in the library also apply to primary sources.

For other types of primary materials, a trip to the archive may be in order. Archives specialize in storing and curating original records for use by governments, institutions, organizations, and researchers. Some very large archives, like the US National Archives in Washington, D.C., or the National Archives of the United Kingdom in Kew, have a clearly defined role as a repository of public records, and their mission is oriented toward maximizing access. Other archives are smaller and may have a much more narrowly defined role. These include archives for specific institutions, such as museums, churches, or hospitals. University libraries fall into this category, as they usually maintain a "special collections" department containing the library's rare books and manuscripts, along with university records and donated collections. Finally, archives are both a physical space and the product of the act of collecting and preserving. Thus, an archive can even include a collection of photos and letters held by families or individuals.

What makes formal archives so special—beyond their larger size and accessibility—is the work of the professional archivists who staff them. Archivists are critical partners of many researchers because they have specific training in the care and maintenance of records, and in cataloguing and managing the custody of materials. This means that they help historians find and use resources, but their work also helps validate the provenance and chain of custody of primary materials. For this reason, it is wise before researching in the archive to contact the archivist and explain briefly the nature of your research, which materials you are interested in accessing, and when you would like to begin your work. Archival items are almost always noncirculating; you must view them in the archive during business hours, so notifying the archivist in advance will make your visit more productive. Archivists will be able to tell you whether items are accessible, and they can prepare them for you in advance of your visit. Since archivists work so closely with their materials, they can also answer questions about the collection and may also be able to suggest other possible sources related to your project.

Although archivists work in accordance with a common set of professional standards, the diversity of archives, both in terms of the repository and the types of materials stored there, means that there are often differences in the ways researchers search for and access resources. For instance, not all archives offer digital databases, and others use different types of classification systems for their collections. For this reason, researchers often locate materials through the use of **finding aids**. Finding aids typically provide a detailed overview of the location of the source in the archive, and they may also have a summary of the item and instructions related to its use. A typical finding aid may include a catalog number similar to a call number, and it will identify the collection in which the source is located. To help locate a source within a collection, a finding aid may also indicate a more specific location, such as the series to which the source belongs. Series refer to specific types of sources. When organizing a collection, archivists sometimes find it easier to place photographs with photographs and correspondence with correspondence, and then within each series to organize items alphabetically or chronologically. Thus, finding aids listing series will then show an identifier for finding the source within the series. These sorts of directions help the archivist locate items within the archive and pull them for review, but they also can help you as the researcher cite the source properly, so it is important to make a note of these indicators for each source. Besides revealing location, finding aids will often provide an abstract or overview of a source, which can be helpful in identifying which sources you wish to review, and they will give guidance on how the source may be used. For example, if there are restrictions on access to certain parts of a collection, that will be noted on the aid.

Increasing amounts of archival material are appearing online through digitization initiatives, and historians are increasingly recognizing the value of carefully vetted digital resources.[26] The United States Holocaust Museum and Memorial in Washington, D.C. (https://collections.ushmm.org/), is just one of a number of large institutions offering public access to their holdings as part of their educational mission. Other projects include collaborative initiatives aimed at offering widespread access to the pooled resources of multiple archives. A key example of a nonprofit collaboration is the Internet Archive (https://archive.org/), which was founded in 1996. The Internet Archive uses crowdsourcing, in which an army of online volunteers grow and develop the collection. Its initial focus was on books, but it has since grown to feature millions of digital items, including a large collection of archived websites. Still other digital archives exist as for-profit commercial ventures. Library vendors like Adam Matthew Digital (https://www.amdigital.co.uk/) sell collections of online materials in thematic packages. And, of course, popular websites like Ancestry.com (https://www.ancestry.com/) sell memberships that connect members to archival materials related to genealogical research. These sorts of initiatives have grown dramatically in the last two decades, though it is still the case that most professional historians should expect to do at least some of their research getting their hands dirty (though maybe under the protection of white gloves) inside a physical archive.

Annotating Your Bibliography

Undergraduates often ask their professors or research mentors what the right number of sources is for a given project. Sometimes instructors dictate a certain number of specific types of sources, or they specify a rule of thumb, such as one source per page of text. Such prescriptive approaches might be right for a secondary-school assignment, where the idea is to demonstrate familiarity with proper citations, but for professional historians, and even for a proper university research project, they are at odds with the goals of answering as fully as possible a research question and resolving a research problem. In these instances, the answer to the "how many sources?" question usually has a very simple answer: all of them! In other words, there is no predetermined limit to the size of a bibliography; rather, the bibliography is determined by the question and by the available sources. Of course, very few projects actually manage to mobilize every conceivable source. Some may be unavailable to the researcher, some may be in an inaccessible language, and still others may simply elude a diligent search. In practice, researchers should build a bibliography that allows them to review the most relevant available sources. A complete bibliography is much more feasible for a historian with institutional funding and years to work, but even undergraduates should strive for the most comprehensive bibliography possible. This makes it imperative to define a manageable research question with tightly defined parameters that permit a reasonably sized bibliography for the allotted time. The structure of the project should thus make it possible to favor the quality of the bibliography over the quantity of sources.

One way to demonstrate the quality of your bibliography is by annotating your sources. An annotated bibliography includes both the source citation and an annotation, or brief description of the source. Annotations enhance bibliographies by providing more details about the sources and by highlighting their connection to the project at hand. Annotations usually consist of no more than 100–200 words addressing the overarching topic, approach, and arguments of a given text. The annotation can also say a word about the author, including their intellectual background and the ways in which their larger body of work relates to the cited text. When you first construct a bibliography, your annotations may be limited to what you can learn about a source from a quick glance, an abstract, or a review. As your research progresses, you can add more detail, incorporating an overview of your evaluation of a particular source and an explanation of how it connects to the historiographic threads you are charting for your project (we will discuss synthesizing and placing sources in Chapter 5). As you move into the primary materials, the annotations can provide descriptions of the type and contents of the source and its importance to the project. While primary source texts such as books or diaries would likely merit a single annotation, it is possible to bundle series of related sources such as correspondence or government records and annotate the lot. With all of your sources, you may wish for your annotation to specify why you selected them for your project.

Your annotated bibliography may seem to be an early step in your research project, but it is nonetheless an important achievement. A high-quality bibliography stands as tangible proof of your training and experience in information literacy. If done properly, the citations show that you are able to identify tertiary, secondary, and primary sources relevant to a specific research topic. The annotations, meanwhile, indicate your ability to assess, evaluate, and synthesize the information. They can also point the way forward for the rest of your project. In Chapter 5, we will learn how to organize and assess your sources, a task for which your bibliography will be indispensable.

History in Practice: Creating Annotated Bibliographies

In the sample below, Bruce Baker has excerpted part of his initial bibliography, which is divided into primary and secondary source sections. At this stage in your research, you may not have had a chance to review the items in your bibliography, so your annotations will not be as detailed, but this example provides a look at a finished annotated bibliography.

Bruce Baker, "The Cotton Kings"

Primary Sources
William P. Brown Papers, Historic New Orleans Collection

> Brown was the cotton broker who successfully cornered the market in 1903. His papers at the Historic New Orleans Collection had never been used. While there was very little in the way of correspondence or detailed

business records covering the day-to-day operations of his brokerage, there were some very useful materials about the evolution of his understanding of crop predictions (crucial for understanding the market) and also extensive scrapbooks of newspaper clippings and ephemera.

RG21: Records of the District Courts of the United States. National Archives and Records Administration, New York.

In 1910, Brown and others again cornered the market, but in this case they were prosecuted in federal court for violating the Sherman Antitrust Act. The records of the US District Court for the Southern District of New York included the trial records, including the grand jury testimony, which provided great detail on the events around the 1910 corner.

Report of the Commissioner of Corporations on Cotton Exchanges, Part I. Washington: Government Printing Office, 1908.

After particularly egregious actions by the New York Cotton Exchange in 1906, the federal government's Commissioner of Corporations did an investigation into the operations of cotton exchanges, focusing on New York and New Orleans. It took testimony from many of the people most knowledgeable about the trade, and it resulted in a five-part report, published over two years, that exposed in detail many of the corrupt practices of the New York Cotton Exchange and how these problems affected farmers and manufacturers.

Secondary Sources

Beckert, Sven. *Empire of Cotton: A Global History* (New York: Knopf, 2014).

This is a vast, global history of cotton in the past several hundred years, making the broad argument that cotton production was significant in India until British involvement crushed Indian industry and instead started the Industrial Revolution in Britain and later other parts of Europe. The cotton that supplied this expanded production came from bound labor, especially enslaved labor in the American South until the Civil War. The study does not focus much on the processes of marketing cotton and on the cotton futures trade.

Hochfelder, David. "'Where the Common People Should Speculate': The Ticker, Bucket Shops, and the Origins of Popular Participation in Financial Markets, 1880–1920." *Journal of American History* 93, no. 2 (Sep. 2006): 335–358.

This article examines the role of information in financial markets around the turn of the twentieth century and the regulation of markets by studying public reactions to "bucket shops" where stocks and commodities were not actually traded, but individuals unconnected to any formal exchange could make what amounted to bets based on price information coming from actual markets.

Levy, Jonathan Ira. "Contemplating Delivery: Futures Trading and the Problem of Commodity Exchange in the United States, 1875–1905," *American Historical Review* 111, no. 2 (Apr. 2006): 307–335.

Levy's article uses controversies over futures trading at the end of the nineteenth century as part of a larger project to understand attitudes towards and financial mechanisms for dealing with risk. It does address some key issues about how futures trading worked, but its main interest is in the effects of futures trading on more abstract ideas about the economy.

Woodman, Harold D. *King Cotton and His Retainers: Financing and Marketing the Cotton Crop of the South, 1800–1925* (1968; Columbia: University of South Carolina Press, 1990).

This is the most comprehensive study of the financial infrastructure and marketing of cotton in the nineteenth and early twentieth century. It discusses at length the relationship between planters and factories in port cities in the antebellum period and the breakdown of this system after the Civil War and its replacement with a system of brokerage. It has very little to say about futures trading, however.

APPLICATION EXERCISE

Start building your bibliography! Concentrate on secondary sources, but if you know of some primary materials, go ahead and add them to the list. For each source, write a brief annotation explaining how the source connects to your initial research question. As you continue your work, you can expect your bibliography to grow and evolve. What you want to produce now is a list of sources that will be sure to help you get started.

Notes

1   American Library Association, "Presidential Committee on Information Literacy: Final Report," July 24, 2006, accessed September 15, 2018, http://www.ala.org/acrl/publications/whitepapers/presidential.

2   Lionel Casson, *Libraries in the Ancient World* (New Haven: Yale University Press, 2001), 31–47.

3   Sharon Chien Lin, *Libraries and Librarianship in China* (Westport, CT: Greenwood Press, 1998), 3.

4   Markus Friedrich, *The Birth of the Archive: A History of Knowledge*, translated by John Noël Dillon (Ann Arbor: University of Michigan Press, 2018), 32.

5   Ibid., 30–58.

6   Kim Leeder and Eric Frierson, eds., *Planning Our Future Libraries: Blueprints for 2030* (Chicago: American Library Association, 2014); Lauren Cohen, ed., *Library 2.0 Initiatives in Academic Libraries* (Chicago: Association of College and Research Libraries, 2007); David R. Moore, II and Eric C. Shoaf, *Planning Optimal Library Spaces: Principles, Processes, and Practices* (Lanham, MD: Rowman and Littlefield, 2018).

7   Erik Brynjolfsson and Andrew McAfee, *The Second Machine Age: Work, Progress, and Prosperity in a Time of Brilliant Technologies* (New York: Norton, 2014), 7–8.

8   Klaus Schwab, *The Fourth Industrial Revolution* (Geneva: World Economic Forum, 2016).

9   Daniel Bell, *The Coming of the Post-Industrial Society* (New York: Basic, 1973), 212; Bell, "The Social Framework of the Information Society," in *The Microelectronics Revolution*, edited by Tom Forester (Cambridge, MA: MIT Press, 1981): 500–49; Fritz Machlup, *The Production and Distribution of Knowledge in the United States* (Princeton: Princeton University Press, 1962).

10 Donald P. Hammer, ed., *The Information Age: Its Development, Its Impact* (Metuchen, NJ: Scarecrow Press, 1976); Wilson P. Dizard, *The Coming Information Age: An Overview of Technology, Economics, and Politics* (New York: Longman, 1982).

11 Eric Schmidt and Jared Cohen, *The New Digital Age: Transforming Nations, Businesses, and Our Lives* (New York: Vintage, 2013).

12 Theodore Roszak, *The Cult of Information: The Folklore of Computers and the True Art of Thinking* (New York: Pantheon, 1986).

13 Frank Webster, "What Information Society?" *The Information Society* 10, no. 1 (2010): 1–23.

14 Roszak, *Cult of Information: A Neo-Luddite Treatise on High Tech, Artificial Intelligence, and the True Art of Thinking* (Berkeley: University of California Press, 1986), *xix*.

15 Roy Rosenzweig, *Clio Wired: The Future of the Past in the Digital Age* (New York: Columbia University Press, 2011), 31.

16 Quoted in Jennifer Howard, "Debate at N.Y. Public Library Raises Question: Can Off-Site Storage Work for Researchers?" *Chronicle of Higher Education* (April 22, 2012). https://www.chronicle.com/article/Debate-at-NY-Public-Library-/131615, accessed October 10, 2018.

17 Bridgett Wessels, Rachel L. Finn, Kush Wadhwa, Thordis Sveinsdottir, Lorenzo Bigagli, Stefano Nativi, and Merel Noorman, *Open Data and the Knowledge Society* (Amsterdam: Amsterdam University Press, 2017), 24–43, 42.

18 David Hackett Fischer, *Historians' Fallacies: Toward a Logic of Historical Thought* (New York: Harper Perennial, 1970), 3–4.

19 Fischer, *Historians' Fallacies*, 10.

20 *The Chicago Manual of Style*, 17th ed. (Chicago: University of Chicago Press, 2017). See also "The Chicago Manual of Style Online," accessed January 10, 2019, https://www.chicagomanualofstyle.org/tools_citationguide/citation-guide-1.html.

21 Kate L. Turabian, *A Manual for Writers of Research Papers, Theses, and Dissertations: Chicago Style for Students and Researchers*, 9th ed. (Chicago: Chicago University Press, 2018).

22 April Grey and Rachel Isaac Menard, "Rethinking Service Models: Mobilizing Library Access for All Platforms," in *Cutting Edge Research for Developing the Library of the Future: New Paths for Building Future Services* (Lanham, MD: Rowman and Littlefield, 2015), 11–22.

23 Abe Korah and Erin Dorris Cassidy, "Students and Federated Searching: A Survey of Use and Satisfaction," *Reference and User Services Quarterly* 49, no. 4 (2010): 325–32.

24 Donald A. Barclay, "The Myth of Browsing," *American Libraries* 41, no. 6/7 (2010): 52–4.

25 Marcus Bull, *Thinking Medieval: An Introduction to the Study of the Middle Ages* (London: Palgrave Macmillan, 2005), 76.

26 Alexandra Chassanoff, "Historians and the Use of Primary Materials in the Digital Age," *American Archivist* 76, no. 2 (2013): 458–80.

Suggested Reading

Blouin, Francis X., Jr., and William G. Rosenberg. *Processing the Past: Contesting Authority in History and the Archives*. Oxford: Oxford University Press, 2012.

Mann, Thomas. *The Oxford Guide to Library Research*. 4th ed. Oxford: Oxford University Press, 2015.

Presnell, Jenny L. *The Information-Literate Historian: A Guide to Research for History Students*. 3rd ed. Oxford: Oxford University Press, 2018.

Rosenzweig, Roy, and Anthony Grafton. *Clio Wired: The Future of the Past in the Digital Age*. New York: Columbia University Press, 2011.

5

Approaching Historiography: Active Reading and Secondary Source Analysis

What we will do in this chapter:

➢ **REFLECT** on the differences between active and passive reading.
➢ **DISCOVER** the principles of active reading.
➢ **APPLY** active reading skills to analyzing and synthesizing secondary and tertiary sources.

Not all reading is the same. If you are like us, you read different things for different occasions. The books on your nightstand or in your beach bag are likely not the textbooks and monographs you read for your classes or for research. Your eclectic reading habits even demand multiple libraries. You might visit a university library for the heavy academic works and a local public library to find books for entertainment and escapism. But what makes bedtime or vacation reading so much different from research reading? It is not simply a matter of fiction versus nonfiction. Rare indeed are the hardy souls who consider Joyce or Tolstoy to be light reading. Nor is it a question of length. Two enormously popular "beachy" books, J.K. Rowling's *Harry Potter and the Deathly Hallows* and George R.R. Martin's *A Game of Thrones*, each stretch to around 800 pages. Ultimately, the real distinction is found in the complexity of a text and in the reader's level of mental engagement. "Beach reads," simply put, demand less brain power. They involve a fairly straightforward narrative or relatively simple exposition that allows the reader to take a more passive role. Indeed, this is precisely what makes light reading such a relaxing activity. It requires some mental energy, but usually just the right amount to keep the mind busy without feeling overburdened. Light reading facilitates an escape from the everyday and thus lends itself well to decompression after a long day or to a pleasant vacation experience.

Research reading, by contrast, requires **active reading**. Like the active learning we discussed in Chapter 2, active reading relies on a greater degree of metacognition to discern an author's intentions and respond to a sophisticated message. Rather than simply following the text in the moment, as you might do with bedtime reading, active reading is a more nuanced process that yields the fuller meaning of a more complex text. Reading may always be good for your mind, but active reading is central to the goal of becoming educated. As you will learn in this chapter, the same active reading skills that are indispensable for success in your university coursework are also required for working with the sources that you have collected for your research project.

Cultivating active reading skills should be a key objective of any university education. But be aware that it takes patience. You may find the process frustrating at first, since you have been reading almost all of your life and probably thought you were pretty good at it. In fact, you probably already possess strong reading skills, but the new challenge is to tackle a larger volume of more sophisticated texts. You may find it initially difficult to accommodate the slower pace that active reading requires. It is important to stick with it, however, because experience shows that even advanced university students often struggle with reading secondary scholarship. They tend to miss the proverbial forest for the trees, focusing on details and premises and missing the overarching arguments within texts. The bad news is that the only way to overcome this shortcoming is to practice. Start with short, simple texts like newspaper articles and Web blogs and then move up to longer periodicals. Collaborate with other students to check your comprehension and discuss your assessments. And use the strategies that we will discuss in this chapter. With time, not only will your understanding of texts improve but your experience will likely boost your efficiency as a reader and decrease the amount of time you need to work through a text. You will find yourself reading not only more effectively but more quickly. Above all, your active reading skills will help you become a more successful student and a much more effective researcher.

REFLECTION EXERCISE

Think about your past and present reading habits. How often do you read each day or each week? What sorts of reading do you most enjoy, and how frequently do you read these types of materials? What types of reading are less engaging or more challenging and why? Thinking back on your reading over the last three years, how would you say that your reading habits and abilities have changed, and how would you like to see them continue to improve?

Activate Your Reading!

Student success textbooks offer a number of mnemonic devices to promote active reading. There is the venerable **SQ3R Method,** which was first introduced in the 1940s by the psychologist Francis P. Robinson.[1] SQ3R involves *scanning* a text before reading, *questioning* it as you go, *reading* the text, *reciting*, or summarizing, the main points, and then *reviewing* your notes. Over fifty years later, Robinson's method is still popular in student success textbooks, but literacy specialists have made some improvements. More recent schemes include Nancy Bailey's **S-RUN-R Method,** which streamlines the process while making it more applicable to sophisticated texts. This approach calls for readers to *survey* the framework of a text, including its title, headers, and any graphs or images, then to *read* the text and *underline* the key points. Readers then return to the text for a round of *note-taking* and later to *review* their notes.[2]

When it comes to extracting and reviewing the information from a text after reading, there are also a number of approaches, but literacy scholars maintain that not all are created equal. Among the methods that they recommend most highly are *practice testing*, in which the reader creates questions to answer from memory at the end of a reading, and *distributed review*, which calls for short review intervals spread over time. Other respectable methods include *self-explanation*, in which the reader paraphrases the main points of a text in his or her own words and relates them to his or her own experience, and *elaborative interrogation*, or the conversion of factual information in a text into questions to answer later. Less effective approaches include simple *summarization*, which calls for the text to be boiled down to a short statement illustrating the main points, and *highlighting* or *underlining* a text without secondary review.[3]

Success guides usually encourage students to choose the reading method that they find most effective. The guides less frequently explain how the methods are essentially based on the same principles. *Specifically, these approaches work as active reading strategies because they all replicate the process of critical thinking.* Indeed, if you think about active reading as a critical thinking exercise, then the principles behind the individual techniques will make more sense. Connecting active reading to critical thinking will allow you to work beyond the simple mnemonic schemes to understand not only the content of individual texts but also the ways in which multiple texts fit together and the ways in which we can apply historical thinking to primary sources. In this way, you can raise your metacognition to the next level and understand the reasons why reading strategies work the way they do, which may help you stick with them as you develop your own active reading skills.

For some texts, the critical thinking components may not be immediately obvious. It can be tough, for example, to see an argument embedded within a fictional narrative or a seemingly straightforward presentation of facts in a nonfiction work. But both fiction and nonfiction texts typically contain elements of both *exposition*, with which they relay information, and *persuasion*, meaning that they lead readers to see a question or an issue in a certain way. Authors may incorporate persuasion through explicit arguments, or they may be subtler, using narrative orientations, selected emphases, or even omissions to lead readers to understand or adopt a specific point of view. At still other times, the authors may be unaware of the ways in which their biases and assumptions add an inadvertent element of persuasion. The fact that different levels of meaning can be embedded within the same text means that reading can occur at multiple levels. We can read superficially, consuming the elements of the text with little reflection merely for information or amusement, or we can employ our critical thinking skills to extract its fuller meaning.

The principal steps that we identified for critical thinking, *analysis, evaluation, construction*, and *synthesis*, also apply to active reading. As we approach texts with the eyes of critical thinkers, there are some slight refinements we must make to accommodate textual arguments. When we analyzed and constructed arguments in Chapter 2, our examples included spoken arguments presented in the moment. With texts, we often face more sophisticated arguments that demand a more detailed analysis and more carefully considered evaluation. The advantage that readers have is the luxury of time. Written arguments are static on the page, meaning that we can more carefully assess the text and take a step-by-step approach.

Active reading	Critical thinking
Prepare / Peruse / Review the text	Analyze
Contextualize	Synthesize
Respond	Evaluate and construct

Prepare: when reading a vacation novel, few bother to prepare. Some may read the back cover or the dust jacket to get a sense of the story, and a few cheaters may skip to the last page to see how a story ends. But most dive right in, starting on page one and letting the narrative wash over them. Active reading demands a little more work on the front end. This includes previewing an abstract, a synopsis, or table of contents. It can involve "scanning" the text, giving the introductory paragraphs a cursory read, looking over the topical paragraphs to get a feel of the structure, and glancing at the conclusions. For larger books, your preparation can lead you to find and read a review of the book in a newspaper or journal. In any case, the goal is to identify the overarching point or argument of the text and ascertain its general structure before beginning your more in-depth reading.

Peruse: After establishing a general sense of the piece, you can read the text more carefully, putting your preparatory work into action by connecting the finer details to the text's premises and arguments. Pick out the specific premises or subpoints that make up an argument and mark them for later reference. You can keep notes in a separate place, but as long as you go back and review later, it is also acceptable to highlight them in the text or make a brief note in the margins (provided that you are willing and able to mark in the pages). Comprehension is key while reading. Keep a dictionary handy to make sure that you understand the vocabulary in the text.

Review: Once you have winnowed the specific premises that constitute the argument, you should review your notes and highlights to crystallize in your mind both the main conclusions of the text and the ways in which the author reached those conclusions. You can do this by converting your highlights and marginalia into separate notes and then reworking those into a summary. As you review, be sure that you fully understand the elements of the text and are satisfied that they fit together to shape the larger argument. If there are parts of the text that you do not understand, you should read those sections again and mark them as questions if you are still confused.

Contextualize: There are different levels to active reading. The first is to read the text in isolation, seeking to grasp its internal argument. The second is more global and calls for you to think about the broader context in which the work was written. One good question to ask yourself when reading any text is "Why was this text written?" In other words, you should attempt to discern what its purpose is, which audiences it seeks to reach, and to which other people or texts it responds. The text itself will likely provide clues. Authors will often state their intentions and will directly address their audiences or those to whom they are responding. You can also sometimes determine the nature of the intended audience by the language and style of the text. If the author writes with very precise, sophisticated language; uses unexplained jargon; and employs copious citations, then the text may be directed more toward specialists rather than the public.

Respond: Comprehending a text is only one part of active reading. In keeping with the principles of critical thinking, you must also evaluate the quality of the argument and then articulate its implications. Are the questions, premises, structural framing, and argument clear in the text? Do the premises and evidence presented in the text adequately support the conclusion? Does the argument satisfactorily respond to the implicit question in the text? Does the argument raise new questions? What affirming arguments or counterarguments can you make in your response?

DISCOVERY EXERCISE

Working with a partner, locate a short nonfiction source, such as an article in a popular periodical, a mainstream online blog, or a syndicated opinion column in a national newspaper. You and your partner will each read the piece independently following the steps above and keeping detailed notes drawn from your process. Preview the text and summarize your sense of the overarching argument and then diagram the argument more fully as you read. How does your assessment change as you read and review the piece more fully? What is the immediate context of the piece, and to what or whom does it respond? Write your own brief response to the argument in which you summarize the piece and articulate your evaluation of the arguments. At the end of your assessment, compare notes with your partner. In what ways did your analyses, syntheses, and evaluations agree or diverge?

(Re)Constructing a Historiography: Working with Secondary and Tertiary Sources

In Chapter 4, you completed a bibliography that included secondary materials related to your initial research questions. To complete the Query Phase of your project, you must now review the sources you have collected in order to ascertain how they respond to your questions. Theoretically, the historical literature should answer your questions completely and comprehensively. In other words, an expert in the field should be fully satisfied that an issue has been laid to rest through existing scholarship. The truth is, however, that this is seldom the case. Historical research is a collaborative enterprise precisely because issues in the past are complex. Either there are gaps in the answers to questions about a historical topic or the available answers have errors or uncertainties. It is also likely that past discoveries have raised new questions to explore. In any case, for almost every historical topic under study in the academic literature, there is always a need for more scholars to push a question further, to correct misconceptions, to offer fresh perspectives, and to explore new possibilities.

This is where you enter the field. Your objective in reviewing the secondary literature is to find a space within the historiography on a topic in which you can make a new contribution. You will then articulate the space that you find as a **research problem** that your project will address. There are different research problems for nearly every topic. It could be the case that very little has been written on your topic or addressed your question, or that some aspects need further exploration, or even that an important aspect of the story has been overlooked. More experienced researchers might identify flaws in interpretations of a topic or outright errors. In any case, your work should address at least one significant problem in order to ensure that your contribution is original and valuable to other scholars in the field. Of course, you do not have to solve every problem at once, and you need not feel compelled to tackle the biggest problems in the field.

In some cases, new scholarship can tackle both small and large questions at once. An excellent example is Christopher R. Browning's *Ordinary Men: Reserve Police Battalion 101 and the Final Solution in Poland.* In this work, Browning used interrogation records from the members of a reserve police battalion who had participated in mass killings in Poland. In one sense, Browning's research problem was quite modest. He was writing the first major history of a single paramilitary unit that had been part of a horrendous set of war crimes. But beyond his narrow subject were two larger questions that he sought to answer about the history of the Holocaust. The first dealt with how the genocide had unfolded in its early stages and the second with the motives of the actual perpetrators. In his review of the literature, Browning found that few prior studies had looked beyond the Nazi leadership to understand how and why the Holocaust unfolded, and those that did usually depended on the recollection of survivors. Browning's study thus offered a rare occasion to understand the perspectives of the perpetrators and thereby made a major contribution to the field.[4]

If some histories emerge from uncharted territory, others develop from research problems found directly within scholarly texts. Four years after Browning's study appeared, Daniel Jonah Goldhagen raised new questions about Police Battalion 101. His follow-up book, *Hitler's Willing Executioners*, contains an example of a research problem based on a disputed interpretation. Using the same set of interrogation documents, Goldhagen challenged Browning's central assertion that a variety of psychological pressures had informed the participation of the German perpetrators. He argued instead that their acts reflected a deep-rooted "eliminationist anti-Semitism" widespread in German culture.[5] His very different interpretation soon launched a vigorous debate among historians, as the vast differences between Browning and Goldhagen's conclusions became themselves important research problems. A number of new studies attempted to resolve the opposing interpretations by closely examining the two historians' work, with many in the end finding fault with Goldhagen's methodology and conclusions.[6]

Scholars wishing to add to the discussion about Holocaust perpetrators would want to be sure to read Browning, Goldhagen, and the other books associated with this debate. In other words, they would need to become familiar with the historiography related to this question. The same is true for any historical topic. If you are to be a part of the academic discussion, then you must know the prior contours of that discussion and find the places where you can say something new. Fortunately, you have already made a good start. When working in the library, you put together a bibliography of the sources most relevant to your topic. Now you must do three more things: prioritize your approach to the bibliography, discern information from each of your secondary sources, and synthesize the historiography.

Reading Your Bibliography

Creating a bibliography is one thing. Working through one is another entirely. Depending on your topic, your bibliography may be quite large. Some topics simply generate enormous bodies of scholarship. There is perhaps no better visual example of this dilemma than the stunning tower of books at the Ford's Theatre Center for Education and Leadership in Washington, D.C. In 2012, the Center erected the tower as a display of the scholarship on Abraham Lincoln. Reaching thirty-four feet in the center of the museum alongside a winding staircase, the books—all 7,000—represent fewer than half of all known scholarly books on the subject.[7]

With such historical subjects, it can be nearly impossible to master the literature, even for a professional. Other topics are more manageable, of course, but even then, it is difficult for novice historical researchers to determine which works are relevant for their research questions or which are deemed most significant within the discipline.

To help with this part of the process, it is helpful to observe three principles to guide your approach to the historiography:

First, when wading through the literature, work from broadest to most narrow. If you are relatively new to a topic, then it makes sense to start with the fundamentals. Using the Lincoln example, if you were writing a research project on Lincoln's influence on the outcome of the Civil War, it would be necessary first to know something about the war and about Lincoln's presidency. So rather than wading into the more specialized treatments, you might begin with a few general histories of the era. These studies, in turn, would likely help you identify the more focused works. You would simply need to follow their footnotes and bibliographies to see which sources they selected.

One particularly helpful way to approach the broader contours of a topic is to consult the relevant **tertiary literature**. Tertiary sources are those that synthesize secondary sources. They include encyclopedia articles, historical dictionaries, and bibliographical works. They can also include short published reviews of books or longer review essays of multiple works. Tertiary sources are great places to start because they provide more condensed accounts of the circumstances and narratives surrounding a topic and also because the authors tend to be seasoned experts who know the literature well and can provide brief sketches both of the broad outlines of a historical topic and of the prevailing points of discussion within the relevant historiography. Finally, tertiary sources are useful ways to identify the most

FIGURE 5.1 *Book Tower Exhibit at Ford's Theatre Center for Education and Leadership. Courtesy of Gary Erskine and Ford's Theatre.*

significant secondary and primary sources and can thereby make wading through the literature that much simpler. Libraries often place some tertiary sources, including encyclopedias and dictionaries, in a special noncirculating **reference section,** where they are always available for consultation.

Tertiary sources are always useful for finding tidbits of information about a topic, and can help you throughout the project. In the Query Phase, however, your overarching objective in working with tertiary sources is to find the best way into the secondary literature. The secondary sources are scholarly works that convey new knowledge or fresh interpretations by analyzing and synthesizing primary research. They include **monographs,** which are single works focused on a single topic or a single aspect of a topic; **anthologies,** which are collections of essays relating to different aspects of a topic, and standalone **articles,** which are shorter treatments about a topic that typically appear in academic journals. The same principle applies when reading secondary sources: start with the broader works to gain insights that will lead you to a more fruitful engagement with more specific research questions.

Second, it helps to work from the most recent secondary and tertiary sources to the oldest. In other words, you should read a work published in 2018 before you read a source published in 1999. This may seem counterintuitive, but it is an effective approach because it makes your survey of the literature progress more efficiently. Each work of secondary scholarship should have a historiographical discussion placing the work within the literature. This means that the works provide an overview of historiographical discussion up to that point. Therefore, rather than starting at the beginning and essentially rebuilding a scholarly conversation from start to finish, you can usually read the historiographical sections of a few recent works and get a sense of what scholars have said about a topic, what questions they have asked, and which works are considered most significant. You can then move backward to older works in a more selective way.

Third, you should prioritize the most relevant sources. Not every book or article about a topic will prove equally useful to your research. Some may address issues that are outside the scope of your question, while others may contain outdated or discredited arguments. In order to be more productive, you should usually privilege the works that are most relevant, which are those that are most likely to yield the information that you need. Relevance in this case can mean a couple of things. It can refer to sources that scholars consider most influential in the field, or to works that deal most closely with the stated research questions. Ideally, you should consider both of these when prioritizing your source, but note that these do not always align. Sometimes an important work in the broad topic area simply does not address your specific question. Usually, a cursory survey first of the title of the work, then of an abstract or summary, and then of the work itself can help you make a judgment call about the order in which you review sources in more depth.

These rules of thumb are not meant to exclude sources; rather, they are intended to help you set priorities. Even before reading the first book, these principles can also serve to guide your approach to the sources in the library. These same criteria of breadth, time, and relevance are factors in deciding which search tools to use, how to construct search queries, and how to organize the results. Every project is unique, of course, and the trick is to know how to balance principles such as these in order to pursue your study most effectively.

APPLICATION EXERCISE

Reorder your bibliography by priority, and use the new list to guide your work plan. In what order will you work through your sources? Provide your reasons for prioritizing your sources as you do.

Analyzing and Evaluating Secondary Scholarship

With your priorities in order, you are ready to work through the individual secondary sources. Here your active reading skills will be put to the test. Experience has taught us that analyzing scholarship is a particular challenge for undergraduates. If you have little experience with journal articles or academic monographs, then your first encounters will demand a great deal of patience. Scholarly texts are more complex than run-of-the-mill periodicals and popular nonfiction books. They lay out painstaking arguments with copious sources and a deep engagement with other scholars. Since you are likely new to the academic conversation, it may be easy for you to miss the larger points of a piece amidst the more minute details. The good news is that the more scholarship you read, and the more feedback you get from your reading, the better your active reading skills will become. Odds are that you will find yourself understanding each source more clearly and working more efficiently. For now, however, you should be prepared to take your time and work very carefully through the material, particularly through the sources most relevant to your project.

Vetting Secondary Sources

In accordance with the practices of good active reading, your process will include some preparatory work before you can dive into the text. The first is to vet the source, examining it critically to confirm its validity and adherence to best practices in the field. This includes verification that the source has clear documentation of its evidence in the form of footnotes, endnotes, or in-text citations, but it also involves an assessment of the author and publisher of the work. In principle, any piece of academic writing can be carefully researched and significant to your project. In fact, to suggest that a text was invalid because the author was not a professional historian would be an example of an *ad hominem* **fallacy**, which occurs when we conflate the argument with the person making it. At the same time, knowing that a trained historian has written a text, that a reputable publisher has edited and produced the work, and that the text exhibits rigorous evidentiary standards can offer a base level of reliability that it is largely free from factual errors or unwarranted arguments.

One of the simplest ways to vet a source is to confirm that it has been published through a reputable journal or academic publisher. Strong research journals and presses have rigorous editorial standards that provide another layer of quality assurance. Many choose to build their reputations by publishing in selected scholarly fields and by building editorial boards populated by field specialists. In recent years, for example, Latin American historians have looked to Duke University Press, Stanford University Press, and the University of Nebraska Press as some of the publishers producing high-quality scholarship in their field. In searching for the right journals or monographs, research libraries are invaluable, because they do their own vetting when choosing the databases and journals to which they subscribe, and they tend to be very careful in selecting the books that they purchase. They also often collaborate with faculty experts who can help them determine which journals and presses are the most reputable and relevant in their respective fields.

For more advanced vetting, researchers sometimes examine the available analytics on an academic journal to assess its relative weight. One such method is to examine an academic journal's **impact factor**, which is derived from the average of citations for recent articles in the journal over the course of one year. The idea is that the higher a journal's impact factor, the more weight its articles have in shaping the academic discussion in their discipline. Researchers often try to publish in journals with higher impact factors, but they are also quick to recognize the limits of this approach. First, impact factors tend to have greater weight in fields like the natural sciences than in history, where scholars publish both books and articles. Second, impact factors often do not account for the preferences of smaller subfields. A journal like *The American Historical Review*, which is widely considered very significant for historians across all fields, carries a five-year impact factor of 2.194, while a more specialized journal like *German History* is rated at a smaller 0.691. But *German History* is highly regarded among historians working on German topics, and thus its impact factor is less critical.

Internet sources pose special challenges. The fast pace of changes to the online landscape has made Web sources a much more common feature of research, but the same pace of change has made quality control quite difficult. The first thing to recognize is that not all online sources are of the same kind. In terms of reliability, there are at least three different classes of Web resources. The first and most reliable are the online versions of print periodicals, journals, and books. Many mainstream newspapers and magazines such as *The New York Times* and *Newsweek* publish their content in digital format, as do most academic journals. An increasing number of print books, meanwhile, are available as e-books that researchers can read online or with the use of e-reader devices. The digital versions carry the same level of quality as their print counterparts, and you can find them in the catalog of your research library or in one of its vendor databases (i.e., JSTOR, Ebsco, etc.).

More academic research is available online and outside the library in the form of **open-access** journals. The open-access movement gained momentum in the early 2000s as a way of making scholarship more widely available to those outside the academy and thus fulfilling a commitment to scholarship as a public good.[8] The problem is that these sources, because they lie outside the purview of libraries, can have dubious credentials. Some open-access publishers, like the journal *International Social Science Review* published by the Pi Gamma Mu International Social Science Honor Society, publish professional academic and student research and use the same basic editorial standards and double-blind peer review processes found in high-quality print academic journals. Others may be less reputable, and more than a few fall into the category of so-called predatory journals that are less committed to academic quality than to an underlying profit motive. These sorts of publications tend to have either no review process or one that is suspiciously accelerated, weak editorial standards, an editorial board with questionable or nonexistent academic credentials, and, most tellingly, a practice of charging authors to publish their work. Because they operate with flashy academic titles and operate in the same space as reputable open-access sources, predatory journals can be hard to spot. One consortium that keeps track is the Directory of Open Access Journals based at the University of Lund in Sweden (https://doaj.org/), which lists over 12,000 journals and allows users to suggest new additions or report suspicious titles. For researchers, the best advice is to be exceptionally cautious and to examine the practices of open-access journals very carefully. Reputable publishers will clearly list their editorial staff along with their submission and review policies on their website. Research assistants at university libraries can also help you determine the rigor of a particular journal.

Then there is the vast array of nonprofessional Web sources, including blogs, personal websites, online videos such as YouTube, and, of course, Wikipedia. These show up with increasing and sometimes disturbing regularity in student work, partly because they are easy to find and easy to digest. The obvious challenge with such sources, however, is that they are almost never peer-reviewed, and they may not display their evidence or reveal complete information about their authors. For this reason, many of these sources are simply not appropriate for a university-level research project, and the few that are demand that researchers be prepared to vet them thoroughly and articulate clearly why they have chosen them. In other words, Web sources, when used at all, should demand more work from researchers and not less. Personal blogs from known professional scholars or journalists may be suitable, but they should adhere to the same level of quality in terms of citations and use of evidence, and even then readers should most likely privilege peer-reviewed and professionally edited sources.

Wikipedia articles, meanwhile, have slowly seen their academic quality grow over time. For light informational reading or for settling a quick bet about whether John Williams's original score for *Star Wars: A New Hope* won an Academy Award, Wikipedia can be a marvelous resource. For research, it is worth noting that Wikipedia articles increasingly display footnotes with sources and include lists of references, but they are nonetheless authored by interested amateurs through **crowd-sourcing**, which involves multiple anonymous authors contributing to each piece and raising questions or objections to particular elements. Some studies have shown that Wikipedia articles can be more accurate than professional, peer-reviewed reference sources, but this is certainly not universally the case, and the absence of systematic controls and known authors means that they still very rarely appear as sources for mainstream historical scholarship.[9] Moreover, readers should be aware that articles may be deliberately vandalized or populated with unchecked factual errors.[10] And Wikipedia essentially prohibits articles based on primary source research and discourages articles with informed opinions on secondary literature, meaning that its utility never rises above the level of a superficial tertiary source. University faculty today may be slightly less inclined to impose bans on such sources, but the rule of thumb should always be that no Web source of this type should go unchallenged and uncorroborated.

APPLICATION EXERCISE

Vet your sources! Review the items in your bibliography, and for each source, write a short statement about its reliability. Have your sources been peer-reviewed and published in reputable journals or with academic presses? Are there questions about any Web sources? If any of your sources do not stand up to scrutiny, briefly explain why you have chosen to remove them from your bibliography.

Reading Secondary Sources

Having prioritized and vetted your sources, your next act of active reading preparation is to distill a sense of the overarching argument and structure of the source before reading. The reason that preliminary reading is such an important step is that it helps you navigate the complex argumentation and evidence employed in a sophisticated academic source. Because historians are often addressing their scholarship to other professional historians, their books and articles make assumptions about what their readers know. For the uninitiated, it can often feel like walking into the middle of a conversation without knowing the full story. At the same time, historical scholarship often mixes analysis, narrative, and theoretical discussion, and this can challenge the expectations of an inexperienced reader. For this reason, the preparation that you do should be aimed at shaping your expectations so that you can distinguish the expository from the persuasive elements and understand how the minor points shape the larger arguments.

In order to understand a text, it can be helpful to understand the author. The author's background, training, and body of research often inform their basic orientation toward the topic about which they are writing. If you were working, for instance, on a study of European nationalist movements, and were reading a book like *Nations and Nationalism since 1780: Programme, Myth, Reality*, a quick review of the author, Eric Hobsbawm (1917–2012), would tell you that he identified himself intellectually as a Marxist. Certainly, you should be prepared for a greatly nuanced study (and you would not be disappointed), but you would know that his perspective is likely to be informed by Marxist theory. This would not be likely to invalidate their arguments, but it can tell you a lot about how they choose their topics, frame their questions, and interpret their results.

For all of your texts, you will want to gain an advance understanding of the main arguments before diving into the minutiae of the text. The best way to prepare is to read a summary prepared by the author, publisher, or by a qualified academic reviewer. This can include abstracts, which provide in just a few hundred words a condensed overview of the topic and argument, and often the research problem, and methodology used in the project. An abstract does not provide enough information to assess whether the research problem is valid or the argument well constructed, but it does give you an overarching idea so that you can later understand more clearly how the pieces fit together. If the book you are reading does not have an abstract, you can usually find a brief synopsis or even read a short book review to get a sense of the same elements. For chapters in edited volumes or articles in special editions of journals, the editor's introduction typically includes a few words about the contents of the individual chapters and a brief explanation of how they fit within volume as a whole.

Another step you can take to prepare a reading is to ascertain the structure of a piece. Structure refers to the way in which a text is put together and the framework in which the author lays out the premises and conclusions. Good historians use a structure that best conveys their argument. Their work may be arranged as a narrative of events laid out in chronological order, a step-by-step treatment of specific primary sources, or a segmented discussion of specific themes, or a consideration of different theoretical or historiographical approaches. Longer pieces may combine elements in order to deliver a more complex set of arguments. A historical monograph may divide chapters by major chronological events but focus within each chapter on a specific theme. In any case, clues to a book's structure are often evident in a table of contents, while articles and book chapters frequently use subtitles to help readers navigate a text.

After preparation comes the actual reading. Here careful note-taking will greatly aid the active reading process. Your notes for each source, and especially for the high-priority sources in your bibliography, should include a full bibliographic citation and an overview of what you have learned about the author, argument, and structure. Then, as you go through the text, you want to do more than simply note the facts, names, and dates that appear in the article; rather, you want notes that indicate how the information in the piece informs the larger arguments. For this reason, the best strategy is to practice **reverse outlining**, in which you take apart each section of the text and show how the parts fit together to construct the overarching arguments. To make a reverse outline for an article or a book chapter, start with the three basic components of the piece: the introduction, the body of the text, and the conclusion. For each of these principal sections, identify their principal elements and then determine how the remaining details support the main points.

Most of the framing for an article or a book will be evident in the introductory section. When perusing a text, you should read the introduction especially carefully and then reflect on it before moving further in the text. The introduction should at a minimum identify the topic and explain why it is significant for academic study. Historians usually can accomplish this task with an opening vignette or quote in the first pages of the reading. The piece may then draw from this opening an initial research question or problem and use it to situate the piece in the historiography. You can often expect the piece to discuss the conclusions of other historians, and you should be careful not to confuse their views with the author's main points. Finally, this discussion should lead the author to describe his or her main question or conclusion and to delineate the methods and sources that the author uses in his or her study.

What follows is an elaboration of the topic in the body of the text. It is in this section that most of the narrative or thematic exposition takes place and in which the author presents his or her primary evidence. To break down the body section, start with the subtitle for the section and then connect the constituent paragraphs to the section. Each paragraph's topic should be evident in the first sentence (also called the topic sentence) of the paragraph. The ensuing components should then elaborate on the paragraph topic. In this way, you can better master the historical facts and details contained within the piece, because instead of simply memorizing them, you are discovering the essential links between the facts and details, on the one hand, and the points that they support, on the other.

Upon reaching the conclusion of a piece, you should look for more than a mere summary of the argument. Conclusions typically gather up the threads of a complex work and affirm the central arguments, but they are also spaces where authors discuss the implications of their work, situate their findings in a broader context, and discuss any evident limitations of their present study. Authors may also propose new questions raised by their results or even suggest new hypotheses for related questions. These may include unsupported claims, but that is acceptable; they are meant to be nothing more than suggestions for future research. Taken together, these concluding elements are meant to sum up the findings in the present work and to suggest ways for future scholars to carry the academic conversation forward. Conclusions typically end with a sense of closure for a particular book or article, but they never close the door on the larger research into a topic.

Embedded within each section of the article or chapter are the citations connecting the text with its evidentiary support. These citations make the act of reading scholarship different from other types of nonfiction, because scholars want to pay attention to both the flow of the text and to the citations sprinkled throughout the piece. A reverse-outlining approach can help you manage the two, because while you are extracting the main points during a first reading, you can focus on the text itself with less regard for the citations. You can then make a second pass through the texts to connect the details to the skeletal frame and assess the use of evidence. At each point, you can determine where the author uses primary or secondary evidence and thereby learn something about the areas in which the text makes original arguments. And you can form judgments about whether the evidence employed is appropriate for the point it is supporting.

It is during this second reading that you can shift from analysis to evaluation. Here the basic rules of critical thinking apply. You want to determine whether the supporting claims in the text are *clear, convincing*, and *relevant* to the argument, and then decide whether they create adequate support for the overarching conclusions. The clarity of the argument should be evident in the text, while the quality of the arguments will require evaluation of both text and citations. Do the authors explain their points adequately? Do they build properly toward their final conclusions? Are their primary sources of adequate quality, and are they sufficient to make the case? And, finally, did the answers provided by the piece raise new questions? In your notes, you should articulate as specifically as possible where a text falls short or where you have questions or are unsure about a particular claim. The point is not to throw rocks at a piece indiscriminately; rather, the goal is to criticize the work of others constructively. Instead of asking what is wrong with a piece of scholarship, you should ask where the piece, and by extension our understanding of the topic, could be improved.

Synthesizing Your Sources

As you interrogate the individual sources in your bibliography, you should be developing a sense of the larger historiography on your topic, as well as the current state of the field, which includes the latest approaches, findings, and interpretations. This calls for you to do more than merely understand your sources in isolation. You must also think about how they link with and even speak to one another. Alternatively, you may find new connections between formerly disparate conversations. The result in either case will be a new *synthesis*, bringing together the principal sources in your bibliography to present a refined research question derived from a research problem evident in the historiography. Synthesis is a form of active reading that demands contextual awareness for each of the sources in your bibliography. In other words, as you discern the argument in each piece, you must also consider how it both stems from and relates to other secondary sources. As you read, keep in mind the following questions:

- *How have the scholars answered the research questions?*: Each source under review should contain material relating to the questions guiding your project. The point is to keep track of the answers they provide, which means analyzing their individual arguments. If a single source does not address the questions or provide meaningful context, then you can likely remove it from the bibliography and move on to the next source. If many books do not address the questions, then you will face an important decision. Should you modify your research question to bring your project more in line with the discussion, or can you justify the significance of your question despite the dearth of secondary literature and move on to your primary sources?
- *Which academic works seem most important in the discussion?*: The bibliographies of secondary and tertiary works are key, because seasoned scholars come to know the most critical works in their areas of research. Moreover, they tend to position their own work *vis-à-vis* the prevailing literature. As you conduct your secondary review, you may notice a list of common works appearing in the conversation, and the sources may even explicitly indicate why some works are especially significant.
- *What sources are most commonly used to answer the questions?*: Be on the lookout for common source bases and be able to explain why some sources are used routinely in the historiography. Do the

individual secondary texts use the sources in the same way, and do they lay the same emphasis on the same primary material?

- *What points of consensus and disagreement are evident?:* As you come to study multiple sources addressing the same questions, you should begin to see areas in which the sources broadly agree and those that are points of contention. Some disagreements may take the form of heated debates, but others may be inadvertently diverging interpretations. Conversely, some forms of agreements may stem from common, unspoken assumptions. Your task will be to see where scholars stand on the material facts surrounding a historical topic and theme, why they may not share the same perspectives, and how their disagreements might be resolved.

- *What are the different areas of emphasis within historical studies?:* Even if they agree on the basic contours of a historical event, not every scholar covers every historical question the same way. Some may take a wider or narrower scope, while others may situate a historical event or trend in a different context. In these instances, differences of opinion might not be disagreements over sources or interpretations, but questions of focus or perspective. It is possible in such instances for multiple historians to make accurate assessments of a topic even if their views do not align. These different perspectives usually reflect changing views over time, and identifying them can help you understand the flow of the academic conversation and frame your own approach.

On to Discovery!: Moving beyond the Query Phase

With a refined question and a defined research problem in mind, you are ready to dive into the primary sources. Be aware that finishing the review of your bibliography does not by any means end your engagement with secondary sources. While working with your primary materials, the odds are good that you will encounter new secondary materials or need additional sources to provide context or evidentiary support for points that arise along the way. Be ready during the remaining parts of the research project to adjust your questions and historiographical claims as you encounter new evidence. Add relevant materials to your bibliography, and for longer projects, be especially mindful of new scholarship that appears while you are working. Be sure to keep your question in front of you as you carry out your primary research. And be ready to use the active reading skills for your primary sources. As we will learn in Chapter 6, they are one part of a battery of skills that you will need for your direct encounter with historical material.

History in Practice: Identifying a Research Problem

In the sample below, Jack Wells analyzes the central secondary source for his project and then connects it to the wider historiography on Christianity in the late Roman Empire. As you will see, Wells places a selection of key historians in dialogue with one another across centuries in order to define the general research problem that will direct his project.

Jack Wells, "Christianity and the Fall of Rome"

Edward Gibbon (1737–1794) produced one of the greatest historical works in the English language. The first volume of *The Decline and Fall of the Roman Empire* appeared in 1776, and five more volumes, which carried the story all the way down to the fall of Constantinople to the Turks in 1453, appeared over the course of the next twelve years. It has been widely admired for the beauty of its prose and for its thorough use of primary sources. Among the reasons Gibbon cited for the cause of the decline was the rise of Christianity. In Volume Four of the work, Gibbon mused about the various reasons for the fall and argued that the worldview and behavior of the Christian Church contributed significantly to the problems Rome was facing in the fifth century. In particular, he noted that Christianity prioritized concern for the next world at the expense of civic virtues, and he believed the wealth of the empire was being directed not to the army that could defend the borders but to a church that turned out to be ambivalent about the fate of the state. Furthermore, he believed that the sometimes-violent religious squabbles caused by Christians distracted the emperors from security and competent administration.[11] This analysis reflects the worldview of the European Enlightenment of the eighteenth century. Gibbon, like his contemporaries Voltaire and Thomas Jefferson, was skeptical about the merits of institutional religion. But, as we shall see later, primary source evidence can be mustered to support the claim. Whether that evidence is convincing is another matter.

There have been plenty of skeptics. Perhaps the most powerful was an Irish historian, J.B. Bury (1861–1927). Bury rejected Gibbon's view, reasoning that Christianity could not possibly be a cause for the "decline and fall" because it predominated in Constantinople as much as in Rome in the fifth century, and the eastern empire was continuing along quite nicely for several more centuries. Instead, Bury preferred to see the fall of the West as the result of "a series of contingent events," which, had the course of history been altered here or there, may have resulted in a completely different outcome for the western empire.[12]

On the other hand, Gibbon's views about Christianity's role in the end of antiquity still have resonances and echoes in modern scholarship. Peter Brown (1935–) prefers not to focus on the issue of "decline" at all. Instead, he prefers to view the transition from the ancient to the medieval worlds through the lens of gradual transformation. Yet he too believes that the Christian Church facilitated the destruction of the western Roman Empire because, in his words, the Church "dissociated itself" from the army and "sapped" its strength.[13] For this reason, a proper understanding of the nature and cause of the western Roman Empire's collapse, and the role of the Christian Church remains elusive.

APPLICATION EXERCISE

Flex your historiography muscles! Choose two sources from your bibliography that deal with similar aspects of your research topic. Prepare a presentation in which you first analyze and evaluate the main points of each source and then synthesize their contribution to your topic. Finally, explain briefly how you would respond to the two sources and how they might thus shape your own approach to the topic.

Notes

1. Francis Pleasant Robinson, *Effective Study* (New York: Harper & Brothers, 1941), 13–33.

2. Nancy Bailey, "S-RUN: Beyond SQ3R," *Journal of Reading* 32 (1988): 170–1.

3. John Dunlowsky, Katherine A. Rawson, Elizabeth J. Marsh, Mitchell J. Nathan, and Daniel T. Willingham, "Improving Students' Learning with Effective Learning Techniques: Promising Directions from Cognitive and Educational Psychology," *Psychological Science in the Public Interest* 14, no. 1 (2013): 4–58.

4. Christopher R. Browning, *Ordinary Men: Reserve Police Battalion 101 and the Final Solution in Poland* (New York: HarperCollins, 1992).

5. Daniel Jonah Goldhagen, *Hitler's Willing Executioners: Ordinary Germans and the Holocaust* (New York: Vintage, 1996), 23.

6. See, for example, Norman G. Finkelstein and Ruth Bettina Birn, *A Nation on Trial: The Goldhagen Thesis and Historical Truth* (New York: Metropolitan, 1998).

7. "A 34 Ft. Tribute: The Lincoln Book Tower," *Ford's Theatre Blog*, accessed August 15, 2018, https://www.fords.org/blog/post/a-34ft-tribute-the-lincoln-book-tower/.

8   Roy Rozenzweig, *Clio Wired: The Future of the Past in the Digital Age* (New York: Columbia University Press, 2011), 118–21.

9   Murray G. Phillips, "Wikipedia and History: A Worthwhile Partnership in the Digital Era?" *Rethinking History* 26, no. 4 (2016): 523–43, 529–35.

10 Rosenzweig, *Clio Wired*, 60–5.

11 Edward Gibbon, conveniently excerpted in "General Observations on the Fall of the Roman Empire in the West," in *The End of the Roman Empire: Decline or Transformation?* 3rd ed., edited by Robert Kagan (Lexington, MA: D.C. Heath, 1992), 28–9.

12 J.B. Bury, *History of the Later Roman Empire: From the Death of Theodosius I to the Death of Justinian*, vol. 1 (New York: Dover, 1958), 308–11.

13 Peter Brown. *The World of Late Antiquity: AD 150–750* (New York: Norton, 1971), 119.

Suggested Reading

Adler, Mortimer J., and Charles Van Doren. *How to Read a Book: The Classic Guide to Intelligent Reading*. New York: Simon & Schuster, 1972.

Shandley, Robert R., ed. *Unwilling Germans: The Goldhagen Debate*. Translated by Jeremiah Riemer. Minneapolis: University of Minnesota Press, 1998.

6

To the Archive and Beyond: Working with Primary Sources

What we will do in this chapter:

➤ **REFLECT** on the nature of historical evidence.
➤ **DISCOVER** how cultivating textual, quantitative, and digital literacy skills helps historians interpret a variety of historical sources.
➤ **APPLY** critical thinking and active reading skills to analyzing, evaluating, and synthesizing primary sources.

Primary sources are the most challenging, but also the most rewarding, part of historical research. They are our direct links to the past, providing the vital clues that allow historians to make discoveries and forge interpretations. In one sense, they are empirical tools, enabling historians to look into the past, and thus serving them in the same way that telescopes and microscopes aid astronomers and biologists. At the same time, however, they are the tangible remnants of the past and thus part of the phenomena historians study. For this reason, there is no denying an element of excitement that attaches to contact with primary sources. The encounter summons a lost time that at once connects us to the breadth of human existence and reminds us of our own ephemerality. Primary sources can evoke episodes of sweeping change affecting millions or invite us more intimately into the private world of another human being.

Historians always strive to maintain a critical distance between themselves as researchers and the historical subjects they study. But they are mindful of the fact that they are studying real people and that the sources they read often connect them to the experiences of individuals. In a series of reflections on archival research, the American historian Beth Barton Schweiger emphasized the ways in which her work impacted her on both a professional and personal level:

To write history is, for me, to make a relationship with the dead. I try to see people in the archives. I take enormous pleasure in this task of recovery and discovery, and in the creative work that follows as I decide how to tell their story. Like the meeting of characters in fiction, these encounters count as a genuine expansion of my experience, offering a perspective beyond the self and the possibility of wisdom.[1]

Schweiger reminds us that while primary sources are treasured opportunities, they are also awesome responsibilities. It is, after all, the historian's task to share that "expansion of experience" with others by interpreting past sources in a way that does justice to historical subjects and the world in which they lived. She acknowledges the dilemma by calling to mind the magnitude of the gulf between past and present: "At best, it seems, I might be able to see the dead only as they chose to represent themselves. At worst, I will only see myself reflected in the records they have left behind."[2]

Primary sources are the best hope of crossing the chasm, but they rarely yield their secrets easily. There are the problems of transcription, of deciphering scrawling handwriting, or converting numerical data into meaningful information. There are problems of translation, of making sense of lost manners of speaking and writing, of forgotten idioms, and of foreign languages and dialects. And, of course, there are the myriad silences, the gaps in the records, and the tenuous links between the questions we have and the information we find. As the historical discipline has developed, its practitioners have worked as a community and in partnership with librarians, archivists, and scholars in other fields to interpret known records and identify new sources.

REFLECTION EXERCISE

Think about all the material possessions and documents that are currently in your bedroom or dorm room. Imagine that scholars from the future knew nothing about the times in which you lived but somehow found your room perfectly preserved. What kinds of things might they conclude about you? About the society that you live in? About your worldview? What problems in interpretation might arise if someone had to learn about you only through the material objects that you have left behind?

Over time, increasing amounts of material have become available to scholars both in physical libraries and archives and online, enabling new types of research while creating new challenges. Among these has been a growing diversity of primary materials. The emergence of "history from below" approaches and a new emphasis on histories of culture have generated new sorts of questions inquiring into the lives of a range of previously overlooked historical groups. And they demand different kinds of sources. Whereas the historians of the nineteenth century expected to work with mostly political records found in state and church archives, today's historians must sometimes go far afield in search of an ever-widening array of primary sources. At the same time, scholars working in a postmodern frame have embraced a so-called **archival turn**, raising questions about the guiding assumptions behind the preservation and cataloging of information.[3] Why, these scholars ask, do we privilege some sources over others? Why do we favor some methods of collecting and curating materials? In what ways might our archival practices be more inclusive of the voices of those marginalized in their own time?

The expanding possibilities for primary research, and the problems that accompany them, are beyond the scope of any single book. Thus, this chapter will focus on two broad aspects of primary sources central to the expanding horizons of the contemporary discipline. The first concerns the relationship between textual approaches and the expanding range of source types. As you will learn, even as historians remain devoted to texts as their principal primary sources, they have also embraced a wide variety of new materials, including visual sources, musical compositions, oral histories, statistical data, and even physical sites and objects. Historians approach these new sources using many of the same core principles involved in interpreting traditional texts. Second, this chapter will introduce you to the broader range of skills required for today's primary research. This includes familiar skills such as information literacy, active reading, and critical thinking, but also new skills connected to quantitative and digital methods. You will discover that as the historical field becomes more dynamic and expansive, so too must the researcher become nimbler and more innovative.

Approaching Primary Source Texts

Whether preserved in libraries and archives or found in museums, private collections, or on the internet, primary source texts are the staples of historical research. From the earliest days of the discipline, historians distinguished themselves from other fields through their engagement with textual records of historical events, and primary texts continue to define historical work. In many ways, the process of finding, preparing, and analyzing primary source texts follows the same rules as those for secondary and tertiary works. But because there are so many different kinds of primary sources, and because the range of possible interpretations is so wide, there are also some unique considerations that apply. Here, for example, are just a few of the most common primary texts:

Autobiographies	Legislation	Meeting minutes	Poetry
Correspondence	Magazines	Memoirs	Published fiction
Depositions	Manifestos	Newspapers	Reports (academic, government, etc.)
Diaries	Manuscripts	Pamphlets	Scripts

Vetting Primary Sources

The first essential quality of any valid primary source is authenticity. Historians must ascertain whether a potential text is indeed what it purports to be: a source derived from a specific time period and historical agent (i.e., a named person, group, institution, government, etc.) and related to a specific historical topic. There have been a few infamous cases in which historians have had to contend with false documents. One of the most well known is the so-called Donation of Constantine, a document attributed to the Roman Emperor Constantine in the fourth century CE and used in the later Middle Ages as a legal basis for papal supremacy within the Christian Church. Only in the fifteenth century did the Italian scholar Lorenzo Valla (1407–1457) show through an analysis of the use of language in the text that the document was a forgery from the eighth century CE.

Modern historians have not been immune to faked documents. In 1983, a German art forger named Konrad Kujau crafted over sixty volumes of counterfeit diaries that he claimed were written by the Nazi dictator Adolf Hitler. This incident revealed not only one of the key challenges of working with primary sources but also the ways in which historians and archivists work together to verify historical documents. In this case, the diaries became a public sensation when the German magazine *Stern* purchased them for a front-page story in April 1983. They had allegedly been found in the wreckage of an Allied aircraft and kept in secret in East Germany. When the diaries came to light, they were instantly controversial, but at first they fooled a number of highly respected historians, including Sir Hugh Trevor-Roper (1914–2003), a noted expert on Nazi Germany and Adolf Hitler. Following the initial excitement of their public discovery, close analysis revealed the diaries to be forgeries. A scheme to sell them to newspapers around the world fell apart, and the forger eventually went to prison for fraud.

In his book *Hitler's Diaries: Fakes that Fooled the World*, Charles Hamilton, a historian and handwriting specialist, explained how scholars unraveled the lies surrounding the documents. According to Hamilton, the documents first raised suspicions through their dubious **provenance**, or point of origin. Many historians flatly refused to believe that they would have survived a fiery plane crash intact. Moreover, the diaries had a poor chain of custody after their purported discovery, meaning that there were few controls over the documents before they came to the attention of historians. Third, the physical character of the documents was in question. Scholars studied the paper, ink, and binding used in their creation and showed how these did not conform to known materials used by Hitler in the 1940s. Fourth, historians expressed doubts about the content and the context of the diaries. The wording and phrases did not match up with known expressions used by Hitler, and none of his contemporaries could recall him keeping such a voluminous diary. And, finally, experts like Hamilton detected discrepancies in the **paleography**, or historical handwriting evidence, that bore telltale marks of forgery.[4]

These same techniques would apply to virtually any primary text, though in the case of the Hitler diaries, scholars benefited from unique access to surviving witnesses and comparable documents that allowed for thorough analysis. For historians working with much older documents, the process can be much more laborious, and doubts about authenticity can linger. Fortunately, it is most likely the case that most of the sources that you will use in your project will be housed in a library or an archive and will have the benefit of careful prior vetting from past historians and archivists. If that is not the case, then you must be prepared to verify the authenticity of your source, to articulate clearly your reasons for using it, and to properly qualify any conclusions you reach on the basis of evidence carrying any degree of uncertainty.

Determining Relevance

If authenticity is the *sine qua non* for any primary source, then relevance is the basis for its priority. As a general rule, the more directly a source connects with a historical issue, the more important it is to the researcher. Relevance often derives from a personal connection to a source. As in the case of the Hitler writings, historians are eager to study historical figures using the subject's own words. In a similar way, a source can be deemed relevant because it expresses a group ethos, as with sources that speak for a village, a political party, or a family. It can relate a spatial connection, as in a source stemming directly from a place under study. And, of course, the relevance of a source is enhanced by its closeness to the time of an event. Reflections from decades after the fact are not without utility, but the vagaries of memory can engender false narratives and muddle key details. For these reasons, historical researchers strive to find as many sources as possible that connect closely to the people, places, and times under study.

On many occasions, direct primary sources are simply not forthcoming, and historians must prioritize indirect sources. This may include half of a two-way exchange of correspondence, recollections written by friends or acquaintances, or contemporary newspaper accounts. At other times, even clear examples of tangential texts may be difficult to find, stretching the interpretative powers of historical researchers and even at times leading them to blur the boundaries between primary and secondary sources. To highlight the innovation required to access some remote periods, we might point to the recent work of the Classical historian Charles Muntz. In his 2017 book, *Diodorus Siculus and the World of the Late Rome Republic*, Muntz took on the perennial challenge of gaining new glimpses into the first century BCE, when the power of ancient Rome was on the rise even as the Republic slipped into an extended period of political crisis. Muntz's approach was to take a fresh look at the writings of the Greek historiographer Diodorus Siculus (90 BCE–30 BCE). Diodorus is hardly a household name these days, but classicists know him very well as the author of the *Bibliotheke*, an ambitious collection of histories of the known world from the beginnings of civilization to the fourth century BCE. Before Muntz's study, many historians regarded the *Bibliotheke* as a third-hand source covering events that unfolded centuries before Diodorus was even born. By contrast, Muntz treats the writings of Diodorus as a primary source for the first century BCE. "Diodorus was not writing in a historical vacuum," Muntz explains, "he was constantly attempting to engage in the intellectual debates of his time."[5] With this idea in mind, Muntz shifts the ways in which scholars traditionally read Diodorus, examining instead the points of emphasis, the buried assumptions, and the overt omissions that inhabited Diodorus' historical synthesis. In this way, Muntz identifies subtle nods toward salient issues in the waning years of the Republic, including the origins of the crisis gripping Rome in the first century and the possibilities of a new political reality in the years to come.

Muntz's take on Diodorus is meant to shed new light not only on the circumstances in which the Greek historiographer wrote his accounts but also on the works themselves. In particular, it showcases many of the best practices that historians use to prepare their primary sources. Among these is an awareness of the authorship of a primary text. As far as possible, historians want to know who created a source and under what circumstances they produced it. Was the source written by a single individual or by multiple authors? Was it written all at once or over a longer span of time? When and where did the authors write the source, and how long did they take to complete it? Crucially, historians also seek to understand the motives behind a text, always asking why the author or authors chose to write the text. Muntz does this by reading the clues that Diodorus provided about his own life and placing those alongside other known writings by Greek intellectuals in the Roman republican period. He is thus able to situate Diodorus within a tradition of growing Greek elite attachment to Rome as a pathway to success and status, which helps explain the allusions that Diodorus makes to Rome as a positive civilizing force.[6]

Determining key aspects of authorship and motive helps the researcher understand the author's inherent biases, which in turn can shape the information contained in the text and the manner of presentation. Historians should be aware that authors involved in specific events may attempt to minimize or overstate their involvement depending on how they see the events reflecting upon their self-image. As time passes, they may be subject to lapses of memory, diminished access to information, or like Diodorus, they may be responding to cultural norms or outside pressures that shape their recollections. These sorts of biases certainly warrant a higher level of scrutiny, and identifying them is important for reading a text, but they should not necessarily disqualify them as valuable sources.

Reading Primary Texts

Aside from his innovative choice of primary sources, what makes Muntz's study of Diodorus so interesting is the way in which he reads the *Bibliotheke*. Rather than taking the volumes of Diodorus' history at face value, Muntz probes the text for its underlying meanings. He disregards nothing, taking special interest in portions of the text previously dismissed by scholars. This includes the mythical elements that Diodorus incorporated into his histories, which even historians who accept his value as a historiographer have tended to overlook. Yet Muntz deftly shows how Diodorus may have chosen his myths carefully to appeal to contemporary audiences and advance his overarching views on the growth of Roman power. For instance, Diodorus retells the mythical journeys of the Argonauts, who sailed to the Eastern Mediterranean and Black Sea region in search of the legendary Golden Fleece. According to Muntz, Diodorus' retelling may well have been intended to connect with Roman expeditions to the same region, with Diodorus suggesting that where the ancient Greeks had failed to civilize the Black Sea, the Romans were destined to succeed. Muntz's suspicions are seemingly confirmed by, among other clues, an analysis of Diodorus' portrayal of the island of Samothrace in the North Aegean Sea, which had become a cult site for contemporary Romans, and by details in the retelling of the Argonaut myth, including portrayals of the demigod Heracles that conformed to distinctly Roman interpretations. "It is likely, then," Muntz concludes, "that Diodorus intended his Argonautica to be seen as endorsing Roman expansion in the Black Sea region."[7] In a larger sense, this new reading of the *Bibliotheke* shows how Diodorus, an ostensible outsider, contributed to a broader view of Roman power as a positive, civilizing force.

As we have seen, these sorts of interpretations depend upon close, innovative reading, requiring skills that would likely elude a less experienced historian. But this should by no means discourage beginners from tackling primary sources. One of the great things about reading historical documents is that it is possible to read them at different interpretative levels. Although you may be a rookie historian, your work thus far has already imparted some familiarity with critical thinking and active reading, so you are well equipped to engage some of these levels right now. You may make a start by attempting a descriptive assessment of the text, including an *analysis of its basic content and explicit claims*. Does the text simply convey information, or does the author exhibit a clear perspective? Does the author seek to persuade a reader to take a certain action or adopt a particular point of view? For some documents, you may find yourself reading to discern argumentation using the same sorts of reverse outlining techniques you employed with your secondary literature. Then your analysis may lead you to make a *critical evaluation of the overt claims in the document*. Are the arguments and premises in the document clear and convincing? Does the structure of the prose properly support the author's position? Are the claims and conclusions logical and informed by appropriate evidence?

Once you analyze and evaluate the explicit arguments and claims in a historical document, you are ready to push to a deeper level, which will call for you to apply your historical thinking skills. Specifically, you will *seek to uncover its implicit claims, underlying assumptions, and layers of meaning*. People in the past—even the relatively recent past—acted, thought, and understood the world in different ways than we do in the present. We see this in Muntz's discussion of the *Bibliotheke*, when he reveals the subtle points embedded within Diodorus' retelling of the Argonautica. In both cases, contemporaries would have read the documents very differently than we would today, and it is up to the historian as far as possible to try and recover to uncover the meanings that documents carried for their creators and contemporaries. When working with individual sources, one useful way to begin unlocking their unique historical elements is to *identify incongruities in your critical analysis and evaluation*. Where in the text do you see points of view that seem unclear or foreign to you? Are there claims with which you do not agree? Does the text exhibit factual errors? Does it make seemingly unwarranted assumptions or extrapolations?

For each incongruity you find in a primary text, you must determine why it is there and what it means. It is, of course, very possible that such instances are nothing more than typical flaws in thinking, but it is also possible that you have identified a moment in which the author of a historical document sees the world in a different way. In those cases, a proper interpretation demands an *understanding of the document's historical context*. Only by knowing something about the social and cultural environment in which a text was created can we hope to establish the referents that inform the text's deeper meaning. There are two ways that historians can establish the necessary context. The first is to turn to the secondary sources. In the last chapter, we learned how to use your secondary bibliography to reconstruct the historiographies of specific topics and gain insight into the state of the academic discussion and find a research problem. As you work with your primary sources, secondary synthesis takes on a new function, allowing you to cultivate broad knowledge about your topic to inform your reading of the primary sources and better situate them within their context.

The second way is to synthesize multiple primary sources. Rare indeed is the moment in which you can make a significant discovery with just a single text. In almost every case, you will need to gather multiple sources, and likely multiple types of sources, in order to answer your research question. Synthesis involves a number of different operations depending on the scope of the research topic and the types of sources available. It can involve such tasks as placing sources in a series, which refers to the order in which documents were produced or meant to be read. Synthesis can also entail using several sources to fill in gaps, looking for missing clues to what transpired in an event. Multiple sources can also allow historians to compare multiple points of view on a topic to create the most accurate account of an event or to determine how different individuals or groups responded. Depending on the questions you are asking, the process of putting your sources together in this way may help you in a number of ways. It may serve to establish a sequence of events, identify patterns cutting across texts, corroborate a narrative of an event, verify a set of circumstances, or dispute a presented account. Each of these outcomes can in turn help us determine cause and effect, to make judgments about why something happened as it did and what its effects and implications might have been. We can thus make interpretations that articulate a priority of causes, revealing the factors that were most significant in effecting historical change. And having access to multiple sources may even provide a wider and longer view of an event or time period that can aid us in spotting historical changes underway that we might otherwise not see with a single source.

As you conduct your textual research, be mindful of the potential of your primary sources, but also *be aware of their limits*. There are things that we just cannot know with the information we have available. New researchers sometimes read too much into their sources. When studying a document promoting an idea or a belief, they can be tempted to see the presentation of an idea as evidence of its broader resonance in public. In fact, reception is a difficult thing to pin down; historians can analyze the content of a document, but without direct statements from contemporary readers, they usually cannot discover with certainty how people responded to its ideas. In other instances, historians may find evidence that a person took a particular action, such as undertaking a journey or participating in a war, but they may not have evidence for what that person was thinking at the time or what motivated him or her to act. Whenever possible, you should mine your sources for every possible insight, but you should also respect the moments when gaps remain and be prepared to qualify the instances in which you are less certain of an interpretation because of your source limitations. Above all, you must always keep your research question in front of you during your investigation. Do not try to force your sources to answer a question with an argument that they are not equipped to support; rather, be willing to let your evidence guide you to refine your question even further so that you can construct a thesis that will have the proper empirical weight and will stand up to scrutiny.

Nontextual Primary Sources

The sorts of limitations that you will no doubt encounter in your project have bedeviled historians since the first days of the discipline. They have also led to some important innovations. Historians today draw upon a variety of source types, including images, musical compositions, oral accounts, physical sites, statistical data, and even material objects. Such unique sources facilitate interdisciplinary investigations, bringing historians into contact with archaeologists, art historians, economists, ethnographers, geographers, and musicologists. The methods required to approach nontextual sources also connect historians with engineers, mathematicians, and natural scientists. Collaborations like these connect researchers to new ways of thinking, new research questions, and innovative applications of research methods and tools. Yet despite the obvious intellectual benefits of interdisciplinary exchange, historians retain a certain element of disciplinary rigor with nondocumentary sources. Specifically, they distinguish themselves by the ways they "read" such sources using many of the same techniques that they use to interpret written texts.

Visual Sources

It should hardly be surprising that historians should take an interest in images. They are, after all, ubiquitous features of human activity. From the enigmatic ideograms carved into stones in the American Southwest to the colorful cave paintings in the caves of Europe, images signal some of the earliest appearances of human culture. They were "textual" long before the invention of text. Closer to our own time, technological innovations and globalization enabled the production of a wide variety of image types presented in brilliant colors and employing materials from all over the world. Below are a few prime examples:

Advertisements	Designs	Manuscripts
Architecture	Digital images	Maps
Banners and emblems	Films	Photographs
Blueprints	Illustrations	Signs

However "realistic" an image may seem, we must take care to remember that there is always an element of artifice. In other words, they represent the world of the past, but they do so through the subjective eye of their creators. For this reason, historians approach images in the same way that they read texts. Where archaeologists examine images in order to discern the features of a human culture, and where art historians focus on the internal developments of artistic style, form, and content, historians utilize images to extract the messages they contain about the immediate contexts in which they were created. We want to know what they can tell us about a particular moment or period in the past. It is a task that leads historians to take a textual approach to images, analyzing layers of meaning as we would a historical document.

Images can also lend themselves to useful historical syntheses. This is how anthropologist Deborah Poole approached her cultural history of the colonial era in South America's Andean region. In her 1997 book, *Vision, Race, and Modernity,* Poole studied what she calls the "visual economy" of Andean society, which included the "organization of production" of images, the "circulation of image objects," and the "cultural and discursive systems through which images are appraised, interpreted, and assigned worth."[8] This meant that she was interested not merely with comparing the content of images but also with historicizing their entire life cycle as cultural products. Her objective was to understand how this collection of images over time, this "image world," contributed to the creation of cultural boundaries and norms that characterized the relationships between native Andeans and European colonizers.

A year later, Poole expanded her work by analyzing images produced by North American visitors to the Andes. Using the 1859 painting *Heart of the Andes* by Frederic Edwin Church, a collection of engravings by Ephraim George Squier, and photographs of Machu Picchu taken by the explorer Hiram Bingham, Poole traced the ways in which Americans depicted the Andes from the mid-nineteenth through the early twentieth centuries. As her work reveals, these images emerged from very different contexts, and their style and content reflected different ways of seeing and representing, but they each informed an "imperialist gaze" that defined the perceived relationship between the American viewer and the Andean landscape. Embedded within the composition of the images were claims to power, whether expressed through the visual language of property in Church's painting, through a "statistical vision" that sought to reduce the Andes to something that could be measured and quantified, or through photos that portrayed the Andes as wilderness and placed them within a vernacular of discovery. Ultimately, she argues that even if the United States never exercised direct control over South America, its most iconic images of the Andes reflected a "visual regime" that, over time and in different contexts, "informed the political culture of U.S. imperialism."[9]

Oral Histories

Just as the invention of photography and film has made it possible to "see" history, so too has the advent of sound recording in the twentieth century enabled the past to speak. As Donald Ritchie has observed, oral history emerged in earnest in the 1970s as part of the movement toward capturing "history from below."[10] Historians like Studs Terkel began interviewing farmers, workers, and other marginalized groups and getting to know their personal experiences. Terkel's 1970 study, *Hard Times: An Oral History of the Great Depression*, included hundreds of interviews intended, on the one hand, to create a pastiche history of the 1930s in the United States and, on the other, to muse on the ways individual perspectives shift over time and merge into collective memory.[11] Today, oral history is a thriving approach concerned with recovering the experiences of people at all levels of society and to preserving contemporary experiences for future generations.

One of the central methodological debates among oral historians concerns the degree to which scholars can "read" interviews as they do textual sources. Because oral accounts relay factual information, make assumptions, and adopt positions about past events, some scholars argue that they are essentially analogous to written sources. Others, however, observe at least two critical points of difference. The first relates to the ways in which oral accounts are created by the interview subject. Memory is a tricky thing for the best of us, and our powers of recall can be eclectic, with events flowing from our heads out of sequence and in odd relationships with other memories. The process of reconstructing a past event often occurs in the course of telling and retelling, and historians must be prepared to untangle memories as they emerge. This raises the second divergence, which involves role of the interviewer. As Ronald J. Grele has observed, "Unlike ... traditional sources, oral history interviews are constructed, for better or for worse, by the active intervention of the historian."[12] Prefatory meetings before an interview, leading questions during a session, and follow-up discussions after can all inadvertently shape a respondent's recollections. Moreover, the setting of an interview may be problematic; whether, for instance, subjects are interviewed one-on-one or in a group setting can change the way the subject remembers.

For these reasons, oral historians have established rigorous methodological practices for their work. Chief among these are efforts to minimize the impact of the historian. This includes making interview questions as open-ended as possible, allowing subjects to engage their memories with minimal interruptions. For deeper studies, such as for life histories, historians work carefully to build rapport with subjects in order to establish trust. They conduct multiple interviews with individual subjects, allowing time for interviewees to pull their thoughts together and to expound after time for reflection. When speaking with more than one subject, historians may create a standard set of questions, striving to avoid leading the subject and instead blending simple baseline questions such as name and demographic information with larger, less restrictive questions that give subjects free rein to recall. After the interviews, of course, historians work to corroborate accounts with other interviews or other types of evidence, and they may follow up with questions meant to clarify answers or to address new information.

As a synthetic exercise, a rigorous oral history approach can pull together a wide variety of experiences related to a major historical event, thereby capturing not only the contours of the event itself but also the ways in which it has since become a part of collective memory. This was Terkel's approach in *Hard Times* and in his 1984 work, *The Good War: An Oral History of World War II*, which tried to capture an American experience that unfolded on a global stage, on both the homefront and the battlefront. In 1992, Haruko Taya Cook and Theodore F. Cook collaborated to produce a similar oral history of the Japanese experience in the Second World War. Their work was especially challenging, first because many of their subjects had suffered traumatic experiences during the war and second because of cultural differences that precluded easy recollections of those years. As Cook and Cook explained, the war was largely absent from the public sphere in Japan, and there were few elements of a national narrative available for subjects to reconstruct their personal memories. The layers of collective memory that did exist included a sense of embarrassment and shame over a lost war or over acts committed during the conflict. The interviewers explain, "This is why many of the stories–particularly of the years of defeat–have the feel of wanderings in a shapeless terrain."[13] Thus, if Terkel faced the dilemma of parsing real experiences from normative attitudes and narratives about the war in the United States, Cook and Cook found themselves working with subjects who had no such guideposts to help them articulate their experiences.

In the course of their work, Cook and Cook found that allowing their subjects to speak in their own time and with few restrictions was the most effective way to allow them to engage their own memories and find a way to relate them. At the same time, however, they found it important to build a relationship with their subjects that would allow them to feel more comfortable expressing difficult emotions:

> For almost all of the people interviewed for this book, the experience of telling about their years at war was an incredibly fresh one, often an extraordinary return to memories held in privacy and silence for up to sixty years. As a consequence, almost *every* interview involved incredible outbursts of emotion. Tears were commonplace—of sorrow, of bitterness or grief, of loving memory, of chagrin or even horror over acts committed .... When we shared their emotions, even cried with them on occasion, they took that as confirmation that they had communicated their own feelings, even expressed gratitude for finally having been able to reveal themselves to another.[14]

Given the methodological complexities of oral history, it is usually the preserve of more seasoned historians. Newcomers to the field may first wish to gain experience in the archives working with textual sources. If you plan to conduct interviews as part of your projects, then we encourage you to first read in more detail the literature on oral history. When working with living human beings, you have an additional set of methodological and ethical responsibilities. For example, it is good practice to get your work reviewed by an institutional review board on your campus that supervises work with human subjects in such fields as psychology and sociology. At the same time, you should know your limits and take special care when working with subjects from different cultural backgrounds or whose experiences include traumatic events. For those sorts of projects, make sure you work closely with well-qualified historians who can act as mentors and research supervisors. Be sure to consult your mentors before approaching subjects or undertaking interviews.

Quantitative Methods

Numbers shape history. We mean this both in the sense that they shape historical events themselves as well as in the sense that they shape the writing of history. A failure to properly interpret numerical data can have dramatic effects on all human actions. In September 1999, just such a miscalculation led to the loss of the NASA Mars Climate Orbiter, which disintegrated over the Red Planet at a cost of 300 million taxpayer dollars. An investigation of the incident revealed that the ground software used to place the craft in orbit had used US units instead of the expected International System (SI) units. As a result of this simple error, the Orbiter was left careening into the Martian atmosphere with a flawed trajectory.

Historians may not always face the same high stakes, but they must also be wary of the ways that the improper use of numerical data can shape their analyses. Numerical data offer historians the seductive possibility of apparent certainty in their conclusions. Numbers are facts, so the theory goes, and facts do not lie. But without care, the supposed certainty of conclusions will prove elusive. This is because numbers, like historical events, do not speak for themselves. They need proper handling before they can be put to use. Failure to do so can lead to consequences less expensive but no less problematic than the destruction of the Mars Climate Orbiter—the writers of history can find themselves with conclusions that their evidence simply will not support.

To look at the controversy that can be caused by incautious use of numerical data, let us take a look at the controversial book, *Time on the Cross: The Economics of American Negro Slavery*, cowritten by Robert Fogel (who later won a Nobel Prize in Economics) and Stanley Engerman. Both men championed the use of social science statistical methods and challenged a standard interpretation of American slavery: that slave-based agriculture in the US South was an economically unproductive and backward system that, because of its inefficiencies, would have inevitably disappeared on its own had the American Civil War not hastened its demise. Fogel and Engerman claimed to show that slave-based agriculture was, in fact, economically efficient and profitable before the Civil War, which meant that it was unlikely that Southerners would have abandoned slavery for economic reasons.

Had Fogel and Engerman stopped there, the book would not have been so controversial. However, relying on plantation records, the authors claimed to show that many of the popular perceptions of slavery were wrong. Among their revisions, they claimed that Southern slaves had better lives than the factory laborers of the North. They suggested that incidents of beatings and sexual exploitation of slaves were rare. Furthermore, they asserted that the slaves actually kept a significant percentage of the wealth their economic activity generated. Lurking under the guise of economic conclusions supposedly supported by raw, inarguable, numerical data was a radical idea: that life for African slaves in the antebellum South was not as bad as people had been led to believe.

How do you use numerical data to prove life as a slave was not so bad? Fogel and Engerman found a Louisiana planter who kept records of the beatings administered to his slaves. His name was Bennet Barrow, and, as the authors explain, "[h]is plantation numbered about 200 slaves, of whom about 120 were in the labor force. The record shows that over the course of two years a total of 160 whippings were administered, an average of 0.7 whippings per hand per year. About half the hands were not whipped at all during the period."[15] The authors then suggested that not all masters applied beatings because of cruelty; instead, they used beatings as a tool to maximize economic efficiency. Fogel and Engerman then moved to a discussion of the incentives, such as future manumission offered to slaves to encourage them to work, and used data to show that the amount of wealth expropriated from slaves by their owners was much smaller than might be expected. "The 12 percent rate of expropriation reported on slave income falls well within the modern tax rate of workers .... Pending a more precise measurement of offsetting services, it seems warranted to place the average net rate of the expropriation of slave income at about 10 percent," which, as they point out, was lower than the modern income tax rate.[16]

Time on the Cross was published in 1974 with great fanfare, including what can only be described as a publicity tour, unusual for a work of academic history. Journalists were told that **Cliometrics**, as this new mathematical-based history was called, was going to revolutionize the historical method and clear up a lot of problems that the old humanistic-based history had not been able to resolve, and many of the initial reviews were favorable.[17] But it did not take long for reviewers to zero in on two main issues with Fogel and Engerman's methods and conclusions, and they did so to devastating effect.[18]

First, they tackled Fogel and Engerman at their strongest point: the apparent unequivocal reliability of numerical data. Remember, numbers do not lie, so how can users of statistical data be wrong? Well, a thought probably occurred to you as you were reading about the beatings administered by plantation owner Bennet Barrow: Is this the only evidence we have about the number and frequency of slave whippings? Apparently it is, and you can see the problem. How typical is Bennet Barrow? Were slaves on smaller farms treated better, or worse? What conclusions can we draw about slavery outside of his plantation and about slavery in years earlier and later? It might be very hard to draw any general conclusions about the frequency of beatings based on this example. Reviewers of the text found numerous examples where grand conclusions about the entire history of slavery were based on very restricted sets of data. Even census data, which Fogel and Engerman used to calculate rates of manumission, were problematic. As reviewers noted, we cannot be sure that census takers were particularly concerned about getting an answer to the exact number of slaves, and it is very unlikely that they counted each slave themselves; instead, they tended to rely on the testimony of the owner. And all of this, of course, overlooks the issue about how we figure out how many beatings is a lot, or whether it really mattered to the slave whether the beating was administered to discipline him or because the beater was a sadist.[19]

The second problem concerned the question of whether a reliance on quantitative methods could free historians from the tyranny of subjective thinking. Fogel and Engerman argued that their data showed that the African slave population in the South were, under the system of slavery, encouraged to be economic go-getters who lived in stable, nuclear family units. Since, they assume, a good life is to have a good standard of living and a nuclear family, the slaves were actually not in such bad circumstances. And they seemed to think because they had shown that African slaves were really economic producers, they were creating a vision of slaves as personally responsible and empowered, a marked improvement over the older Reconstruction-era stereotypes. Reviewers, however, were unimpressed. They pointed out that there might be other aspects of a good life, such as a sense of agency and the right to make one's own economic and personal decisions, that trumped any supposed level of economic well-being.[20] Thus, the reviewers observed that bias creeped in not only because Fogel and Engerman used problematic data but also because they brought their own set of starting assumptions into the work.

The result has been that, in spite of the initial fanfare, *Time on the Cross* did not have the transformational effect on the discipline that the authors hoped. Yet, at a larger conceptual level, the cliometricians had a point. Properly handled, arguments based on quantitative date can indeed allow historians to make powerful arguments.[21] So how should the data be managed? First, you should begin by going back to the question you are trying to answer. Would quantitative data help you formulate an answer to the question? If so, what kinds of data? And most problematically, do such data exist? If not, is it possible to obtain or locate the data? In many cases, sadly, the answer will be no, particularly for students of premodern history. But if such data are available, then you will need to direct your attention to gathering it. This may be as easy as looking up information that is neatly and accurately presented in census tables or as time consuming and painstaking as going to archives and collecting, counting, and recording pieces of information one by one to assemble a database.

Second, you should recognize that quantitative data need to be handled the same way you would handle other kinds of historical evidence. Before accepting any information at face value, you need to be certain that you understand the context in which it was obtained and the limits within which it can be interpreted. As we saw above, even apparently solid sources of data, such as a government census, must be carefully considered before being accepted as accurate. Wills, tax records, bills of sale for land or other property, all can provide useful information for social and economic historians. But you must remember that not everyone in, say, the eighteenth-century English colonies would have been able or even interested in making a formal will, that not all wills would be complete, and that not all wills from the era would survive, so difficult and perhaps even insurmountable difficulties may crop up that prevent you from being able to draw general conclusions from your data. You need to be prepared from the beginning to field questions about why your readers should take your data as accurate and representative.

Once you have a data set that you believe will support your conclusions, you need to perform the proper statistical operations on it to get the information you need. Sometimes this can be simply through taking an average, but even taking averages can be complicated. The most common way to find the average of a set of numerical data is to add up all of the values and then divide by the number of values that you have; this is known as the **mean value**. If, say, you wanted to find the average value in cash willed by the residents of a New England town in the early nineteenth century, you would find the total value of all of the cash bequests in their wills and divide by the total number of people whose wills you have collected. The average you collect, however, could be grossly distorted and misrepresentative of the whole because of a few outliers, numbers that fall far outside the rest of the set. This would be the case if one or two of the wills included people who were either unusually rich or unusually poor. You may therefore prefer to find a **median value**, which is the value at which half the sample you took lies above and the other half lies below a median line. This method will reduce the effect that one or two outliers have on your data set. So, if you have a data set of fifty, your median value would be the value in which twenty-five people left more cash in their wills and twenty-five left less. Finally, you could choose to find the mode or **modal value**, which is the number that most frequently occurs in your data set. If five out of your fifty wills left cash bequests of five dollars, while all other dollar values occurred four or fewer times, your modal average would be five dollars. Statistical tests also allow you to give the **range**, the difference between the largest and smallest number in your set, which can help you determine the spread of a set of data. Others can help you find the **reliability** of your calculations, which indicates how consistently they yield the same answer, and the **validity**, which estimates how effectively your tests measured what they set out to measure.

Once you have your database and have performed the relevant statistical operations on it, you need to analyze it to draw defensible conclusions from it. A few words of warning for how you should handle your data. Wherever possible, you should avoid introducing bias, whether conscious or unconscious, into your handling of the data and into your conclusions. Conscious bias can influence your data handling, particularly if you have a hypothesis that you are hoping to confirm. There may be a temptation to massage the data so that it more strongly supports the hypothesis. For instance, using our study of cash bequests above as an example, you might hypothesize that the number of bequests in wills was higher than previously thought. Therefore, you might select a method of averaging that gives the highest number, rather than letting the qualities of the data determine which method of averaging best represents the evidence. This kind of behavior will only undermine the force of your argument, when attentive and skeptical readers see what you are up to. Unconscious bias is much harder to guard against. It will require careful and skeptical handling of your raw data before you evaluate it. You might try putting yourself in the place of a skeptical reader and ask yourself how you can be sure your sample of data has been fairly collected and is truly representative; if you have trouble defending your own database, you need to be careful in your conclusions.

You also need to beware of jumping to conclusions. Establishing a **correlation** is often a long way away from establishing a causal relationship. If, say, you want to argue that increased cash bequests in wills was a cause of increased consumer spending, even if you establish that both cash bequests and consumer spending were rising in the nineteenth century, you cannot state that rising *bequests* caused an increase in spending. Increase spending might, in fact, be caused by other economic factors, such as a large general growth in the economy, which would also cause the amount of cash bequests in wills to go up. As you can see, statistical data must be carefully handled before it can be used to establish causal connections and might never be able to do so completely.

Finally, you need to present the data so that your reader can understand and evaluate your argument. You may think that, if you have gathered the data properly and performed the required statistical analysis, the burden should be on the reader to evaluate your work. This is not the case. As you now know, embedded in the historical craft are all three of components of the ancient liberal arts of grammar, logic, and rhetoric. While knowledge of the first allows you to communicate clearly and knowledge of the second allows you to formulate defensible historical arguments, it is your mastery of the third that will allow you to persuade your reader to hang around long enough to accept the force of those arguments. Muddled presentation will be interpreted as muddled thinking. So, when presenting quantitative data, you must take care to think about how best to provide your reader that data so he or she can check your work. Pie charts, bar graphs, dot plots, box plots, and even tables of raw data should be provided and placed in appropriate sections of your work. Often historians will provide simple visual aids in the main part of the text and then provide a good sampling of raw data in an appendix, so that the main narrative is not clogged with numbers but the reader can still get easy access to the quantitative information that supports the thesis.

From the above information, it is clear that historians must possess the skill of quantitative literacy, the ability to confidently understand, analyze, and interpret numerical data. This may mean taking courses in statistics, social science quantitative methods, or both. Often a chorus of groans goes up when we talk about the importance of quantitative literacy to our students: "But I'm not good at math! That's one reason I like history." In the twenty-first century, however, as historians, citizens, and consumers, we are constantly bombarded with numerical data, and we therefore cannot avoid basic quantitative literacy if we want to do our jobs well.

Digital Methods

With each passing year, historians, along with other scholars in the humanities, find themselves drawn into the realm of digital scholarship. In fact, when you used library databases to locate your project sources, and when you employ productivity software to write your essay and present your results, you too are engaging in digital scholarship. Historians may seem like they are behind the times, but in many ways, they have long been at the forefront of the Digital Revolution. A handful of historians used the unwieldy early computers of the 1950s and 1960s to facilitate statistical analyses, but interest increased markedly by the end of the 1970s, as the availability of microcomputers coincided with the height of popularity of quantitative history and raised a host of new possibilities for demographic, economic, and statistical studies of the past.[22] In the early 1990s, as the internet was just beginning to emerge as a central information technology, historians like Roy Rosenzweig (1950–2007) were creating the framework for integrating digital tools into historical research, teaching, and public outreach. Rosenzweig's Center for History and New Media at George Mason University wrestled with issues related to the use of digital records as historical sources, the presentation of history online, and the ways in which information technologies facilitated new relationships between professional scholars, amateur historians, and the broader public.[23] It was, in short, among the first to begin discussing the promise and the challenges of so-called digital history.

In the intervening decades, digital history has grown in tandem with the wider field of "digital humanities," which is a broad term that applies to a method of scholarship employing both computing technologies and digitized sources and to a field of study that, in the words of Anne Burdick and others, "asks what it means to be a human being in the networked information age."[24] As the technology has improved, so have the range of possible applications for scholarship. Today, digital history includes not merely the preserving, archiving, and utilization of sources online; it has opened up new historical questions and ways of analyzing and interpreting data. Perhaps most significantly, digital methods have come to function as what Shawn Graham, Ian Milligan, and Scott Weingart have called the "historian's macroscope." They refer to the possibility of using digital methods to analyze so-called big data, much larger sets of information that may span a longer time period of time, a larger area of the world, or a much more voluminous aggregation of primary sources.[25] The digital toolkit that they describe corresponds to the tremendous growth in the amount of digitized information and the processing power of modern computers, and it has informed the emergence of new subfields in history adopting larger spatial parameters (such as global history) or longer time horizons (as with so-called big history or deep history).

In many ways, practically every historian engages in some sort of digital history. When you accessed library and archival databases to find your primary and secondary sources, and when you read some of your sources via the World Wide Web, you used digital methods aimed at organizing vast amounts of available scholarly resources. Even when you take notes, plan your essay, and write your results, you are likely using word processing software to create historical interpretations and presentations. In order to be successful with these tools, you first had to possess basic computing skills, including a familiarity with the Web and fundamental operational knowledge of common software programs. If you so choose, you can build on these essential skills in a number of ways. Most simply, you can learn how to operate additional software, including database applications such as Microsoft Access, Tableau, or even simple online databases like Airtable. These apps will allow you organize and analyze large data sets to find patterns across many sources or to locate information more quickly within sources.

If you wish to push forward from there, you can learn other, more specialized applications, such as those used for **text mining**, which involves deep searches within large bodies of texts for very specific sets of information. One very simple way that you can try text mining now is to use the Google Ngram Viewer (https://books.google.com/ngrams). When you enter one or more search terms or items (n) into the viewer, Google displays the numbers of incidents of n that appear in its collection of digital books over time. This can be very useful if you are researching a term whose meaning may have changed over time. When, for instance, we searched for sources on climate change in Chapter 4, we may have learned that, according to the Ngram Viewer, incidents of the phrase "climate change" are rare before the 1980s, which means that we would have to draw on different search terms to locate sources related to that topic to understand how the concept emerged from earlier decades.

Other types of specialized software enable researchers to model data in various ways. **Modeling** describes the ways in which data and the resulting interpretations are organized and presented using digital means.[26] This can include **data visualization** techniques, which refer to representations that enable people to see patterns or connections within and among data. Through the use of visualization software, scholars can represent data in a number of ways, whether in a linear fashion as in a timeline or a PowerPoint slide presentation; spatially, as on a map; or schematically, as in a diagram. Visualization techniques have made it possible for scholars to engage in far-reaching **network analysis**, which explores the intricate, often hidden connections among groups. Initiatives such as the Historical Research Network Research group spearheaded by Marten Düring and the "Mapping the Republic of Letters" Project at Stanford University have benefited a great deal from visualization techniques.[27] Other projects, like the Trans-Atlantic Slave Trade Database (http://www.slavevoyages.org/), led by David Eltis at Emory University, inspired a visualization tool designed by Andrew Kahn of *Slate* magazine that allows viewers to see representations of actual slave ships crossing the Atlantic in a time-lapsed display.[28] Through the use of this site, visitors get a sense of the sheer enormity of the slave trade over several centuries as they watch hundreds of ships traverse the map to the New World. At the same time, viewers can manually pause to explore the records available for each ship, thus gaining a sense of the individual human stories of those involved in this massive, long-running historical event. The result is both a valuable research aid and a powerful tool for teaching a critical epoch of world history.

In recent years, historians have increasingly recognized the value of digital methods and have begun incorporating them into mainstream disciplinary practice. In the near future, it is likely that more and more new historians will undergo more advanced training, with many going beyond simple software training to learn programming skills that will allow them to design and implement their own software applications. In other instances, historians with backgrounds in traditional qualitative or quantitative methods may find themselves in new collaborations with programmers, software engineers, and data analysts to answer historical questions arising from the latest trends in digital research. It may not be likely that digital scholarship will completely supplant older forms of primary source methodology, but it is almost certain to become a fixture within the practice of history that may very well add a permanent layer to the required skill set for the next generation of historians.

DISCOVERY EXERCISE

How have historians used different kinds of primary sources in your topic area? Find at least one secondary source that makes use of nontextual sources related to your research question or research topic, whether images, oral histories, or quantitative data. How did the historian read the source, and what sorts of things did he or she learn that we might not otherwise know from traditional primary texts?

Conclusion: The Cycle of Discovery

Whatever specific primary sources you find or methodological approaches you use to "read" the past, your process of discovery will likely shift from leading you to an initial conclusion to establishing a final argument that answers your research question. This does not happen all at once but unfolds gradually in steps depending on the complexity of your project. As you begin to undertake your research, you will most likely take an **inductive approach**, following the evidence in your primary sources. It is especially important early in your primary research to listen to your sources with an open mind and not make hasty prejudgments about what you will find. At the end of this process, however, you may be in a position to form a **hypothesis**, a preliminary conclusion based on your first encounters with your evidence. As your research progresses, your hypothesis may in turn allow you to adopt a **deductive approach**, in which you measure your early hypothesis against your later findings. This will lead you to corroborate your discoveries wherever possible against other sources, seeking to confirm or reject your hypothesis. If your evidence demonstrates that your suppositions are accurate, then you will have reached your final argument, and that means that you will be ready to transition from the Discovery Phase to the Presentation Phase of your project. In the next three chapters, you will learn how to write up your results, how to apply proper ethical practices to your work, and other ways to share your scholarship with your peers.

History in Practice: Interpreting Primary Sources

Below are two examples of examinations of primary sources, the first from a text and the second a visual source. In the first example, Jack Wells reveals how the addition of contextual information can transform a seemingly innocuous statement into a powerful hint of the author's underlying motives. In the second, Bruce Baker shows how a simple scene captured in a photograph can yield several interpretations and point the way toward further research.

Jack Wells, "Christianity and the Fall of Rome"

Let's take a look at a primary source that might, at first glance, seem to offer little insight into a history of the "Decline and Fall" of the western Roman Empire. It comes from Book nineteen, chapter twenty of St. Augustine's (354–430) *City of God*:

> Meanwhile, and always, the supreme good of the City of God is everlasting and perfect peace and not merely a continuing peace which individually mortal men enter upon and leave by birth and by death, but one in which individuals immortally abide, no longer subject to any species of adversity. Nor will anyone deny that such a life must be most happy, or that this life, however blessed spiritually, physically, or economically is, by comparison, most miserable.[29]

This seems somewhat philosophical or theological and does not at first seem very promising as a source for historians. What does it mean? Well, its basic theme would appear familiar to many Christians, or, for that matter, any people who believe in a happy afterlife. Basically, Augustine is saying that earthly peace does not hold a candle to the permanent and perfect peace of heaven, no matter how wonderful peace in this world might seem.

Let's put this statement into its context. *City of God* is more than just a philosophical and religious treatise; it is a polemic designed to counter criticism of Christianity. In AD 410, Alaric and the Visigoths sacked the city of Rome. This shocked the Roman world. As Augustine makes clear in the beginning of the work, it did not take long for pagans to find a reason for this disaster: the Romans had turned away from the gods that had made them a powerful empire. Some pagans were saying that the spread of Christianity had doomed Rome.

Augustine wants to rebut that idea and attacks the problem from several directions. One way he does this is to contrast the earthly city with the city of God. In this particular passage, his meaning is clear. Any peace or happiness that we find on Earth, even if it were to last us our whole lives, is insignificant compared with the peace we will get if we can make it to heaven. The conclusion that would follow is that we should not worry so much about our earthly condition. The imperfect earthly city may have peace. Or it may be sacked by the Goths. Either way, the fate of the earthly city should not preoccupy us. We should focus on getting to the City of God.

When combined with other sources, such as Sulpicius Severus' *Life of St. Martin of Tours*, in which the soldier-saint states, "I am Christ's soldier; I am not allowed to fight"[30] you can see how some might argue that the Christian worldview is incompatible with the civic virtues that Rome needed to defend its empire.

Bruce Baker, "The Cotton Kings"

FIGURE 6.1 *Photograph of the cotton docks at Norfolk, Virginia, c.1890. Library of Congress, Accessed January 29, 2019, https://www.loc.gov/item/2016795438/.*

This photograph (brought to my attention by one of my students as part of a class assignment) shows bales of cotton on a dock at Norfolk, Virginia, probably in the 1890s. I was writing an essay about how the circulation of small quantities of loose cotton had supported an elaborate underground economy in New Orleans in the 1870s. Much of the controversy over these bits of cotton depended on whether they had accidentally fallen, and were thus fair game for anyone who chose to pick them up, or whether people had deliberately stolen handfuls of cotton from the bales. In this photograph, we can see why that distinction was so hard to make. The bagging that covers the bales is damaged and ragged. There are also many pieces of cotton already lying on the ground, exactly the sort of thing that nobody objected to people taking. The people in the photo are also worth noting. Three men use hand trucks to move bales, while two others lounge off to the side in a way that may have been suspicious to the businessmen concerned about pilfering on the docks. There are thus multiple ways to interpret the photograph, and we would need additional evidence to lay the controversy to rest.

APPLICATION EXERCISE

Find at least two primary sources—textual, visual, oral, or quantitative—that are related to the same event or theme, and prepare a report of your analysis and evaluation of each source. Your report should include the following:

1) a description of the contents of the source, including any claims or arguments it contains;

2) an assessment of any areas of incongruity that you find based on the above stated questions and techniques;

3) a statement of the ways in which your primary sources fit together to form a synthesis.

Notes

1   Beth Barton Schweiger, "Seeing Things: Knowledge and Love in History," in *Confessing History: Explorations in Christian Faith and the Historian's Vocation*, edited by John Fea, Jay Green, and Eric Miller (South Bend: University of Notre Dame Press, 2010), 60–80, 61.

2   Ibid.

3   For the postmodern roots of the archival turn, see Jacques Derrida, *Archive Fever: A Freudian Impression*, translated by E. Prenowitz (Chicago: University of Chicago Press, 1995). On the implications of the archival turn for historians, see Antoinette Burton, ed., *Archive Stories: Facts, Fictions, and the Writing of History* (Durham: Duke University Press, 2005).

4   Charles Hamilton, *The Hitler Diaries: Fakes that Fooled the World* (Lexington: University of Kentucky Press, 1991), 72–4.

5   Charles E. Muntz, *Diodorus Siculus and the World of the Late Roman Republic* (Oxford: Oxford University Press, 2017), 26.

6   Ibid., 3–6.

7   Muntz, "The Argonautica of Diodorus Siculus," *TAPA* 148 (2018): 331–60, 355.

8   Deborah Poole, *Vision, Race, and Modernity: A Visual Economy of the Andean Image World* (Princeton: Princeton University Press, 1997), 9–11.

9   Deborah Poole, "Landscape and Subject: U.S. Images of the Andes," in *Close Encounters of Empire: Writing the Cultural History of U.S.-Latin American*

Relations, edited by Joseph M. Gilbert, Catherine C. LeGrand, and Ricardo D. Salvatore (Durham, NC: Duke University Press, 1998), 107–38, 131.

10 Donald A. Ritchie, *Doing Oral History: A Practical Guide*, 2nd ed. (Oxford: Oxford University Press, 2003), 23.

11 Michael Frisch, "Oral History and *Hard Times*," *Oral History Review* 7 (1979): 70–9. Reprinted in *The Oral History Reader*, edited by Robert Perks and Alistair Thomson (London: Routledge, 1998), 29–37.

12 Ronald J. Grele, "Movement without Aim: Methodological and Theoretical Problems in Oral History," in *The Oral History Reader*, edited by Robert Perks and Alistair Thomson (London: Routledge, 1998), 38–52, 42.

13 Haruko Taya Cook and Theodore F. Cook, *Japan at War: An Oral History* (New York: The New Press, 1992), 12–13.

14 Ibid., 13.

15 Robert William Fogel and Stanley L. Engerman, *Time on the Cross: The Economics of American Slavery* (New York: Norton, 1974), 145.

16 Ibid., 156–7.

17 Charles Crowe, "Time on the Cross: The Historical Monograph as Pop Event," *The History Teacher* 9 (1976): 588–630.

18 For the most detailed and trenchant critique, see Herbert G. Gutman in "The World Two Cliometricians Made: A Review-Essay of F+E=T/C," *The Journal of Negro History* 60 (1975): 53–227, and republished as *Slavery and the Numbers Game: A Critique of Time on the Cross* (Urbana: University of Illinois Press, 1975).

19 Gutman "The World Two Cliometricians Made: A Review-Essay of F+E=T/C," 53–227.

20 Roger Ransom, "Was It Really All That Great to Be a Slave? A Review Essay," *Agricultural History* 48 (1974): 578–85; Paul A. David and Peter Temin, "Capitalist Masters, Bourgeois Slaves," *Journal of Interdisciplinary History* 5 (1975): 445–57.

21 For a more thorough discussion of quantitative methods, see Konrad H. Jarausch and Kenneth A. Hardy, *Quantitative Methods for Historians: A Guide to Research, Data, and Statistics* (Chapel Hill: University of North Carolina Press, 1991), which with the exception of its somewhat outdated take on using computer technology remains a reliable introduction.

22 Richard J. Jensen, "The Microcomputer Revolution for Historians," *Journal of Interdisciplinary History* 14, no. 1 (1983): 91–111.

23 Roy Rosenzweig, *Clio Wired: The Future of the Past in the Digital Age*, Introduction by Anthony Grafton (New York: Columbia University Press, 2011).

24 Anne Burdick, et al., *Digital Humanities* (Cambridge, MA: MIT Press, 2012), *vii*. Quoted in Eileen Gardiner and Ronald G. Musto, *The Digital Humanities: A Primer for Students and Scholars* (Cambridge: Cambridge University Press, 2015), 4.

25 Shawn Graham, Ian Milligan, and Scott Weingart, *Exploring Big Historical Data: The Historian's Macroscope* (London: Imperial College Press, 2016).

26 Burdick et al., *Digital Humanities*, 18–19.

27 Düring, Marten, "Historical Network Research: Network Analysis in the Historical Disciplines," *Historical Network Research*, 2017, accessed December 10, 2018, http://historicalnetworkresearch.org.

28 Andrew Kahn and Jamelle Bouie, "The Atlantic Slave Trade in Two Minutes," *Slate,* June 25, 2015, accessed December 10, 2018, http://www.slate.com/ articles/life/the_history_of_american_slavery/2015/06/animated_interactive_of_ the_history_of_the_atlantic_slave_trade.html.

29 St. Augustine, *City of God*, edited by Vernon J. Bourke (New York: Image Books, 1958), 468.

30 Thomas F.X. Noble and Thomas Head, *Soldiers of Christ: Saints and Saints' Lives from Late Antiquity and the Early Middle Ages* (University Park, PA: The Pennsylvania State University Press, 1995), 8.

Suggested Reading

Dougherty, Jack, and Kristen Nawrotzki. *Writing History in the Digital Age*. Ann Arbor: University of Michigan Press, 2013.

Gutman, Herbert G. *Slavery and the Numbers Game: A Critique of Time on the Cross*. Champaign: University of Illinois Press, 2003.

Jarausch, Konrad H., and Kenneth A. Hardy. *Quantitative Methods for Historians: A Guide to Research, Data, and Statistics*. Chapel Hill: The University of North Carolina Press, 1991.

Ritchie, Donald A. *Doing Oral History*. 3rd ed. Oxford: Oxford University Press, 2014.

7

Academic Integrity and Ethical Research

What we will do in this chapter:

➢ **REFLECT** on the roots of ethical practices in the academy.
➢ **DISCOVER** the professional standards of conduct for historians.
➢ **APPLY** ethical principles to the practice of research.

After weeks or months of solitary study, late nights in the library, and long hours at the computer, it can be easy to forget that research is a collaborative enterprise. The research may feel lonely, but historians never work alone. They are part of a wider discipline committed to the study of the past. The disciplinary community has its rare moments of tangible togetherness, at conferences and workshops that bring scholars together a few times a year. But what truly forges a sense of unity each day is a common set of ideas and values that translate into shared practices. Among these, perhaps none are more important than those concerning ethics. The ethical standards of the historical discipline derive from sound critical thinking processes and serve to ensure the quality of research findings and delineate the ways in which historians work together effectively.

Ethical principles play a crucial role in all academic disciplines and are handed down to the students who study them in the university. Many of these commitments overlap across disciplines and comprise the academic integrity policies of higher education institutions. The precise rules and sanctions may differ slightly from institution to institution, but in general, all universities expect students to represent themselves honestly, to treat their peers and professors with respect, and to verify that the products of their learning are authentic and original. Finally, both professional and student researchers are expected to produce results that are reproducible, meaning that other scholars could reasonably expect to follow their methods and sources and arrive at similar results.

Few would disagree that these expectations are reasonable and even noble. Yet a number of studies over the last few decades have revealed startlingly high numbers of sanctioned violations of academic integrity and even higher rates of self-reported dishonesty. The actual rates vary across surveys due to differences in the methods and parameters of various studies, so there is no precise data on how many students are actually violating academic standards, but the aggregate picture suggests that dishonesty is disturbingly common. In the 1990s, Donald L. McCabe and Linda Klebe Treviño conducted three of the most-widely cited studies using a set of integrity criteria established by William J. Bowers in 1964.[1] They revealed that overall rates of self-reported academic dishonesty remained largely consistent from the 1960s to the 1990s, and they were consistently high. Between 74 percent and 87 percent of respondents in their three major studies reported committing an academic integrity violation in at least one of nine categories. Among the most common infractions were incidents of **plagiarism**, which involves representing as one's own the words or ideas of another person. Approximately 50 percent of respondents admitted to copying material from another source without attribution.[2]

The reasons why students engage in acts of academic dishonesty vary widely. Scholars have studied factors such as age, gender, academic standing, and involvement in extracurricular activities on ethical decision making, but they also acknowledge that the resulting correlations do not necessarily identify a "type" of student more likely to cheat. More fruitful studies have focused on the circumstances that lend themselves to dishonesty. This includes institutional conditions that create opportunities for cheating, contextual factors such as financial stresses or grade pressures, and cultural factors, such as family upbringing or perceptions of the acceptability of cheating in university courses.[3]

The problem is by no means limited to students. Researchers across a number of disciplines, including historians, have committed ethical violations in their scholarship. In his survey of prominent cases of scholarly dishonesty, historian Peter Charles Hoffer has shown how unique pressures within the discipline have been partly to blame. The lucrative potential of publishing on certain popular historical topics and the politicization of other topics have tempted a handful of scholars into falsifying primary sources, plagiarizing secondary sources, or even inventing details of their personal backstories.[4] In such cases, the failure to respond to inherent pressures can be a product of poor training or of bad habits developed while still a student. This suggests that professional behavior depends on a solid ethical foundation at the university level, which makes proper training and practice in the classroom all the more essential.

The research suggests that institutions can do a great deal to promote ethical behavior by cultivating a "culture of integrity" in universities. This can include articulating institutional values and connecting them to the routine work of learning in the classroom. McCabe and his colleagues stress that values must be more than simple, negative directives toward "law and order," with a singular focus on enforcement of rules; rather, they should be framed "aspirationally" toward, among other things, "fairness," "trust," and "respect" in a positive way that includes students as agents of promoting integrity on campus.[5]

In this chapter, we will argue that one of the best ways to *act* more ethically is first to learn how to *think* more ethically. To that end, we will show you how practicing solid **ethical reasoning** can raise awareness of the root principles that underlie academic integrity policies at the university and the ethical guidelines within scholarly disciplines that safeguard the quality of research. This, you will find, is key to understanding why academic integrity policies and ethical research practices matter. It can also inform the strategies we use to uphold the integrity of our work and avoid inadvertent violations.

Fundamentals of Ethical Reasoning

On its own, the word "**ethics**" does not refer specifically to a particular right or wrong. Instead, it refers to the ways in which we conceive and act upon notions of right and wrong. To be "ethical," then, means adhering to a moral ideal or concept, or to act in accordance with a defined system of right and wrong. The academic study of ethics is a preserve of philosophy and as such involves the evaluation and construction of moral arguments.[6] In this way, ethics intersects with critical thinking. Recall the definition of critical thinking that we have used in this book, which involves making decisions about what to believe or do. The decisions that we discussed involved concrete choices: if I put on a coat, then I will be warm. Ethical practice is similarly connected to critical thinking in that we must make choices based on evidence. The difference is that the choices are informed by notions of whether the acts, effects, and beliefs implicated in a choice are inherently "good" or "bad." Since moral concepts stem from human perceptions, there is no empirical way of proving them. For this reason, *ethical reasoning operates as a form of critical thinking, but it does so within the context of preconceived ethical concepts and systems.*

The underlying ideas and beliefs make ethical reasoning possible by providing a set of general premises that support more specific conclusions. For example, if you see a man on the street unknowingly drop a wad of cash in front you, basic critical thinking would tell you that you can collect it, say nothing, and have the money, but you would risk getting caught. Or you can return it to the man who dropped it and move on with your life, but you would have lost the opportunity to spend the money. These facts, however, will not tell you much about whether taking the money is the right thing to do. If, however, you adhere to a specific system, for example a Judeo-Christian ethical system, then you may be willing to accept without further evidence that it is wrong to steal. In this case, the right choice for you will be obvious.

Ethical reasoning skills play an important role in the work of historians and other scholars, because they provide a useful framework for analyzing the decisions of others. Historians can use ethical reasoning to explore the origins and consequences of the choices of historical agents, the underlying assumptions that informed notions of right and wrong, or ideas about the good life and perceptions about the proper roles of individuals in past cultures. At the same time, professionals and students alike can employ ethical reasoning skills for the way in which they conduct their work, that is, in order to comprehend and assess academic integrity policies and principles of professional ethics.

As a quick primer, we will identify three sets of fundamental concepts that shape views of academic integrity and research ethics. To understand how they work, we will use them to analyze the following hypothetical scenario:

> Andrew is a second-year undergraduate taking a course on nineteenth-century British history. He is in the middle of a final exam that involves a take-home essay to be completed by the next day. One of the main required essay prompts is proving particularly troublesome, since it covers material that Andrew neglected to study thoroughly. The instructions included with the exam expressly forbid collaboration with other students, but it so happens that Andrew's friend Kaitlyn took the course last semester and wrote an essay on a similar question. Andrew mentions his dilemma to Kaitlyn and weighs whether to ask for a copy of her response before he begins to write. Kaitlyn, meanwhile, deliberates over how best to help her friend.

As we analyze the choices that Andrew and Kaitlyn must make, we can conceptualize three pairs of concepts, each operating along an imaginary spectrum.

Axis 1: Absolutism and Relativism in Ethical Systems

The scale of the dilemma facing Andrew and Kaitlyn hinges above all on the degree to which their acts represent a breach of the rules. This raises a question about the flexibility of a given ethical system. One the one hand, some systems adopt a position of **moral absolutism**, which means that we may not break the rules under any circumstances. What is right in these systems is always right, and what is wrong is flatly wrong. Many religious systems operate this way. In the Judeo-Christian traditions, the Ten Commandments are literally written on stone to signify their inviolability. There is little wiggle room with blanket statements like, "Thou shalt not steal." On the other hand, other systems are not as clear. When visiting an art museum, maybe you have seen one of those "suggested donation" boxes in the vestibule. Technically, entrance to the museum is free, but maybe there is a hint that the right thing to do would be to give some money. But giving depends on whether you have any money or are in the giving spirit. It is, in short, a system committed to **moral relativism**.

Absolutism and relativism rest on opposite ends of a conceptual axis because many systems have varying degrees of rigor. When driving a car, the rules for driving include road signs and signals that prescribe proper driving behaviors. Drivers are always expected to stop for traffic lights when the light is red and to wait until the light is green to proceed. This is ostensibly a hard-and-fast rule that aims to protect all drivers. But, then again, it is not always the case, since drivers may make a right turn against a red light when there is no crossing traffic. In that sense, the rules are relative, and the right action depends upon the conditions.

For the most part, academic integrity rules fall on the absolute end of the spectrum. In principle, there are no excuses for violations. In practice, however, there are hints of relativism. For example, institutions often make exceptions to certain rules for students with special learning needs. Some test-takers may earn a time extension or have access to otherwise-prohibited notes if the university or the professor agrees that the students have exceptional learning needs. In the case of plagiarism, a professor may overlook a poor example of paraphrasing or an improper citation if it appears certain that the student committed the violation out of error rather than intent. In these sorts of cases, the intent of the integrity rules is to safeguard the quality of the academic work and to help students learn and exhibit their best work. Thus, there is some flexibility with the rules as long as accommodations preserve the underlying goals of the system.

With respect to the British history final, however, if Andrew and Kaitlyn elected to collaborate on the exam, they would knowingly be violating the stated conditions of the test. But they would not be breaking the rules for the sake of wanton criminality; rather, they would be treating the rules as relative in order to earn Andrew a higher grade. In this instance, they would be practicing a specific form of relativism known as **situational ethics**, which, according to the ethicists Louis P. Pojman and James Frieser, "states that objective moral principles are to be applied differently in different contexts."[7] Andrew and Kaitlyn would both probably say that they almost always follow the rules, but that in this case the difficulty of the exam question and the risk to Andrew's grade create conditions that demand extraordinary action.

Situational dilemmas can be the font of many fascinating ethical discussions, but this case simply is not one of them. The reason that Andrew and Kaitlyn's situational ethical argument is flawed is that it violates not only the rules but also the spirit of the system behind the rules. Collaborating with a peer to find the right answer for an essay question does nothing to help Andrew learn, nor does it allow him complete his best and most authentic work. It only offers the hope of artificially raising his score on the exam, which is supposed to be a numerical assessment of his actual performance. It thwarts any honest assessment of his performance in the course and misrepresents his knowledge. Most likely, both Andrew and Kaitlyn know that their potential decision relativizes the academic integrity policy, so we have to push further to understand their ethical rationale.

Axis 2: Altruism and Egoism in Ethical Motives

Another way we might analyze Andrew and Kaitlyn's ethical problem is to consider the personal motives that inform the underlying ethical question: *Should we collaborate to earn a higher score on the final exam?* Motive often comes down to the distinction between **egoism**, in which one is focused on the interests of the self, and **altruism**, in which one is oriented toward others. On the far end of this spectrum are the so-called ethical egoists, who hold that the right thing to do is to act in accordance with their own interests, while on the other end of the spectrum are the pure altruists, who always make choices that favor others, even at the expense of themselves.[8] These, of course, are hypothetical extremes, since few if any individuals inhabit the radical ends. But one's actions can definitely shade toward one or the other end of the spectrum. If Andrew chooses to cheat on his exam, it is because he believes that doing so will improve his grade. Whether he is conscious of it or not, his assumption is that earning a good grade for himself is more important than following the prescribed rules. Perhaps he will attempt to ensure that his collaborator goes undetected, but generally his decision lands squarely on the egoist side of the spectrum. By contrast, Kaitlyn's decision would be motivated more by her interest in helping her friend, even at personal risk to herself, thus placing her more on the altruistic side (even if she believes that preserving her friendship is in her own best interest). In any case, both would still be committing an ethical violation.

When assessing their options, it is important to point out that theirs is not necessarily a mutually exclusive choice. There is a way that the two could act ethically and still benefit both themselves and each other. At first, it can be difficult to locate academic honesty on the egoism–altruism spectrum. In the case of final exams, doing the right thing may come at a cost for the individual without a clear benefit for anyone else. In fact, academic honesty falls right in between egoism and altruism because it benefits both self and others. It does so directly in a negative sense, in that following the rules precludes the possibility of getting caught and facing sanctions. More importantly, it has a positive, indirect benefit in that it upholds a culture of integrity for the course and the university, which enhances the quality of the students' grades and their diploma. If outsiders knew that cheating was rampant at a particular institution, then they might be inclined to think less of the value of a degree from that institution when evaluating their credentials or when making hiring and promotion decisions. Seen from this perspective, an honest grade, even if it is less than stellar, possesses more egoistic value for Andrew in the long run than one corrupted by academic dishonesty, and altruistically it ensures that other students who follow in his wake will enjoy the benefits of a quality degree.

Axis 3: Actions, Ends, and Ethical Orientations

Alongside underlying motives are the orientations behind ethical decisions, whether they are aimed at the *rightness of an act* or the *rightness of an outcome*. We can represent this aspect of an ethical argument on a spectrum between **teleological** and **deontological ethics**. Teleology, you may recall, comes from the Greek word *telos*, meaning "end." As an ethical concept, teleology suggests that our actions or beliefs are good when they produce good results. If Andrew and Kaitlyn decide to work together to feed Andrew the answers to the exam, it is in part because they judge the rightness of the action to be dependent on the right end, which for them means walking away with the best possible grade. By contrast, a deontological decision would rest on whether the act of collaborating was itself right or wrong. If one or both students decided not to collaborate, it would be in part because at least one of them observed that cheating is against the instructions of the exam and thus wrong.

The vast majority of ethical decisions fall somewhere between the radical extremes of deontology and teleology. We might argue that in this case, the best choice would be one that strives to align the perception of the best outcomes with adherence to the right actions. To steer Andrew and Kaitlyn in the proper direction, we would first recognize that the rules are clear, and the students' actions should therefore uphold them. At the same time, we would suggest that they reconsider their ultimate goal. Instead of seeing the grade as an end in itself, and striving toward producing work of the highest quality and authenticity, they would inevitably choose not to break the rules of the test. Seen from this perspective, Andrew might not be too pleased with his score, but he and Kaitlyn would at least be more at peace with their decision.

Making Ethics a Priority

You may have observed that in the case of Andrew's British history final, doing the right thing will come at a cost. Because he is not prepared for the questions, any sense of academic honesty will mean a poor showing on the examination. He may recognize the long-term value of a quality degree, but in the short-term grades matter, and this will undoubtedly put pressure on him to commit an integrity violation, particularly if he feels the chances of getting caught are meager. Indeed, studies show that the desire to "get ahead" is paramount in decisions to commit integrity violations.[9] Students facing looming deadlines or who are unprepared for time-sensitive assignments may treat them as extraordinary conditions demanding uncharacteristic responses. Under normal circumstances, these students would not knowingly violate academic integrity rules. In the back of their minds, they no doubt want to see themselves as honest and upstanding students; it is simply that the outside image of their performance takes precedence. The problem is that this same motivation seems more prevalent at the moment of the violation than at the beginning of a course of study, when a student could take steps to avoid an ethical predicament, such as attending class faithfully, seeking legitimate assistance from professors, and practicing better time management. When that occurs, time pressures become a convenient excuse for unethical choices after the fact.[10]

Preventing these sorts of unfortunate circumstances demands an appreciation for ethical work as a comprehensive priority. This requires the proper knowledge, attitudes, and skills. Institutions and professors have a responsibility to promote a positive view of ethics by integrating clear and visible messages in course and curriculum design and in the process of student advising and mentorship. Students meanwhile should expect to familiarize themselves with the policies of their disciplines and institutions and view the practice of ethics as an inseparable element of university learning alongside studying, reading, and writing. And they should recommit themselves at the beginning of every course and project to upholding academic integrity. When students face pressures, they must be willing to seek help, to accept the consequences in cases where they fall short, to put integrity above grades, and to learn from mistakes. Finally, as we will see in the last section of this chapter, students can apply various techniques to guarantee that their research and writing meet ethical standards.

REFLECTION EXERCISE

Write your own statement of ethics. Using the terminology described in this chapter, make an argument in which you explain why ethics is important to you and how you intend to keep ethical practices at the forefront of your university work. In what ways do your ethical commitments conform to an egoistic and teleological view of ethics?

From Academic Integrity to Research Ethics in History

One of the long-term benefits to ethical practice at the university level is that the experience prepares students to be ethical professionals. Just as academic integrity is integral to the mission of a university, so too do codes of ethics serve to define professional fields and academic disciplines. The specific rules may differ from field to field depending on their unique objectives, but they nonetheless rest upon overarching values that align with university academic integrity codes. This means that learning to uphold academic integrity policies is an essential element of future professionalism.

Academic integrity commitments also bring students into closer contact with the disciplines that they study. Indeed, ethical practices are a prerequisite for membership in any scholarly community. Along with research tools, methodologies, and domains of inquiry, they are defining features of a discipline. By attesting to the reliability of academic research, they lend disciplines their aura of authority and build trust among their constituent scholars. Without these practices, the production of knowledge within a discipline would lack credibility, and the bonds that unite a disciplinary community would swiftly wither.

Within the discipline of history, articulating and upholding the values, goals, and ethical practices of history are the responsibility of every institution associated with the discipline, but the central guidance comes from the major disciplinary associations. In the United States, the lodestar of the field is the American Historical Association (AHA), which maintains a *Statement on Standards of Professional Conduct*. This document declares that historians seek above all to "investigate and interpret the human past," and it makes clear that the audience of historical scholarship includes both professionals in the discipline and the wider public. When defining the discipline, the AHA includes a very open-ended and welcoming statement on membership, defining it as a "self-conscious identification" with the disciplinary community. There are, in other words, no governing boards that act as gatekeepers for the field. History is a public endeavor, and membership is consequently widely open to the public. For those who choose to identify themselves as historians, the AHA expects that they will follow the standards of the discipline, which include the utilization of "learned practice" and adherence to the field's ethical guidelines.[11]

The AHA identifies at least five core values that aim to make historical inquiry as accurate, as truthful, and as inclusive as possible. Paramount among these is the notion that all scholarship be pursued with an attitude of "trust and respect" for both fellow scholars and members of the public.[12] At the heart of this principle is the authority that historians hold as dedicated researchers of the past. Preserving that authority hinges on making interpretations that are trustworthy. If historians act from explicit bias or solely for personal gain, then their peers and their audiences have little basis for relying upon their judgments. Furthermore, no historian can interpret the past alone; new historical knowledge hinges on the discoveries and interpretations of others. For this reason, historians must be able to rely upon each other, and they must work collegially to cultivate the professional relationships that facilitate new discoveries.

In order to uphold its overarching values, the AHA stresses the importance of "honoring the integrity of the historical record," which means writing about documents, artifacts, and other primary sources as they actually appear and not misrepresenting existing evidence or "fabricating" evidence that does not exist. Historians must properly document any evidence they use so that other researchers can verify the results and utilize the sources for future studies. The organization also expects "acknowledging one's debts," which calls for historians to recognize when they borrow words or ideas from other scholars. Finally, the notion of "trust and respect" means that historians must "welcome diverging points of view," accepting that not all scholars will agree with one another on interpretations of the past, and seeking to find the best interpretations through "constructive criticism" that uses the techniques of critical thinking to assess different perspectives.[13]

Taken together, these values overlap with university integrity policies in that they seek to uphold the accuracy of human inquiry, research and knowledge production, and the credentials of the scholar. The expectation is that both students of history and professional historians will present their reflections and interpretations of the past in a way that is faithful to the evidence, responsible to those to whom they are indebted, mindful of its contributions to the larger mission of historical inquiry, and respectful in their engagement with others' ideas and writing. Moreover, both students and professionals must represent themselves accurately in their work, and in their résumés and curriculum vitae. They should never inflate their credentials or misrepresent their record of research and writing.

Making ethics a priority in academic work and understanding the principles, values, and standards that underlie scholarly disciplines are two important ingredients to ethical research. A third essential component is the application of strategies to conduct ethical research. In order to be faithful to the evidence, to acknowledge properly the debts of colleagues, and to thereby build trust and show respect for research subjects and peers, historians must exercise care in the collection and presentation of evidence.

DISCOVERY EXERCISE

Assess the integrity practices of your university. What are the institution's main policies and enforcement strategies? For example, does the university have an honor code, an integrity monitor, or some other system? What are the stated expectations of students, faculty, and administrators? How do students learn about integrity policies and what roles do they play in the enforcement process? Finally, to what extent do university's education and enforcement of academic integrity reflect negative or positive approaches? In what ways, in your view, might your university improve its approach to promoting a "culture of integrity" on campus?

Taking Notes

Avoiding ethical problems in essays hinges on proper notes, and these in turn rest upon a consistent note-taking system. Good historians come to appreciate the value of writing things down carefully. Your notes are indispensable not only for collecting evidence from your sources but also for developing your own ideas. There is no right way to take notes; the particular approach that you take depends on personal preference and experience. Some hardy historians continue to use old-fashioned methods, stacks of note cards or collections of spiral-bound notebooks. Others have embraced more modern, digital methods, making use of software applications like Evernote, Google Keep, or Microsoft OneNote. Any system that works for you is a good system, so long as you take heed to record information thoughtfully and systematically.

When extracting information from sources, whether they be primary documents or secondary texts, your notes should include a full citation and a note of where you can find that source should you need to consult it again in the future. A secondary monograph drawn from the library needs a note that includes a call number so that you can find it quickly. Similar care must go into the information drawn from the text. When writing down material from a specific passage, you want to ensure that you do not accidentally plagiarize material later. The way to avoid this is to make it a rule either to quote the information exactly as you find it in the text or otherwise to **paraphrase** it carefully, meaning that you reiterate the idea or intent of a text or passage entirely in your own words. In practice, you will probably include both quotes and paraphrases. If a passage looks like a good candidate for quoting in the text, then write it down verbatim in quotation marks. *Under no circumstances should you take a note without paraphrasing or quotation marks*; otherwise, you run the risk of confusing paraphrases and quotes and of accidentally transferring a passage into an essay without proper attribution. At the end of each note, you should include a reference indicating the page number or other relevant document location in parentheses.

It is perfectly fine to interject your own thoughts or questions while taking notes, and it can be a good practice to think with your texts while you are working. But you do not want to be sloppy when intermingling your ideas with those of the authors with whom you are working. You need a way to distinguish your own words. To accomplish that, you can vary your font style. When making a personal comment, use bold letters or italics, or change the color or size of the font. Always be consistent and use the same differentiated font elements across all of your notes.

Once you have completed your notes, find a safe place to keep them for the long term, whether that is in a box, on a shelf, or in the cloud. If questions arise about your work down the road, or if another student or scholar has questions beyond your immediate essay, you may need to return to your original notes months or even years later. Think of your notes as part of the permanent record related to your history project and treat them accordingly.

Citations

When you enter the Presentation Phase of your project, you will need yet another system to give proper credit to your sources and to present the evidence for your arguments. For the most part, historians use the *Chicago Manual of Style*, which cites sources in footnotes at the bottom of a page or endnotes placed at the end of an essay. Beyond their placement, footnotes and endnotes are essentially the same, providing a reference to the source and the location in the source where the cited material is found (i.e., a page number or dated entry). Scholars who wish to verify your work or conduct follow-up research should be able to use your footnotes to find the same information you used in your essay.

With footnotes and endnotes, the references are numbered sequentially throughout an essay or a book chapter. The reference number appears at the end of the sentence or sometimes at the end of an independent clause where the cited information appears. The footnote number appears as a superscript number just after the punctuation mark and after the closing quotation mark when citing a quote. In other words, with most word processing software, writers can simply place the cursor at the position on the page where the citation number is to appear and use an insert menu on the toolbar or taskbar to "Insert Footnote." The software will then take the writer to the bottom of the page or end of the document to complete the citation. Writers will usually want to give the footnote a smaller font; if the body text is a twelve-point font, then create the footnote in the same font style (i.e., Cambria or Times New Roman) and then set the footnote text to a ten-point font. This helps readers distinguish between the text and the references. Below is an example of a cited quote from Sven Beckert's *Empire of Cotton: A Global History*:

> As Sven Beckert explains, "Cotton, the nineteenth century's chief global commodity, brought seeming opposites together, turning them almost by alchemy into wealth: slavery and free labor, states and markets, colonialism and free trade, industrialization and deindustrialization."[1]

---

[1] Sven Beckert, *Empire of Cotton: A Global History* (New York: Vintage, 2015), *xix*.

The first time you cite a source using Chicago or Turabian Style, you must provide a full citation. If the same source appears later, however, then a shortened citation including the author's last name and an abbreviated title and page number will do. So, our quote from Beckert, if it appeared as a second citation of his book, would appear as "Beckert, *Empire of Cotton*, page number."

When deciding on how best to place a citation, it is acceptable to cite several sentences or even an entire paragraph together with a single footnote as long as the information in the section comes from the same source. If there are multiple sentences in a passage from multiple sources, or if your own ideas appear in the middle of the section, then more than one footnote may be in order. When using a direct quotation, the footnote should appear immediately after the quote. When two or more quotes appear back-to-back from the same source, however, then multiple citations may be needed, but only if the quotes come from different pages.

Paraphrasing and Quoting

The center of any historical research essay is your interpretation of past evidence. It thus stands to reason that the majority of the essay should contain your words. Nevertheless, there are key moments in any essay in which you will want to quote the exact words of an outside source. Certainly, you should avoid using quotations as filler or to repeat a point needlessly, but you will almost certainly find opportunities to use selective quotes to strengthen your case. In his guide book, *How to Write a Thesis*, the Italian historian and novelist Umberto Eco maintains that there are two main situations in which you should include a quote. The first is when you take "quotes from a text that you will interpret," and the second occurs when you take "quotes from a text that you will use to support your interpretation."[14] This means, on the one hand, that when you are making an argument about a specific passage, you should include a quote to show readers a key portion of the text you are analyzing. On the other hand, when you need proof or reinforcement for your argument, a quote can clarify and bolster your point.

When deciding what to quote from a text, you should look for passages to best convey the particular point you wish to make or that best illustrate the material you are attempting to analyze. Since you can always paraphrase content from a text, you should choose passages that express a point succinctly or that express an idea in more precise or more eloquent words than you can muster in a paraphrase. In general, you should limit your quote to the essential elements of a passage, limiting yourself to three sentences worth of material. If that proves impractical, then you must use a block quote, which is a passage set apart from the main text and incorporated in a slightly smaller font.

In most cases, material from other sources will enter your essay through paraphrasing. Again, a paraphrase is an idea or a passage translated into your own words and then cited in your essay. Paraphrasing is useful not only for translating key passages from other texts but also for condensing the ideas of much larger bodies of text, such as summarizing the contents of an article or book. In any case, you should strive to put paraphrased material as completely as possible into your own words; if you find it too difficult for some reason to fully alter the original text, because the right words fail you or you are at risk of losing the original meaning, then you should consider using a direct quote. To see how this works, let us return to the quote from Sven Beckert about the global history of cotton:

Original Citation

As Sven Beckert explains, "Cotton, the nineteenth century's chief global commodity, brought seeming opposites together, turning them almost by alchemy into wealth: slavery and free labor, states and markets, colonialism and free trade, industrialization and deindustrialization."[1]

---

[1]Sven Beckert, *Empire of Cotton: A Global History* (New York: Vintage, 2015), *xix*.

This passage is quoted verbatim using quotation marks and a footnote citation. It is just short enough to fit into the text without requiring a block quote. Notice that the text also alludes to the author. In general, you want to avoid placing an unintroduced quote, which appears with quotation marks but gives readers no immediate clue to whom it refers.

Now let's see a first attempt at paraphrasing. This one, you will see, is poorly done, and represents a violation of academic integrity rules. We have placed the words taken directly from the original text in bold font:

First Attempt: Plagiarism

Cotton, the nineteenth century's highest commodity, **brought opposites together, turning them** into fabulous **wealth: slavery and free labor, states and markets, colonialism and free trade, industrialization and deindustrialization.**

This passage makes a minor attempt to modify the original text, but dropping a word here and changing a couple of words there still leaves 85 percent of the original text, still a clear case of plagiarism. The violation is exacerbated by the absence of a citation. In the next attempt, things improve somewhat:

Second Attempt: Poor Paraphrasing

Cotton, an important **commodity,** harmonized **seemingly opposite** ideas: **slavery** and wage earnings, imperialism and **free trade, industrialization and deindustrialization.**[1]

---

[1]Sven Beckert, *Empire of Cotton: A Global History* (New York: Vintage, 2015), *xix.*

A professor looking at this passage would likely determine that the student tried to avoid plagiarism, but still left a shoddy paraphrasing borrowing many of the original words and the essential structure of Beckert's sentence. In the very least, the citation has returned, so clearly the student has attempted to give credit, but still needs to work on this passage a bit more:

Third Attempt: Better Paraphrasing

As Sven Beckert has observed, **cotton,** by harmonizing new and old means of production and distribution, became a key trade product and a paramount economic success story in the **nineteenth century.**[1]

---

[1]Sven Beckert, *Empire of Cotton: A Global History* (New York: Vintage, 2015), *xix.*

In this final version, the in-text attribution and the citation are present, which is good because the idea in the sentence is a particularly central and highly original point in Beckert's book. At the same time, the only words that carry over from the original text are "cotton," and "nineteenth century," which have to remain because they identify the topic of the discussion. The student has rephrased everything else and has even changed the structural arrangement of the ideas. Given the precision and importance of the original, it is probably the case that Beckert's sentence deserves a full quotation, but this paraphrase certainly passes muster.

Institutional Review Boards

Historians as a rule strive to show respect to their research subjects, and they make it their business to exercise great care when entering their lives and telling their stories. In most cases, historians do not have to worry too much about offending or harming their subjects. After all, their subjects are usually long deceased. There are times, however, when a project includes an interview or otherwise involves the participation of a living person, and when that happens, a different set of ethical standards applies. Working with human subjects is familiar to psychologists, sociologists, and other social scientists who regularly work with living human populations, and over the last century, their disciplines have developed rigorous safeguards to protect the rights, sensibilities, and physical and mental well-being of their subjects. Oral historians frequently work with these same considerations in mind, and like their colleagues in the social sciences, they cooperate with the ethical review protocols at their institutions.

Since the 1970s, federal law in the United States has mandated these sorts of institutional review boards as a way to evaluate human and animal research projects to verify adherence to ethical standards. For human research specifically, the boards are important mechanisms for guaranteeing that human subjects understand the nature of the studies in which they participate and that they are able to give informed consent. They also seek to make certain that the parameters of studies are not likely to cause unintentional harm to subjects. Things are a little different in the United Kingdom, where all research is subject to ethical review, but where oral histories are generally granted blanket exemptions.

There is widespread agreement within academic communities that institutional review boards serve a valuable purpose, but there are unique challenges that confront scholars in specific fields like history and anthropology. The ethicist Michael Montag and the historian Rachel Vagts have detailed the complaints that humanities and social science scholars have raised against a system of ethical review that was largely created to serve the needs of the natural sciences and thus applies ethical standards less suited for the methods of other fields.[15] For example, they have pointed to requirements that interview subjects remain anonymous, which is a sensible requirement for a clinical study but much less so for a historical account addressing a specific group of individuals. They have highlighted instances in which review boards have demanded complete transcripts of questions and answers before an interview, which is difficult for historians and anthropologists who wish to give their subjects space to expound on an unpredictable range of topics.[16]

In an attempt to accommodate the concerns of board members, adhere to national standards, and still preserve the unique methodological requirements of live interviews, the Oral History Association maintains its own rules, outlined in a 2009 document, "Principles and Best Practices of Oral History." The guidelines cover all phases of an encounter with a subject, from the steps needed to prepare for an interview to the proper way to archive transcripts and recordings. Along the way, the document makes recommendations for dealing with the thorniest issues related to IRB requirements for social science research. To address the question of anonymity, for example, the document suggests that interviewers meet with subjects before a formal recording session in order to discuss the appropriate information about the project and discuss with subjects their rights and obligations before and after the interview. Interviewers are expected to explain the options for anonymity, the scope of access to recordings, and come to agreement on any off-limits topics or interview ground rules before conducting the interview, giving the subjects the option to opt out if they so choose. With respect to the dilemma with pre-approved questions, the standards state, "Interviewers should prepare an outline of interview topics and questions to use as a guide to the recorded dialogue."[17] This means that the historian need not provide precise questions in advance, but they should be able to provide an overarching sketch of the interview and be willing to share outlines, releases, and project statements to the institutional review board for approval before formally approaching the subjects for an interview.

If you are considering an oral history project, then before you begin the Discovery Phase of your project, you should consult with your research mentor and determine the prior obligations for submitting your work for review by an institutional review board at your university. It is possible that your project may be exempted from oversight under federal regulations in the United States, but those exemptions derive from the boards themselves, so you should expect to submit a project overview, identifying yourself as the lead researcher, or **principal investigator (PI)**. Following these protocols not only keeps you and your research supervisor on the right side of university policy and US law; it also demonstrates your commitment to respecting the people who appear in your study and whose history you intend to explore.

Ethical from Beginning to End

The marks of your commitment to ethics appear throughout your research. In the text itself are the selected quotes and paraphrases from primary secondary texts, in footnotes at the bottom of every page there is a nod to the scholarly works upon which your own contribution relies. These elements of your essay are critical as both exhibitions of your evidence and as acts of "acknowledging your debts" in keeping with the standards of the discipline. But, as we have stated, ethics also begins at the beginning. This is true of your commitment to academic integrity on the first day of a new course, and it is true in your essay. For longer papers, such as undergraduate theses or dissertations, it is customary to include a formal acknowledgements section at the very beginning of the work. Since not every debt that you incur in the course of a research project belongs in a footnote, the acknowledgments section is a space for identifying the many unsung heroes whose support and encouragement made your project possible. The archivists and librarians, the colleagues who lent advice to help you find answers, the peers who lent their eyeballs to help you find typos, and of course your mentors are among those who merit recognition and thanks. It is also very important to acknowledge any grants, fellowships, or institutions that provided funding or materials for your research.

If ethical work counts among your values from the start, then it should remain so at the end. As a final ethical act, in the spirit of gratitude for the help you have received and in following the discipline's call to be of service to peers and public, we might encourage you to pay your debts forward. As you build expertise in history and in your topic area, and as you become more practiced with the practices of sound research, be willing to help those who come after you. Be generous with your knowledge and experience. Avoid feeling territorial about your research area, and instead welcome those who wish to expand their understanding of your topic. Ethical historians participate in the academic discussion within their field through their original research contributions, but also through constructive feedback on the work of colleagues and students. Be frank with your advice and honest with your criticism, but maintain a charitable approach that sees your peers as fellow historians who, like you, are trying to make a positive contribution to our understanding of the past.

History in Practice: Paraphrasing Sources

Below is a lengthy quote that Jack Wells wants to use in his essay, because it contains an important interpretation of the role of depopulation in the decline of the western Roman Empire. But, as the example shows, quoting is not always the best solution.

Jack Wells, "Christianity and the Fall of Rome"

In writing about the role of Christianity in the collapse of the empire, it helps to tackle the alternative explanations. That is what makes this passage from J.B. Bury so important, because it refutes depopulation as a potential cause of Rome's decline. The problem is that the passage itself is a little unwieldy. For instance, Bury refers to Gibbon, but only indirectly, and the basic point about depopulation is couched in a slightly larger discussion about the causes of decline. Thus, I would want to paraphrase most of the passage and perhaps find one or two choice statements that are clear and that drive home the author's point.

> The explanations of the calamities of the Empire which have been hazarded by modern writers are of a different order from those which occurred to witnesses of the events, but they are not much more satisfying. The illustrious historian whose name will always be associated with the "Decline" of the Roman Empire invoked "the principle of decay," a principle which has itself to be explained.

Depopulation, the Christian religion, the fiscal system have all been assigned as causes of the Empire's decline in strength. If these or any of them were responsible for its dismemberment by the barbarians in the West, it may be asked how it was in the East, where the same causes operated, the Empire survived much longer intact and united.

Consider depopulation. The depopulation of Italy was an important fact and it had far-reaching consequences. But it was a process which had probably reached its limit in the time of Augustus. There is no evidence that the empire was less populous in the fourth and fifth centuries than in the first. This "sterility of the human harvest" in Italy and Greece affected the Empire from its very beginning, but does not explain the collapse in the fifth century. The truth is that there are two distinct questions which have become confused. It is one thing to seek the causes which changed the Roman State from what it was in the best days of the Republic to what it had become in the age of Theodosius the Great—a change which from a certain point of view may be called a "decline." It is quite another thing to ask why the State which could resist its enemies on many frontiers in the days of Diocletian and Constantine and Julian suddenly gave way in the days of Honorius. "Depopulation" may partly supply the answer to the first question, but it is not an answer to the second ....[18]

APPLICATION EXERCISE

Try your hand at paraphrasing. Paraphrase the quote above in your own words so that it is clearer and more concise. Which one or two short quotes from the original would be appropriate to include and why. Compare your paraphrasing with a partner and discuss your respective choices.

Notes

1   William J. Bowers, *Student Dishonesty and Its Control in College* (New York: Columbia University Bureau of Applied Social Research, 1964).

2   Donald. L. McCabe, Kenneth D. Butterfield, and Linda Klebe Treviño, *Cheating in College: Why Students Do It and What Educators Can Do about It* (Baltimore: Johns Hopkins University Press, 2012), 35–50.

3   Randy L. Devereaux and Beverly A. McCloud, "Circumstances Surrounding Cheating: A Questionnaire Study of College Students," *Research in Higher Education* 33, no. 6 (1995): 687–704.

4   Peter Charles Hoffer, *Past Imperfect: Facts, Fictions, Fraud–American History from Bancroft and Parkman, to Ambrose, Bellesiles, and Goodwin* (New York: Public Affairs, 2007).

5   McCabe et al., *Cheating in College*, 172–4.

6   Louis P. Pojman and James Fieser, *Understanding Ethics: Discovering Right and Wrong*, 8th ed. (Belmont, CA: Wadsworth, 2016), 1–3.

7   Ibid., 43.

8   Ibid., 82, 87.

9   Mark G. Simkin and Alexander McLeod, "Why Do Students Cheat?" *Journal of Business Ethics* 94 (2010): 441–53.

10   Henning et al., "Reasons for Academic Honesty and Dishonesty with Solutions: A Study of Pharmacy and Medical Students in New Zealand," *Journal of Medical Ethics* 40, no. 10 (2014): 702–9.

11   American Historical Association, *Statement of Standards for Professional Conduct*, https://www.historians.org/jobs-and-professional-development/statements-standards-and-guidelines-of-the-discipline/statement-on-standards-of-professional-conduct (accessed December 10, 2018).

12   Ibid.

13   Ibid.

14   Umberto Eco, *How to Write a Thesis*, translated by Catarina Mongiat Farina and Geoff Farina (Cambridge, MA: MIT Press, 2015), 156.

15   Michael Sontag, "Research Ethics and Institutional Review Boards: The Influence of Moral Constraints on Emotion Research," *Politics and the Life Sciences* 31, no. 1 (2012): 67–80, esp. 68–70.

16   Rachel Vagts, "Clashing Disciplines: Oral History and the Institutional Review Board," *Archival Issues* 26, no. 2 (2002): 145–52.

17   Oral History Association, "Principles and Best Practices for Oral History," http://www.oralhistory.org/about/principles-and-practices-revised-2009/ (accessed December 10, 2018).

18   J.B. Bury, *History of the Later Roman Empire: From the Death of Theodosius I to the Death of Justinian*, vol. 1 (New York: Dover, 1958), 308–9.

Suggested Reading

Hoffer, Peter Charles. *Past Imperfect: Facts, Fictions, and Fraud in the Writing of American History*. New York: Public Affairs, 2014.

McCabe, Donald L., Kenneth D. Butterfield, and Linda K. Treviño. *Cheating in College: Why Students Do It and What Educators Can Do about It*. Baltimore: Johns Hopkins University Press, 2012.

Pojman, Louis P. 2016. *Ethics: Discovering Right and Wrong*. 8th ed. Boston: Wadsworth, 2016.

Turabian, Kate L. et al. *A Manual for Writers of Research Papers, Theses, and Dissertations, Ninth Edition: Chicago Style for Students and Researchers*. 9th ed. Chicago: University of Chicago Press. 2018.

8

Writing like a Historian

What we will do in this chapter:

- ➤ **REFLECT** on the place of narrative in historical writing.
- ➤ **DISCOVER** stylistic techniques for writing about history.
- ➤ **APPLY** strategies for creating outlines and writing proposals, essays, and abstracts.

History and Narrativity

History is one of the best fields of study for learning how to write. In the assignments that attach to your history courses, and especially in your research projects, you can expect opportunities for learning to write with clarity, power, and style. Sometimes, we believe that students and faculty alike overlook this unique benefit. By now, you probably know all too well that historians are readers: books, articles, documents, and even art, music, and photographs; if it concerns the past, no form of "text" is off-limits. Less commonly observed are the degrees to which historians are also prodigious writers, and the ways in which they have certain advantages that mold their powers of composition. For one, they work with particularities, meaning that they are writing about something concrete. Other social scientists write mostly about patterns and generalities, while neighboring humanities fields spend more time wrestling with highly theoretical or abstract concepts, demanding a level of precision that can affect the accessibility of their texts. Historians, by contrast, can engage big ideas or thorny issues, but they invariably anchor those with discussions of specific people, places, or events. Even when historians themselves wax theoretical, they are always writing about real human beings. Natural scientists also write about the physical world, but they must deal with natural phenomena, processes that operate over deep time, that occur across galaxies or down to the microscopic level. There are, of course, terrific science writers, but historians have the advantage of connecting readers with other people, presenting life events that may be peculiar by dint of their historical difference, but are nonetheless familiar on a human level.

Historians are also favored as writers because they read, and they read a lot. Among the things that they read are the works of other historians who themselves are great writers. Within every subfield of history, there are touchstone books whose titles are familiar to every advanced student. These are the ones that appear at the top of the doctoral exam reading lists and whose authors are revered as towering trendsetters in the field. Above all, these are the books that stand the test of time. They remain relevant long after their authors have retired and even as new scholarship appears on the shelf. In many cases, the touchstone books are as important for their style as they are for their content.

One such book, popular among historians of modern Germany, is *Germany from Napoleon to Bismarck, 1800–1866,* by Thomas Nipperdey (1918–1992). This was the first of a two-volume history of German history from 1800 to 1918. The title may not be particularly exciting, but there are several reasons why Nipperdey's study is so highly regarded. It is, first of all, a magisterial study of the social and political developments that shaped the German-speaking lands. With its pages chock-full of data on demographics and economics, it paints a far-ranging statistical picture of the transformations that characterized the nineteenth century. Crucially, it is also artfully written. Nipperdey launches his 700 pages with a particularly famous and deceptively simple first sentence: "In the beginning was Napoleon."[1]

With this short opening line, Nipperdey accomplishes three important goals. First, by evoking the first lines of both the Book of Genesis and the Book of John in the Bible, Nipperdey sets up his account as an origin story for the German nation-state, thus framing the first seven decades of the nineteenth century as a narrative shaped by war, revolution, and reform. Second, by centering his account on Napoleon, an outsider, he rejects older historiographical traditions that portrayed the ascendance of the Prussian-centered Empire as the heart of the story and the natural outcome of centuries of historical development. Very tellingly, Nipperdey ends his narrative not in 1871 with the formation of the *Kaiserreich* (the German Empire), but in 1866 with the defeat of Austria. This terminal date suggests a reframing of German history. "It was," in his words, "the end of an era which had lasted nearly a thousand years," but its denouement was not the emergence of the Kaiserreich, but the exclusion of Austria from its former domains in Germany.[2] The result was not the conclusion of Prussia's natural triumph, but the decline of older, polyglot empires and the final rise of a nation-state system, whose consequences would echo through the twentieth century. At the same time, Nipperdey takes equal aim at a more recent historiography that lays the blame for the tragedies of the twentieth century dramatically at the feet of the nineteenth. He decouples the era from modernization theories casting it as a root cause for the emergence of the Nazi dictatorship. He closes his study with no less a powerful statement: "The future was burdened and overshadowed, and it was, as always, fated. But it was open."[3]

These statements, sweeping and authoritative as they are, bookend Nipperdey's third achievement, which is the story that he tells. He manages to take all the ponderous detail and data that he collected for this period and weave it into a cohesive narrative to which readers can relate and that imparts a sense of broader meaning on the events that transpired in the years before the establishment of the German Kaiserreich. His is a story of Germans reacting to the mighty historical tides crashing around them: the great powers of England, France, and Russia invading Central Europe and conspiring to reshape the continent; the political and industrial revolutions, whose initial spark ignited in faraway cities but soon swept across Europe; and of course the towering figures of Napoleon Bonaparte and Otto von Bismarck, who held in common an uncanny talent for seizing control of events and bending them to their will to effect massive historical changes and build powerful empires. We might take issue with Nipperdey's conclusions or even his framing of the period, but there is no denying that he tells quite a tale.

There was a time when the historical discipline thoroughly embraced narrativity and eloquence in its study of the past. Historians in the late nineteenth and early twentieth centuries saw themselves telling very human stories, and their sense of intellectual authority emboldened them to make sweeping interpretations about their subjects. Take, for example, the work of the Dutch historian Johan Huizinga (1872–1945), whose most famous book, *The Autumn of the Middle Ages*, looked through the lens of culture to narrate the final century of medieval Europe. Huizinga explained the transition between the Middle Ages and the modern era not as a sudden series of economic, political, or military events but as a gradual diminishing of medieval cultural forms. His story uses the seasonal changes of autumn as an analogy, as when the leaves first erupt into brilliant color before withering and gradually falling away. It was an apt analogy for the late Middle Ages, when particular ways of "craving a more beautiful life" grew more pronounced in the fourteenth century with increasingly defined customs, magnificent fairs, and deeply elaborated art, before giving way through repetition to something new.[4]

Huizinga's book appeared in 1919 and was translated into several languages between 1924 and 1932. It was popular in part because it resonated with historians in the early twentieth century, a time when the discipline was finding new avenues to explore, using the wider temporal lens of the *longue durée* in order to examine deep structures. But his work remains relevant today, receiving its first full English translation only in 1996. New generations of historians continue to admire its erudition and eloquence. For just a small sample of Huizinga's skill, read the opening to his first chapter, which sets the stage for a European society on the cusp of a slow but inevitable transition:

> When the world was half a thousand years younger all events had much sharper outlines than now. The distance between sadness and joy, between good and bad fortune, seemed to be much greater than for us; every experience had that degree of directness and absoluteness that joy and sadness still have in the mind of a child. Every event, every deed was defined in given and expressive forms and was in accord with the solemnity of a tight, invariable lifestyle. The great events of human life—birth, marriage, death—by virtue of the sacraments, basked in the radiance of the divine mystery. But even the lesser events—a journey, labor, a visit—were accompanied by a multitude of blessings, ceremonies, sayings, and conventions.[5]

With these opening lines, Huizinga engages in a bit of literary world-building with an eye for generality and an assuredness that can only come from years of patient study.

Perhaps paradoxically, just as Huizinga's work was reaching a broader audience in the 1930s, the appetite for literary style and narrative approach began to fall out of favor among historians. The Annales School, to which Huizinga bore some affinities, nonetheless came to eschew narrative in favor of static, structural approaches. At the same time, the popularity of Marxist approaches in the middle decades of the twentieth century led many Western European and American historians on searches for underlying dialectical processes and for the members of an unsung, faceless working class. In the 1960s and 1970s, the cliometricians similarly pushed a scientific approach to history that favored numbers over names and statistics over stories. Finally, the postmodern turn of the late twentieth century called into question the truth claims of literary conventions in historical writing, pushing historians to retreat into the safety of hard facts and figures. The collective upshot of these trends was that the narrative tradition of history was pressured from opposite poles: from one side, it was rejected by a turn toward seeing history as a social science discipline stressing the search for scientific truth, and, on the other side, it was assailed by a postmodern current in the humanities expressing skepticism of truth altogether. With the falling interest in narrative came a concomitant decline in the value of literary style and elegance in historical writing.

It was the English historian Lawrence Stone (1919–1999), a frequent foil to the British Marxist community, who was instrumental in the "revival of narrative" in the 1980s and 1990s.[6] Stone made his case in 1979, in the years after the student movements of the 1960s had undermined cozy notions of consensus that buttressed past Marxist, capitalist, and even scientific worldviews. The desire to assert the voices of the marginalized—women, minorities, postcolonial subjects—engendered a fresh appreciation for the more personal, and particularistic emphases of traditional historical storytelling. Stone suggested that similar revolts had unfolded among historians in the following decade. He maintained that scholars had become "widely disillusioned with the economic determinist model of historical explanation" characteristic of Marxism and skeptical of the "mixed record" offered by cliometrics. Moreover, he observed a fresh hunger for culture and for an understanding of individual agency in historical change.[7] With these observations, Stone heralded a broad disciplinary shift that did not preclude social science methods but that added possibilities for such approaches as microhistory, the history of everyday life (*Alltagsgeschichte*), and gender history, along with the cultural and linguistic turns of the 1980s. Embedded within these movements was a partial restoration of the value of history as a constituent of the humanities.

Seen from this angle, the structure of Thomas Nipperdey's history of nineteenth-century Germany fits with this return to a humanities focus. But its attention to macro-historical trends and its use of quantitative data remain tied to social science methods. Consequently, Nipperdey's work is a key example of the blending of currents from twentieth-century historiography. In a tacit nod to the postmodern challenge, Nipperdey positions his account against two major "master narratives" in German history: the nationalist narrative celebrating the triumph of Prussia and the modernist narrative bemoaning the early harbingers of the Third Reich. Yet by explaining the rise of the German nation-state as a reaction to immense forces of revolution, he did not shy away from his own sense of narrative order on the events of the nineteenth century. In other words, Nipperdey rejects the idea of master narratives, but he embraces the tradition of crafting metanarratives. The difference is that where the former aspires to locate a grander truth about history, the latter simply attempts to make an overarching statement about the past that is plausibly true. There is no claim, therefore, to final truth in a metanarrative, only logical consistency. The result is a way of talking about the past that is both informed by facts and conveyed as narrative.

This, we would argue, comprises a final advantage for the history writer. It is that the discipline of history has a foot in both the social sciences and the humanities, and in terms of writing, it draws from the best traditions of both. It is staunchly empirical, weaving together a variety of types of evidence to see the past from different perspectives, through distinct lenses, and across variable time scales. And it is firmly rooted in the humanities, embracing narrative conventions and a range of styles to tell human stories. The resulting hybridity allows historians to be at once precise and elegant and to have the methodological and compositional space they need to capture the breadth and variety of their subjects. As Lawrence Stone explained, "History has always had many mansions, and must continue to do so if it is to flourish in the future."[8] Decades later, his words continue to ring true.

REFLECTION EXERCISE

Find your favorite history book, or, if you have not discovered yours, ask a friend or professor to recommend one. Assess its quality as a written text. What makes the book a successful piece of writing? To what extent does the book create a narrative, and how effectively does it blend narrative with empirical data? How does this book make you think about your own historical writing?

Striking a Balance

When we discussed active reading in Chapter 5, we made the point that learning to read at a university level is challenging in part because you have already been reading for years. Writing is likewise not exactly a new skill. Thus, it makes little sense for this textbook to try and teach you the finer points of grammar and syntax. If you feel like you need to improve those elements of your writing (and, if we are being honest, all of us could stand a refresher from time to time), then we recommend that you enroll in university-level composition courses, including courses at the advanced level, and that you always make use of writing resources and tutoring on your campus. We also suggest that all students acquire a writing handbook and keep it alongside a dictionary and a *Turabian's Guide* on a personal reference shelf (we do).

Beyond the basics, there are specific improvements that you can make with an eye toward writing like a historian, that is, in a way that honors the best traditions of both the social sciences and the humanities. Writing between these two disciplinary traditions is akin to standing astride a balance beam. On one end is the very precise, formal, and empirical language familiar to scholars in the social sciences and on the other is the more stylistic writing of the humanities. Writing history should ideally place you more or less at the fulcrum. If your words shade too closely to the former end, you risk falling into an overly formal, clinical style that can obscure the human dimension of your research subjects. If you drift too far the other way, however, your paper risks becoming too informal, undermining its authoritative tone, losing its empirical focus, and obscuring its arguments. The challenge is to preserve a style and tone in your writing that is befitting the subject of your research project. Some works may rest slightly to one side or the other, but in general, they should establish a sense of balance between the two.

DISCOVERY EXERCISE

Before reading any further, set a timer for ten minutes and quickly write an essay describing a historical event you have studied recently. It could be an essay about the events surrounding your research topic or a brief description of an event you have encountered in a book or class lecture. Use a freewriting approach. Keep moving forward with your text, ignoring factual accuracy, grammar errors, or citations. When you have finished, set your essay aside and read the suggestions below.

To help you achieve the right tone, there are a few simple practices you can adopt in your writing:

Be consistent with verb tense: Verb usage can be very tricky when writing about history. The people and groups about whom you write lived in the past, but their stories sometimes unfold in a chronological narrative that feels like it is running in the present. And then there are the secondary sources, which were written years and even decades in the past but whose arguments still speak directly to us today. Taken together, these elements of a historical project can lead to an awkward bundle of simple pasts and present perfects that can bewilder a reader and leave them feeling unmoored from any sense of time. To avoid this dilemma, the key is to be consistent with the ways in which you use your verbs. You need not use the same tense throughout a paper, but you should try to use the same tense for similar situations. When relating events from the past, you should use the past tense. When discussing the past from the perspective of a historical figure, you should employ the past perfect, unless the past action is ongoing, in which case you would use the past perfect continuous (also called the past perfect progressive). All three are on display in this example:

> In May 1795, the pirates returned to the island. [simple past] They had buried their treasure there two years earlier, [past perfect], and had been returning every three months to add to their booty. [past perfect continuous]

The passive voice should be avoided: Most sentences are active, meaning they have a subject that performs an action impacting a direct object ("The candidate won the election.") and sometimes involving indirect object ("That speech won the election for the candidate"). Some sentences, however, adopt a passive voice when they switch the roles of the subject and the object. Thus, we could transform the sentence, "The candidate won the election," into a passive sentence simply by rephrasing it this way: "The election was won by the candidate." In some cases, the subject drops away altogether: "The election was won," or "The journey was completed." Using the passive voice is by no means a mortal sin, but it can be unwieldy and awkward to read. Scholarly writers employ passive voice to stress the action while diminishing agency. Their goal can be to distance themselves from an action if they are the subject and thereby maintain an air of clinical distance, as in the sentence, "An analysis was conducted on the census of 1890." Or a writer may implicitly reduce the unique identity of a subject and in this way grant a particular act an air of generality, as when a scholar explains, "A decision was made to formulate a new policy." This works in some social science writing, but history writing is stronger when it emphasizes the particular, and thus focuses on the subject. If they read the sentence, "A decision was made," historians would want to know who made the decision, because they would want to know when, how, and why they made it.

Avoid colloquial language: When we use colloquial language, as when we have a conversation or write informally, our sentences become peppered with shortcuts. We may use idiomatic expressions familiar to friends, we may employ jargon shared among professionals, we may abbreviate, and, of course, we are likely to use contractions. There is nothing wrong with informal elements in normal, day-to-day writing, but the problem with using them in formal writing is that they lack clarity and precision. They can confuse readers who are unfamiliar with the meaning of a shared colloquialism or who do not know the jargon of a particular field or specialty. Moreover, colloquialisms set the wrong tone. Academic writing should be clear and precise, but also professional. A scholar who has put a lot of work into a project and gained a measure of authority on a particular topic should write with authority. By avoiding idiomatic language and contractions, you give an essay the feel of a serious piece of scholarship.

Write in your comfort zone: When shooting for a formal style to lend your writing a polished look and authoritative quality, it is important not to go overboard. Inexperienced writers sometimes try too hard to adopt a formal tone in order to appear "scholarly." What they are really trying to do is bolster their argument with their style. The result can be a variant of what David Hackett Fischer calls "*argumentum ad verecundiam*," or the **fallacy of inappropriate authority**, which attempts to persuade a reader through a false appeal to authority.[9] If the writer couches an argument in academic-sounding language, the thinking goes, then the reader will be more likely to accept it. Certainly, the right style and language are essential to understanding and appreciating an academic argument, but they can only do so insofar as they help improve the piece's clarity and precision. In fact, an overly formal paper can actually make a paper less clear because it can obscure an argument with inaccessible language, or the level of writing can simply muddle the message. For this reason, as you try to balance humanities and social science writing in history, and to maintain an equilibrium between formal and informal style, you should stay within striking distance of your comfort zone. This does not mean that you cannot challenge yourself and try to grow as a writer, but you should not adopt a style that is not natural to you. You can, for instance, expand your vocabulary through your work, but be mindful of words whose connotations you may not fully comprehend, and always be wary of words you find in a thesaurus that you have not checked against a dictionary.

Be concise: Undergraduate writers often worry about the length of their papers. They may have a prescribed page length or word count and worry that they will not have enough material to meet the requirement. Indeed, this highlights a shortcoming of page requirements. While they are usually well intentioned and reflect the typical parameters of a successful research essay, they nevertheless impose an artificial standard that may not conform to the demands of the student writer's main argument. It is fair to say that a paper that is too short will likely lack enough empirical evidence or a sufficiently nuanced thesis. But it is just as likely that a student will feel compelled to stuff his or her paper with fluff in order to reach the desired length. Such papers might include excess verbiage, ponderous sentences rife with comma splices, and tangential elements not directly connected to the thesis. Also common are the dreaded redundant sentences, in which the paper repeats claims across multiple paragraphs in an effort to stretch the length of the paper, to compensate for weak evidence, or in a misguided attempt to label the arguments. The result is a paper that requires a reader to sift through the extraneous elements like a prospector panning for gold in search of the nuggets of crucial information.

Wherever possible, we encourage you to write concisely, avoiding unnecessary words, phrases, and elements. Focus instead on writing the things that are necessary to framing, explaining, and proving your main arguments. This is a practice that should guide your writing, but should also be a part of your proofreading and editing processes. Just as a filmmaker always leaves some extra footage on the cutting-room floor, so too can you go back and shave off the bits of your paper that appear redundant or otherwise nonessential.

DISCOVERY EXERCISE

Go back and review the essay that you wrote at the beginning of this section. How many of the issues described above appeared in your writing? Exchange your essay with a partner and try to spot the incidents of passive voice construction, problematic verb tenses, colloquialisms, and overly labored or unclear language. For each example, make a correction list and write some ways that you could repair any problematic sentences.

Planning Your Essay

Beware the blinking cursor. Present at the opening of every word processing document, this indicator rhythmically beckons you to unleash your writing but also chides you when you have nothing to say. Its persistent flashing is like a siren call to get started, but it is the last place that you want to begin your writing process. There is a lot to be said, of course, for activities like brainstorming, for letting your thoughts run wild and coalesce in order to glimpse the look of your final paper. And experienced writers come to appreciate freewriting, an open-ended, forward-moving foray onto the page that draws a crucial line between the processes of writing and editing. Neither of these activities, however, should be confused with launching a paper cold, or for beginning with the blinking cursor. Whatever your writing style, you must learn that proper writing requires proper planning. Essays demand structure, and structure demands respect for the essay as a whole. This is especially the case when writing an essay centered on a strong, carefully constructed argument. For this reason, when applying your goal planning skills to the Presentation Phase of your research project, you must give yourself time to plan, to outline, and to find the right structure for your essay.

Most guides recommend that you begin with the outlining process, of setting down Is and IIs and As and Bs and so on, but the problem is that outlining assumes structure without content. We have seen more than a few student outlines that begin with "I. Introduction" and end with "IV. Conclusion" without really telling us much about what they contain. In reality, the first thing you need to do, before worrying about where things go, is to decide what belongs in the essay. These are the *elements* of your paper. Start by making a list that begins with your main argument. Below that, write down plainly your research question, your research problem, and your conclusions. Once you have these on paper, you can write down the other elements that are required to elaborate, explain, and ultimately to prove your argument.

Having spelled out the elements you need for the outline, you can determine the proper sequence. For this task, let's use a helpful analogy. Imagine a team of horses pulling a stagecoach. The horses are the elements in the essay, and the coach is the main argument. This serves as a reminder of the essential relationship among the components of an essay. Specifically, the horses attached to the coach must pull their weight and work together as a team. This means first that the components of your paper must all be directly related to your argument; otherwise, your horses are not attached to the wagon and instead are running loose in the lane. Second, it means that the components must be arranged in a logical sequence, lest they become confused and pull the coach into a ditch. Just as each horse has its own place in the line, so too must the elements of your thesis follow in logical order one after the other.

The same principles also apply to each individual paragraph. As you begin to construct your outline, you should designate the larger elements in your paper, which are the ones that are indispensable to the overarching argument, with Roman numerals I, II, III, IV, and so on. Lay these out in the sequence, whether chronological, thematic, or analytical, that most cogently develops the argument. Then, for each Roman numeral section, create subsections marked alphabetically, A, B, C, and so forth. In an essay, these are the paragraphs in which you will elaborate on the individual elements. It is crucial that you design **topical paragraphs**, meaning that each will deal with a single topic. When describing your As, Bs, and Cs in the outline, write out each label as a complete sentence that may serve as a **topic sentence** in the essay. Beneath the topic sentence, identify the related parts of the paragraph as subheadings 1, 2, 3, and so on. Just as you did for the larger paper, make sure that these elements are all necessary and relevant to the paragraph topic. Be specific and try to write in complete sentences to make your points as clear as possible.

From this point, you may find yourself needing further subheadings: a. b. c. d., i., ii., iii., iv., and possibly even more. In any case, make sure that you avoid identifying one subheader without other subheaders. In other words, your outline should not include a subheader A without a subheader B, or subpoint 1 without subpoint 2. If you find yourself with a single element that requires no further explaining or adjoining elements, then it is probably the case that the piece in question either fits in with another, larger component or is less relevant to the project.

Outline carefully, but remember that the outline is not the final paper. During the writing process, you may very well see places where you need to elaborate further or perhaps cut something that seems extraneous. Also, you may find a need for light research to fill in gaps. In all cases, however, the outline should guide the direction of the paper and ensure that your horses are pulling the coach. If it helps, think of your readers as passengers, and when assessing your plan for clarity and completeness, be mindful of any missing elements or leaps of logic that may give your readers (i.e., your passengers) anything less than a smooth ride.

The Products of Writing

At long last, your research is (mostly) done, your horses are in a row and hitched to the coach, and that pesky cursor on your computer is no longer blinking; rather, it's winking, because you are ready to write! The act of writing up your results moves you into the final segment of your project, the Presentation Phase. Actually, the boundaries are not as discrete as you may imagine, and in fact, you have secretly been writing the whole time. In the course of your research reading, your careful note-taking, and your planning process, you have been formulating a response to your research question. It is likely that little soundbites may have been forming in your head, and the presumptive structure of your project has been falling into place. You have been writing your essay without even sitting at the keyboard. The renowned writing specialist Joan Bolker calls the sum of these virtual moments the "zero draft," which she defines as the "moment where it becomes possible to imagine, or discern, a shape to your material, to see the method in your madness."[10] The "zero draft" is pregnant with all the possibilities of your written project. It is not a first draft, exactly, because you have not committed yourself to placing real words on the page.

Even your first draft does not appear overnight. For many researchers, putting the proverbial pen to paper happens throughout the research process. Scholars begin crafting their work early by putting together proposals for research funding or for early peer review. The proposals in turn inform the shape of the future essay, and then an abstract comes together to capture a snapshot of the whole. Thus, just as the Query and Discovery phases of your project can overlap, so too does the Presentation Phase weave itself into the whole, emerging at the end hopefully to yield a finished project.

Writing Grant Proposals

The bad news is that research can be very expensive. Acquiring books and articles, purchasing computers and software, and traveling to libraries and archives require resources. But there are two bits of good news. First, history research is cheaper than most. Historians typically do not need millions of dollars to buy lab equipment or pay for postdoctoral assistants. We would gladly accept millions, of course, but generally our funding needs fall within the range of mere hundreds or a few thousand. Books are cheaper than gas chromatographs, and we typically do much of the work ourselves without the need for outside assistants. The second bit of encouraging news is that there are many potential sources of funding in the form of grants, fellowships, and travel awards. Some sources of funding are available within the historian's home institution in the form of **internal funding**. Resources from outside agencies, government entities, nonprofit agencies, or corporate and private donors constitute **external funding**. In the United States, the National Endowment for the Humanities, which provides a variety of grant opportunities for historians, is a good example of an external funding agency. In the United Kingdom, the Arts and Humanities Research Council is the primary funding agency, along with the Economic and Social Research Council and the British Academy. Both internal and external grants are important for conducting research, though universities tend to expect faculty to pursue outside funding, and they sometimes incentivize faculty who apply regularly and reward those who secure outside resources as part of the faculty review process.

The end of the Query Phase is typically the moment when most researchers are ready to apply for funding. As we mentioned, the elements of the Query

Phase, particularly the shaping of a research question and the engagement with secondary sources, go on throughout the research process, but at some point, researchers determine that they have a clear idea of the primary sources needed to answer their question. At that moment, they are ready to seek support for access to the primary materials, whether that entails a trip to an archive, quantitative data collection, or field interviews. The grant proposal thus stands as the first written product from a project. In it, the researcher will encapsulate his or her findings during the Query Phase of the project and delineate the findings anticipated during the Discovery Phase.

Most grant applications share common features, even if the details can vary widely. Different grant agencies may stipulate lengths, formats, and content expectations for specific grants or fellowships. Some grants that are unique to individual libraries or institutions will likely want the applicant to explain in detail the expected use of the institution's resources. Other entities may want applications that specify how the project conforms to a mission statement or philosophy. There are, however, some general principles that apply to most grant applications that can help you structure your own proposal. First, you should assume that grant reviewers do not understand your topic as well as you do. This means that you must be prepared to explain what the topic is and why it is important for research. Second, you must expect to identify the research question and situate it within the existing literature. When describing the research problem, the key is to help the reader understand why this problem merits attention and resources. Third, the proposal must describe what you as the researcher will do to address the question, including the sources you will investigate and the methods you will use. This also means that you will need to state how the resources for which you are applying will help you carry out your investigation. Finally, the proposal must include a sense of the outcomes you expect to achieve at the end of the project. In the natural sciences and social sciences, these are sometimes known as the **deliverables** of a project. Beyond these points, some grants require a clear budgetary statement and a timeline of how the project will unfold and when it will be completed.

When weaving these elements together into a proposal, style and structure matter. Essentially, you need to be able to introduce your topic to a lay audience without denying yourself space to talk about the more sophisticated elements of your specific contribution. If your proposal sets up your project properly, it will introduce an unfamiliar reader to the importance of your topic, lead him or her to the original contribution you wish to make, and hopefully attract the reader's interest along the way. Fortunately, there are some useful structural strategies that can frame the proposal in an accessible and engaging way.

For one example, look below at the sample proposal. Mary, the author, was researching an undergraduate thesis on the history of narrative filmmaking in Germany and Italy after the Second World War. Given the narrower parameters of a senior project, Mary wanted to focus on the work of two particular directors, but she was concerned that her readers might not know very much about the importance of film in postwar Europe or the role these directors played. Thus, she opens her proposal with a wider view:

The end of the Second World War ushered in a new era that entailed not only the reconstruction of shattered cities but also the reordering of politics and society across Europe. Perhaps nowhere was this process more momentous than in the former Axis countries of Germany and Italy, which experienced the challenges of widespread homelessness and hunger, polar shifts in politics, and in the case of Germany, a period of division and danger on the front lines of an emerging Cold War. Beyond the obvious physical scars, the end of the 1940s and the beginning of the 1950s signaled a dramatic shift in the cultures of the respective countries, as Germans and Italians faced the challenges of the immediate future while confronting the enormity of crimes committed in the recent past. As this project will argue, much of this process played out on the silver screen. For decades, Europeans had flocked to theaters to see the latest feature films and escape from everyday life. Now Germans and Italians used the fictions of the same medium to face the realities of the postwar world and to imagine alternatives to the world that had come before.[11]

Notice that Mary's introductory paragraph begins with a fairly broad statement about the end of the Second World War. Its scope, however, is not too grand. She does not begin with dreaded clichés like "Throughout history … " or "Since the beginning of time … " Historians as a rule detest such statements in part because they are so hackneyed but mostly because they are simply not true and because they preclude the possibility of historical change, which as you know is the historian's stock-in-trade. Instead, Mary prudently keeps her opening statement linked to the topic at hand, zooming out just enough to provide a starting point that readers would understand and accept, and that they would likely agree is an important historical issue. From there, Mary's second sentence steps down just a bit, moving from the end of the war in Europe to a more specific focus on Germany and Italy. The paragraph narrows a shade further in the third sentence by mentioning the more specific moral and psychological "challenges" that the two countries faced. At this point, Mary is in a position to raise the issue of film and thereby move readers to her precise research area.

In this way, Mary's first paragraph follows what we might call a *funnel approach,* starting from a larger point familiar to readers and winnowing down gradually to the core of the project. She surmised that readers would accept her more general claims about the importance of the Second World War and would then follow her reasoning to appreciate the significance of her study within that context. There are other structural devices she might have used. She could, for instance, have introduced the topic from the opposite direction, using a *reverse-funnel approach* that started with a specific example, such as a specific film, and then worked outward to connect it to the larger themes she wished to explore. When choosing your own approach, think about the needs of your project, and above all the needs of your readers, what they know, what they need to know, and what will likely help them understand the importance of your project.

Crafting Introductions and Conclusions

One of the added benefits of preparing a proposal for your project is that you rehearse the framing elements that you can use to introduce your final essay. It is likely that your project will evolve as you conduct your research, but many of the overarching themes and questions will stay the same. For this reason, it is not uncommon for the introduction of an essay to grow from the language of the proposal. One of the differences will be length. As a rule of thumb, introductory sections need be no longer than roughly 10 percent of the total paper. Thus, if your total essay runs twenty pages, you should cover the introductory elements in the first two pages or so. It is not a firm rule, but it helps to keep it in mind so that you do not give in to the temptation to overload the introduction. You want to avoid stuffing the entire argument in the first couple of paragraphs, or of including too much detail in a structural overview of the larger essay. Introductions only set the stage, identifying the topic, the research question and problem, and then pointing the way toward the essay's approach and main argument. Adding much more than this runs the risk of making the introduction overly dense and inaccessible.

Another key difference between your essay introduction and your initial proposal will appear in the way you describe your project. In the proposal, scholars seek support for research that is not yet completed. They are thus obliged to talk about their projects in prospective terms, focusing on the questions that they are posing and the materials that they intend to investigate. Proposals frequently describe research actions using the future tense, "This project will undertake an archival study … " or "This project will answer the following questions … " Essay introductions, by contrast, arrive after the research is completed. They set up a finished project and therefore can abandon the hypothetical language of the proposal. It is not inappropriate to lay out questions rather than answers at the beginning of an essay, but the introduction should at least confidently allude to the answers, using the past or present tense to describe research actions and saving the future tense for allusions to results in the essay, "This paper will show … " or "This essay will reveal how … "

If the main arguments were not clear in the introduction, then they must become so in the conclusion. The conclusion thus acts to gather the piece and sum up the arguments. But conclusions can also be more than mere summaries. Upon reaching the conclusion, the essay has hopefully made its case and met its empirical burden for proving the argument. The final section of the paper should tie any loose ends. It might address any limitations for the study and anticipate any potential points of criticism. Bear in mind that the arguments should be sound within the parameters you have defined for the project (time, place, particular cases, etc.), but the conclusion can be frank about potential blind spots created by the narrow parameters of the study. In other instances, it might acknowledge shortcomings of the available source base or of a particular method and offer thoughts on what future finds could show. These statements should never undermine the argument; rather, their goal is to point the way forward for future researchers.

The conclusion is also the appropriate place in the essay to discuss the implications of a study beyond its findings. This means that the final paragraphs can draw inferences about the study's contribution and make general observations based on the study's more specific perspective. It can step beyond a prescribed geographic location or add an epilogue to the study's time horizons. Here the burden of proof is lower than with the main argument, because in this respect the conclusion is only suggesting rather than proving. The goal once again is to inform scholars who may wish to build projects adding to the discussion.

Finally, the conclusion should provide a sense of closure to the piece. If you were writing an essay about home interiors in nineteenth-century New England, it would be strange to end the essay with a line like, "This changed the American interior for the next century. Home interiors in Australia were also interesting." A reader, jarred by the sudden change of topic, would immediately flip the page over looking for the rest of the discussion. A proper conclusion cannot drop in unrelated or extraneous material without contextualization or elaboration. In this case, the author should probably focus on the case at hand and let Australia be for now. One better strategy for closing a piece might be to create a sense of symmetry with the introduction. This does not mean simply repeating the information from the introduction; instead it implies returning to that information with a fresh perspective. If the first paragraphs posed the question, then the conclusion can posit an answer. If the introduction used a particular example, the conclusion might circle around to the example to make its final points. In any case, readers should feel that the essay is done when they read the last sentence.

Writing Abstracts

Curiously, the very first thing that readers are likely to see is the last thing that you want to write. The abstract is a short description of your entire project and often appears at the beginning of a thesis or dissertation or at the top of an article. Its purpose is to encapsulate in the most condensed language possible the topic, problem, methods, arguments, and overarching contribution of your project. Abstracts have strict word limits depending on the length of the project. For an article or thesis paper, an abstract probably should run between 250 and 500 words. Book abstracts and dissertations can run longer, sometimes stretching to 1,000 words. Given their brevity, they are not the place to rehearse the details of a narrative or the premises that support an argument. There is no burden of proof in an abstract, so you simply make sure that your abstract captures the main point and, if space remains, offers a brief statement of the implications or the larger significance of a study. The result might look something like this actual sample from an article published by Bruce Baker in the journal *American Nineteenth Century History*:

> This study examines an 1887 lynching in Pickens County, South Carolina, in which a black mob lynched a white man for the rape and murder of a black girl. Two members of the mob, both African-Americans, were eventually convicted, but a massive petition campaign led the Governor to pardon them. The study relies largely on coroner's inquests for the murder victim and the lynching victim, court records, and newspaper articles. It suggests that the anomalous nature of this lynching prompted many people to consider and debate exactly what justified lynching and what role race was to play in those justifications. Since the lynching occurred at the very point when lynching victims were becoming overwhelmingly African-American men, the insights provided into contemporary views on lynching are all the more valuable.[12]

Finally, you should select some **keywords** so that other scholars will know how to locate your project while doing their secondary searches. Five to ten keywords are usually sufficient, and they can include the specific sites, people, events, or ideas that you discussed at length in your paper. Make sure that at least one of your keynotes addresses the topic that you have researched. The rule of thumb is to include only the terms that are relevant to your conclusions. If you have more potential terms than keywords available, prioritize by asking yourself which keywords most closely correspond to your essay's conclusions. If you need help identifying keywords, you can consult your library staff, who have experience with research classifications.

From Writing to Editing

Even if writing a piece of this length and complexity is a new experience, you will quickly discover habits and practices that are unique to you. Each individual has his or her own process, with preferences for where the individual writes, when he or she writes, how long, and under what conditions. We do not wish to interrupt the process of discovering your process, but we might impart a few bits of closing advice that deal specifically with how to move from your "zero draft" to your first draft and on to the polished final product.

First, try to separate the writing and editing process. Word processing software is terrific, alerting you to spelling and grammar errors, allowing you to make changes on the fly, and even making it easy to cut and paste whole lines and paragraphs. But it is also incredibly distracting. Whatever your writing process, it probably does not ideally include frequently pausing to fiddle with a piece of text or second-guessing yourself in the middle of a paragraph. You most likely are at your best when your writing is able to flow from your mind to the page. If so, then our advice is to allow yourself to have a first draft. Stick to your plan, but focus on moving forward. Then, upon reaching the end of a section, go back and edit carefully what you have written. Be willing to rewrite weak pieces and excise portions that are tangential or disconnected from your main argument. When preparing your work, think of the writing and editing processes as distinct phases, and carve out blocks of time for both.

By the same token, editing is not always the same thing as proofreading, but both are essential for the success of your paper. When you have completed your essay, which means you have written the full piece and edited its content, you should then proofread the whole. If possible, have a friend or peer read over the piece, but never place the full burden on them. You must take final responsibility for the accuracy of your paper. To ensure this, there are two steps you can take. The first is to give yourself distance from your project so that you proofread it with fresh eyes. After you finish writing, let your piece lie fallow for a day or so if possible. Take a break and get some rest, and then come back to your paper for a final review session. Second, to be certain of the clarity of your piece, read it to yourself aloud. Sometimes things make sense to us as they are making their way to the page, but then sound nonsensical when spoken.

Finally, know when to let a piece go. The closer we get to our research, and the longer we spend on a project, the harder it seems to submit the final essay. We become fixated on achieving a level of perfection that precludes us from reaching a sense of closure. As a result, researchers can become paralyzed, leaving great projects unfinished. For this reason, it is often essential to seek outside help. Sharing drafts with peers and mentors is a great way to keep things moving. Research supervisors worth their salt know the difference between good projects and perfect ones, and they can often provide concrete advice about the last steps needed before submission. Strong feedback from peers, meanwhile, can reassure those who are reluctant to hit that final send button. But, in the end, the author has to be willing to accept a product as finished. It helps to remember that no single research essay is ever the final word on a topic, and that you or others like you will come back and continue the investigation. In that sense, a "finished" work is only finished for now, but not forever.

History in Practice: Planning an Essay

Below we see how Jack Wells planned the first body portion of his essay on Christianity's role in the fall of the western Roman Empire. He has finished his research into his primary question and has stated his central argument. On the planning sheet, Wells identifies two key elements that he will need to include in the paper in order to explain and prove his argument, and he has fleshed them out using his research notes. In the outline, he places the elements in the desired sequence that allows him to build his argument logically and to lay out each point as a coherent topical paragraph. Notice that Wells has created a topic sentence for each main point and has been careful to note places where a quote is in order. The outline that emerges describes the principal ways that historians have explained the role of Christianity and then compares that with the evidence found in two major primary sources. Though the full paper is not depicted, it seems likely that in the next half of the paper, Wells will show the ways in which the sources challenge the historiography, which will enable him to prove his thesis. This is an appropriate sequence, because by first showing the ways in which the sources support the historiography, Wells can explain why older historians thought as they did, and he can anticipate any objections to his own view. By then placing his counterpoints at the end, he makes it clear that his own view is a response to Gibbon and other historians.

Jack Wells, "Christianity and the Fall of Rome"

Before writing my paper, I took some time to do some planning:

Research question: Is there any evidence that the spread of Christianity contributed to the collapse of Roman Authority in Western Europe in the fifth century AD?

Thesis: Although the evidence is mixed, the weight of the evidence does not show that the spread of Christianity or the Christian Church materially affected the collapse of the Roman Empire in the West.

Element: Some historiographical sources looked at Christianity as a culprit in the fall of Rome. What specific points did they make?

- The traditional perspective of Edward Gibbon.

Gibbon lists a number of financial and political distractions caused by the growing power of the Church, including the rejection of heretics, the focus on doctrinal disputes, and the diversion of money to Church institutions. He also suggests that the Church created a new set of virtues at odds with the security needs of the empire.

- The more recent perspective of Peter Brown.

Some scholars continue to follow Gibbon's line of thinking. Peter Brown thinks in particular that the Church weakened the Roman commitment to the army.

Element: In what ways do the primary sources under review here agree with the points in the secondary literature?

- The perspective of St. Augustine's *The City of God* on the sack of Rome.

St. Augustine argues that the sack of Rome was less tragic than it might have been, as the earthly city of Rome is simply less significant than the heavenly city of God: Christians need to recognize that it is the latter that merits our concern and attention, not the former.

- The perspective of Sulpicius Severus' *Life of St. Martin of Tours* on the Roman army.

Severus gives a picture of Roman military life that is largely incompatible with the life of a Christian saint. St. Martin clearly does not like to be a soldier, prefers the cultivation of his soul to defending the empire, and wants to get out of the army and lead a more Christian, spiritual life (Sulpicius Severus, *Life of St. Martin*, ch. 4).

Next, I laid the elements out in sequence in an outline:

I   Introduction (omitted in this sample)
II   Topic sentence: A number of scholars have suggested that Christians and their institutions contributed to the collapse of imperial authority in the western Roman Empire
    A   Edward Gibbon argued this (Kagan, *Fall*, 28–9).
        1   He argued that the Church promoted Christian virtues that were not in accordance with the virtues needed to defend against the barbarians.
        2   He argued that money that could have gone to pay for defending the empire went to priests and nuns.
        3   He argued that the squabbles among Christians distracted the emperors from the real crises, affecting the empire
        4   He argued that persecution of heretics created internal opponents of the regime.
    B   Peter Brown also suggested this (Brown, *World of Late Antiquity*, 119).
        1   He suggested that one cause of the western Roman Empire's collapse was the increased separation between the Church on one hand and the army on the other.

2   Though not intentional, the Church was one institution that "unwittingly sapped the strength of the army and the imperial administration."

II   Topic sentence. There is some primary source evidence that would support this.

A   Sulpicius Severus' *Life of St. Martin of Tours* illustrates Brown's point about views of the army.

1   Martin, because of his devotion to Christ, was anxious to be released from his duties as a soldier so he could serve God, because it was not right for a soldier of Christ to fight.

2   Thus, it seems Christians believed that defending the Empire was morally wrong because it involved killing.

B   St. Augustine's *The City of God* shows some evidence of the negative Christian view of Rome.

1   Augustine wrote to exculpate Christians for the blame of Rome's sack by Alaric in 410.

2   He argued that it was basically irrelevant that evils have befallen an earthly city; instead, the purpose of humans is to earn admission to that more important heavenly city.

3   He implied that Christians should not particularly care whether Rome or the Empire is conquered or not, which would suggest that they would not be particularly anxious to defend it.

APPLICATION EXERCISE

Plan your paper! Write an outline for your essay that identifies your principal argument(s) and lays out the sequence of elements in a logical structure. Use complete sentences to identify each point on your outline.

History in Practice: Achieving Closure

There are no hard and fast-rules for concluding a paper, but the effect must be a sense of closure. In the sample below, Bruce Baker explains how the final sentences of his book attempted to wrap up a lengthy monograph.

Bruce Baker, "The Cotton Kings"

At the end of *The Cotton Kings*, we summed everything up with this sentence: "The power of government and regulation to establish practices that benefitted all market participants, and helped make the price of cotton more accurately reflect the actual real-world conditions of supply and demand, is a power worth preserving, remembering, and celebrating." This sentence was a payoff statement, expressing the importance of the general findings of our study. But, in a nod toward the complexity of business history, we could not resist giving the last word to one of the people about whom we wrote, quoting, "I do not know whether I have made that clear to you or not. It is clear to me, but sometimes I get a thing so clear to myself that I cannot explain it to anyone else."[13]

APPLICATION EXERCISE

Write a sample introduction paragraph and conclusion paragraph that you could use in a research proposal or in your final essay. Annotate your paragraphs to show the structural choices you made, the elements that you elected to include, and the ways in which your paragraphs (1) establish the importance of the topic in the introduction and (2) achieve a sense of closure in the conclusion.

Notes

1   Thomas Nipperdey, *Germany from Napoleon to Bismarck, 1800–1866,* translated by Daniel Nolan (Princeton: Princeton University Press, 1996), 1.

2   Ibid., 704.

3   Ibid., 715.

4   Johan Huizinga, *The Autumn of the Middle Ages,* translated by Rodney J. Payton and Ulrich Mammitzsch (Chicago: University of Chicago Press, 1996), 30.

5   Ibid., 1.

6   Georg G. Iggers, *Historiography in the Twentieth Century: From Scientific Objectivity to the Postmodern Challenge* (Hanover, NH: University Press of New England, 1997), 97–100.

7   Lawrence Stone, "The Revival of Narrative: Reflections on a New Old History," *Past and Present* 85 (1979): 3–24, 8–10.

8   Ibid., 4.

9   David Hackett Fischer, *Historians' Fallacies: Toward a Logic of Historical Thought* (New York: Harper Perennial, 1970), 283.

10 Joan Bolker, *Writing Your Dissertation in 15 Minutes a Day* (New York: Owl Books, 1998), 49–50.

11 Mary McDade Casteel, "Student Undergraduate Research Fellowship Proposal: 'Reel Images of Postwar Life: Narrative Films in Italy and Germany, 1945–1951,'" University of Arkansas Office of Nationally Competitive Awards, https://awards.uark.edu/_resources/downloads/surf-history.pdf (accessed December 10, 2018).

12 Baker, "Lynch Law Reversed: The Rape of Lula Sherman, the Lynching of Manse Waldrop, and the Debate over Lynching in the 1880s," *American Nineteenth Century History* 6, no. 3 (2005): 273–93.

13 Bruce E. Baker and Barbara Hahn, *The Cotton Kings: Capitalism and Corruption in Turn-of-the-Century New York and New Orleans* (New York: Oxford University Press, 2016), 143.

Suggested Reading

Eco, Umberto, and Francesco Erspamer. *How to Write a Thesis.* Translated by Caterina Mongiat Farina and Geoff Farina. Cambridge, MA: MIT Press, 2015.

Jensen, Joli. *Write No Matter What: Advice for Academics.* Chicago: University of Chicago Press, 2017.

Strunk, William, Jr., and E.B. White. *The Elements of Style.* New York: Pearson Longman, 2009.

Sword, Helen. *Stylish Academic Writing.* Cambridge, MA: Harvard University Press, 2012.

Zinsser, William. *On Writing Well: The Classic Guide to Writing Nonfiction.* New York: HarperCollins, 2006.

9

The Outcomes of Historical Research: What You Can Do for History

> *What we will do in this chapter:*
>
> ➤ **REFLECT** on how historical study connects the past and the future.
> ➤ **DISCOVER** how your historical research can be a cultural and social good.
> ➤ **APPLY** oral presentation techniques to sharing your research.

In the summer of 1989, the Cold War was reaching the end of its fourth decade. The United States and the Soviet Union had made some meaningful gestures toward arms control and a return to détente, but there remained otherwise no end in sight to the polarizing standoff between East and West. Thus it was something of a surprise when the political scientist Francis Fukuyama published an essay declaring that a sea change was at hand, one that he claimed would not only mark the end of the Cold War but would more profoundly signal the "end of history."[1] With this provocative phrase, Fukuyama argued that Western liberal democracy was on the cusp of an ultimate triumph over Communism that in a grander sense would conclude its centuries-long march to victory as the ultimate system of political and economic order across the globe. The achievement of liberal supremacy, Fukuyama boldly asserted, would banish the central geopolitical conflict and a primary cause of historical change in the modern era.

Fukuyama was certainly right about the end of the Cold War, which began its swift demise with the fall of the Berlin Wall only a few months after his article appeared. But critics were quick to pounce on the implications of his claim about history. As the post–Cold War era unfolded, they pointed to the resurgence of national conflicts, the rise of Islamic radicalism, and the appearance of new populist authoritarian movements as signs of a continuing dynamic of change and conflict. History, they observed, is quite persistent.

For his part, Fukuyama conceded the point, arguing that he was "misunderstood" on the matter of history and was instead making a "normative" claim about "liberal democracy as the best available system."[2] In more recent years, Fukuyama has very much incorporated the notion of historical change into his work, charting how notions of identity have prevented the full flowering of the liberal democratic order he trumpeted in 1989.[3] Yet the boldness of his original title, however intended, has invited a tremendous amount of discussion and critique about the potential ends of history, mostly discrediting the possibility. For some scholars, such ideas are best relegated to the realm of utopian thought.[4]

The idea of an "end to history" may thus be fanciful, but it is nonetheless intriguing. The discussion seems to activate latent fears that present-day societies may come to disregard history, if not as finished, then as irrelevant. History's visibility in the present, its place in school curricula, and its general presence in contemporary discourse always hinges on perceptions of its relative worth. The fear seems to be that should present-day peoples come to feel disabused of the power of historical change in their own lives, the result could be a broad dismissal of history as a necessary subject of study. There is, indeed, an interesting corollary between social views of history and psychological perceptions of the self. In one 2013 study, a team of psychologists led by Jordi Quoidbach surveyed thousands of people of all ages about their perceptions of how they expected themselves to change over time. The researchers concluded that even when respondents acknowledged changes they had experienced in the past, they still tended to "underestimate the extent to which their personalities, values, and preferences will change in the future."[5] The result, they argue, was an "end of history illusion," which we can extend both to individuals and to the societies to which they belong. The consequences can be significant. Quoidbach and his team noted that a lack of perceptions of change had the potential to result in "suboptimal decisions" related to future planning. This means that people risk making bad choices about their futures absent a realistic sense of how they may unfold.[6]

We would suggest that the same is possible on a cultural level, meaning that notions of the "end of history" raise important questions about the relationship between the past and the future. And thinking about the future is a particularly timely undertaking for students and scholars nearing the end of a major historical research project. Without historical consciousness, there can be little sense of the future. This is because we draw upon the differences between past and present to conceptualize anticipated differences between present and future. Once people begin neglecting historical difference, then they lose that critical model for understanding a different future.[7] It becomes more difficult to view the future as an object of wonder and imagination.

The proverbial door swings both ways. On a very fundamental level, history as a field of study can no more exist without a sense of the future than it can without the memory of the past. In a literal sense, the moment that humanity ceases to exist, history will indeed come to an end. But more figuratively, if humanity were to stop imagining the future in different terms from the present, that is, if people lost interest in tomorrow and no longer envisioned forthcoming changes for their descendants, then their need for history as the study of change over time would correspondingly decline. We might say in short that the relationship between the historical past and the speculative future is one of mutual dependence. It is people living in the here and now who afford history its fundamental value, and the reason that we should is in no small part because doing so lends worth to our own tomorrows.

This idea is important to bear in mind as you complete your research project. After weeks, months, or even years of studying, thinking, researching, and writing, your project is itself about to become an artifact of the past. Soon, it will no longer be that big essay or thesis on which you are working; instead, it will be that project you finished last semester or last year. It may be tempting to push it aside, to shove it in a drawer somewhere and forget about it. But before you consider your history to have reached its end, think for a moment about the possibilities for your work to have ongoing value. It can facilitate how we think about the past, and in this way, it has the potential to resonate into the future. In this chapter, you will learn about some of the grander outcomes that may not come immediately to mind. Specifically, we will discuss some ways that you can present your research and improve the quality of your work through engagement with peers, while at the same time participating in the broader work of the disciplinary community, enhancing our knowledge about the past, and making a meaningful contribution to the future of history.

REFLECTION EXERCISE

In Chapter 3, you created a value inventory and set for yourself some long-range goals. Now it is time to revisit those values and goals and think specifically about, first, how they have changed over the course of your research project and, second, how they might change further deeper into your own future. Write a short essay in which you describe the ways you anticipate both you as an individual and your community to have changed over the next ten years. Of course, no one can predict the future exactly, but you can write about the experiences that you believe are most likely to shape you and your priorities. At the same time, you can also think about how your community or the community where you anticipate living down the road (whether you define that as a city or country) will be different. Finally, how do these anticipated changes shape the decisions you and others in your community should make over the next decade? To what extent do these sorts of reflections lead you to modify your goals?

History as a Cultural and Social Good

For the moment, you may be focused on some of the immediate benefits from your finished work. It is certainly no small thing that your term paper or thesis may secure a strong grade in a course, fulfill the requirements of a degree, or merit honors standing. Beyond these critical outcomes, it is also worthwhile to pause and consider the more indirect ways in which your research can make contributions, to the discipline of history, to the broader field of the humanities, and from there to contemporary society and culture. From the outset, you worked to narrow your historical topic and research questions; now is the time to look up once again to those original horizons and see the larger impact that your work may have.

Preserving and Interpreting the Past

History is by no means the exclusive domain of the historian. The moment that you complete and share your research, you participate in a massive undertaking to preserve the past for present and future generations. Academic historians are an important part of this enterprise, joining the ranks of archaeologists, architects, archivists, librarians, museum curators, and many other professionals whose work serves to protect and display the legacies of past human cultures and societies. There are a great many more amateurs who play a critical role, including collectors, government officials, historical re-enactors, philanthropists, schoolteachers, and volunteers, whose hobbies, personal interests, and sense of public duty lead them to keep historical objects, sites, and events in the forefront of cultural memory. Without these individuals, historians would have no audience, and they would struggle to find the resources to support their research.

The principal way in which historians contribute to this broad cultural undertaking is through their work to interpret the past. Regardless of whether historians study the most recent decades in a local community or remote centuries in a far-away land, their work shapes the relationship between past and present. And even if their primary focus rests on an accurate understanding of historical societies within the context of their own time, they nonetheless assure the continued visibility and utility of the past today. While their partners may do more to safeguard the tangible remains of the past and to make it available to people in the present, it is the historians who shape and convey the meaning of the past through a commitment to rigorous research and critical engagement. In this way, historians join their professional and community partners in bringing the past into public discourse with a particular responsibility to make certain that the discourse adheres to the truest possible understandings of past examples.

Putting the Present in Perspective

Public engagement with history is essential both for seeing the past in the proper light and for understanding the conditions of the present. When guided by thoughtful and rigorous academic interpretation, discussions of history can illuminate contemporary problems and orientations toward the future. As Jo Guldi and David Armitage have argued, historians are more than mere sages writing of foregone times; they are indispensable participants in shaping the present. They have the unique ability to lend long-term perspective to conversations about present-day conditions. Or at least, according to Guldi and Armitage, that is what they should be doing. In *The History Manifesto*, these two historians offered a trenchant critique of the historical discipline's failures to engage fully in this crucial public role. They complained that historians in recent decades have withdrawn from the public sphere into overly specialized projects directed at practitioners of their own narrow subfields. Their penchant for specialization has allegedly diminished the scale of their studies, leading to a phenomenon of "short-termism" that undermines the value of long-term historical perspectives. Historians, they allege, "ceded the task of synthesizing historical knowledge to unaccredited writers and simultaneously lost whatever influence they might once have had over policy to colleagues in the social sciences, most spectacularly to the economists."[8]

When they appeared in 2014, Guldi and Armitage's complaints generated some debate among historians, with some scholars raising questions about their statistical data and rejecting the allegations of historian disengagement.[9] Yet most can agree that their observations about embracing a "return to the *longue durée*" and especially their call for a new "public future for history" remain laudable goals.[10] It is important for historians to remember that even if individual historical studies may draw more interest from professionals, the aggregate effect of disciplinary research has a lot to offer the world at large, both in terms of the salient issues of our day and in terms of general wisdom framing our perceptions.

We might identify three critical perspectives derived from the aggregate contributions of historical research. The first of these, **historical contingency**, refers to the ways in which events or trends rely upon the particular circumstances of the time in which they occur. It is a concept stressing the uniqueness of the moment, showing how ideas, beliefs, and identities are not universal or everlasting, but are the products of human culture. They emerge from decades or even centuries of change and continue to evolve into the future. The more we recognize historical contingency in the past, the better we can see its impact on our present. We begin to see our own assumptions in their proper context and can thereby challenge and change them.

Perhaps the most common example arises with gender relations. Even powerful intellectuals like the French philosopher Jean-Jacques Rousseau (1712–1778) were apt to misinterpret ephemeral cultural norms of masculinity and femininity as universal truths about the roles of men and women. In his 1762 work, *Emile, or On Education*, Rousseau famously prescribed different educational experiences for boys and girls based on the idea, "confirmed by experience," that "each is the complement of the other." Specifically, Rousseau argued, "The man should be strong; the woman should be weak and passive."[11] He failed to see that the characteristics he ascribed were not immutable but reflected a social order reinforced from a young age. By the twentieth century, the shift away from a singular focus on elites allowed historians to disrupt such thinking by highlighting the variety of women's experiences over time. Historians have thus taken part in cultural and social changes that today reveal Rousseau's supposedly "universal" views as in fact antiquated and patriarchal.

History can disrupt, and it can also reassure. The flip side of historical contingency is **historical continuity**, which stresses the things that remain stable across long periods of time. This was a particular fascination for the historians of the Annales School, whose writings about the *longue durée* emphasized different rates of change, moving beyond the sorts of swift transformations wrought by wars of conquest or by new discoveries to unearth the slower metamorphoses beneath the surface of a civilization, such as the gradual development of trading networks or the centralization of state power. Recognizing continuities is important in part because they place present-day problems in perspective. Without a sense of what has come before, it can be easy to misinterpret a challenge as something unprecedented, to mistake a problem for a crisis. Students of history, of course, find it replete with examples of cynics declaring the troubles of their day as a signal of the end times. Sometimes these perceptions are informed by mystical or religious beliefs, as when the radical Anabaptist Jan Matthys (1500–1534) went to war in the German city of Münster and wound up decapitated, all in the belief that the apocalypse was nigh. At other times, a more secular faith in modern novelties can inspire dread, as in the case of the doomsday preppers who saw a potential software glitch as the herald of civilization's imminent demise during the so-called Y2K scare of 1999.[12]

The real danger of losing historical perspective in this way is that radical perceptions produce radical actions. If one thinks that the world is about to end, then one tends to behave as if there is no tomorrow. A mature understanding of the challenges faced by past societies can reveal to us the proper scale of our own. We can draw upon the experience of the past to prepare for new problems, but those same experiences should caution us about seeing our woes as unlike those faced by people in the past. In this way, the study of history can calm nerves and keep us from losing our heads.

Resorting to past problems and calamities reveals a third overarching use of the past, as **historical analogy**, moments that we can compare across time and use as examples for the present. In the first chapter of this book, we went to great lengths to disabuse you of the simple notion that history runs the risk of repeating itself. The past is past and never comes again. Yet even if it is not inevitable, the past can nonetheless be familiar. As the historian Timothy Snyder explains, "History does not repeat, but it does instruct."[13] People in the past asked questions, faced challenges, and devised solutions that we can recognize and learn from today.

We have already seen how Niccolo Machiavelli made historical lessons the center of *The Prince*, his book of counsel for a hypothetical ruler. More recently, Snyder takes the same approach to advise citizens of the twenty-first century. In his 2017 book, *On Tyranny*, Snyder pulls together a wealth of comparative study of dictatorships from the last century to provide guidance on how to recognize the conditions that precede the rise of authoritarian regimes and how to respond both before and after a new tyrant appears. He recognizes in his own day the seeds of new populist authoritarian politics in countries around the world and hopes to provide a means for ordinary citizens to learn from the past and take appropriate action. Snyder is clear that no case will precisely mirror that of another, but he highlights such commonalities as the breakdown of truth in media, the atomization of individuals, and the dehumanization of defined enemies as elements shared across cases and thus apt to appear in future cases in some modified form. Reaching back even further, Edward J. Watts' *Mortal Republic: How Rome Fell into Tyranny* offers a new glimpse into the fall of the Roman Republic, with a clear focus on its relevance to the present. "No republic is eternal," he suggests. "It lives only as long as its citizens want it. And, in both the twenty-first century AD and in the first century, BC, when a republic fails to work as intended, its citizens are capable of choosing the stability of autocracy over the chaos of a broken republic."[14]

At times, Snyder and Watts' advice may seem to veer back to the writings of George Santayana by calling for historical vigilance as a safeguard against the resurgence of past dangers. But remember that Santayana wrote in the context of a widespread belief in progress, whose trajectory hinged on staying the course and not making the mistakes of the past. By contrast, Snyder and Watts argue against seeing a convenient linear trajectory to history, pushing their readers instead to see the future as open-ended and as likely to pivot toward darkness as to justice. In relegating the specter of past dictatorial regimes to useless history books, Snyder claims, "We allowed ourselves to accept the politics of inevitability, the sense that history could only move in one direction: toward liberal democracy .... In so doing, we lowered our defenses, constrained our imagination, and opened the way for precisely the kinds of regimes we told ourselves could never return."[15]

It is not all gloom and doom. Beyond their capacity to warn, the perspectives we receive from history can also thrill and inspire, recalling moments when individuals beat the odds or when communities came together to aspire to great achievements. To note just one example, we see this in a recent spate of works on the history of space exploration, in Jeffrey Kluger and Robert Kurson's accounts of the Apollo space program in the 1960s,[16] or in Margot Lee Shetterly's *Hidden Figures*, which tells the story of the African American women mathematicians who helped make space flight possible.[17] Four decades after human beings last set foot on the Moon, histories of past achievements can be an especially welcome reminder of future possibilities. They just might one day help spur us once again to strive for the heavens.

History and the Humanities

For all our differences, and for all the ways in which people in the past seem out of reach or irrelevant to our lives today, it remains true that the one universal thing we share with our forebears and with each other is a common humanity. Every work of history should remind us of this simple yet crucial fact. In all the varied ways that it lives up to this charge, history takes its place among the panoply of fields, including studies of art, language, law, literature, music, philosophy, and religion, that comprise the humanities. You can thus see your contributions to history as adding to our engagement with the humanities, with studying the past in order to enrich our much larger consideration of ourselves as human beings.

It is surprising to see how easily we can lose sight of these fundamental achievements. Yet in recent years the value of history and, by extension, the greater worth of the humanities seem to have fallen into a much undeserved state of disrepute. Funding is generally down in both the United States and the United Kingdom, and some institutions have moved to eliminate entire history programs.[18] These moves correspond to a widespread criticism of the humanities from pundits and politicians as no longer relevant to the economic mission of today's universities. As the historian Nigel Raab observes, "Although history and related pursuits have introduced fundamental changes in worldviews, they have been portrayed as an extravagance when set against more practical pursuits such as marketing, medical science, or engineering."[19]

In response, a number of public advocates have joined humanities scholars in mounting a robust defense of the humanities.[20] At the same time, they have made attempts to explain how and why the public discourse about the humanities has so stubbornly adopted misleading or even mistaken views. Among the most frequently mentioned reasons is the poor visibility of the impact of humanities fields. When debating the merits of one field of study over another, the average person can readily see the benefit of practical biological, chemical, or engineering research leading directly to new manufacturing materials or life-saving drug treatments. With the humanities, by contrast, it is much more challenging to connect the dots between a history of the Merovingians or a new interpretation of cyberpunk literature and any lucrative present-day benefits or future outcomes. To address this dilemma, the champions of the humanities work to raise awareness about what Raab calls the "hidden value of the humanities," the ways in which research connects indirectly, in unexpected or surprising ways, to the development of our cultural norms and assumptions.[21]

One of the reasons outsiders struggle to see the extended impact of history and the humanities is that they try to extrapolate benefits from individual projects and thereby miss the proverbial forest for the trees. One might be forgiven for looking at a single work of history or philosophy or comparative literature and wondering about its value to an employer or taxpayer. Indeed, more savvy critics have complained that one of the perennial problems with humanities research is "overspecialization," on the one hand, which means that scholars zero in too much on narrow topics, and "overproduction," on the other, suggesting that researchers write so much scholarship that it can appeal only to a handful of specialists.[22] But such views seem uninformed on the way research operates, and they ignore the fact that no work of humanities scholarship stands alone. As you have learned, research is a collaborative enterprise. Scholars write in dialogue with another, and they at times emphasize the finer points of their subjects, but they always do so with much larger goals in mind. Their efforts are shared, and so are the fruits of their labor. The value of humanities research lies not simply with a single work any more than it rests within one employment sector. The benefits are cumulative, and to judge it otherwise is to confuse its methods and practices with its grander outcomes.

There are at least two ways that professional historians and student researchers can raise the profile of the humanities and extend their benefits beyond the ivory towers of academia to the larger public. The first is to make clear the ways in which individual research projects inform larger questions and issues. When you learned how to design your projects in this book, you probably started with a big question and narrowed it down to a more manageable size in the course of your research. As you near the end of your work, it is time to come back to that starting point and think about the contributions you have made. It may also be the occasion to widen your horizons even further. In Chapter 3, for example, we used a sample question dealing with the origins of the First World War. The question itself is much too large for a single essay to handle, but even if you only focused on developments in one country, on a single person, or on an isolated theme related to the conflict, it is important to articulate how your conclusions provide a piece of the mosaic that helps us answer the larger question. As a historian, your work help us understand an extremely pivotal period that affects us even today. At the same time, as a humanities scholar your research is part of a larger effort to grapple with salient questions about how and why wars begin.

The second step is to share your work widely. If you have committed yourself to serious research, and you and your mentors are satisfied that you have arrived at some meaningful conclusions, then it is incumbent upon you to bring it to light for your peers, for other historians, and for the public. Writing your results in an essay, thesis, or book is one way to do it, but there are others. In the next section, we will learn some of the key ways that scholars place their work within the academic discussion.

DISCOVERY EXERCISE

Describe the larger contributions of your own research. In what ways does it have the potential to shape perspectives? What broader issues are at stake in your chosen topic, and how do your conclusions inform our understanding of those issues?

Presenting and Publishing Research

During the Presentation Phase of a project, there are many ways for historical researchers to share their conclusions. Many opportunities are specifically geared toward the public. Depending on the particular audience that historians wish to reach, they may pass along their findings in public policy briefs, in museum exhibitions, on websites, or even in interviews or consultations on films. Every historian should embrace opportunities for public engagement, but before a historian ventures out into the public sphere with a shiny new collection of research findings, he or she should first share the results with academic peers. Doing so gives the historian an opportunity to respond to professional feedback so that the work is as complete as possible and that its contribution meets its fullest potential.

At the heart of professional presentation is **peer review**, in which one or more scholars assess the quality and accuracy of another scholar's work. Peer review is important first because it allows the practitioners of the discipline to verify that a potential contribution conforms to the methodological and ethical standards of the discipline. This matters because poor research with dubious practices can not only thwart the discipline's mission of informing the broader public but can also discredit the discipline as a whole and diminish its claim to academic authority. Second, a rigorous peer-review process gives fellow experts a chance to weigh in on the significance of a work's contribution to the field. In this way, disciplinary colleagues and future researchers can be assured of the essential quality of new scholarship. Errors are always possible, but the system has been historically successful and today acts as a linchpin of the broader enterprise of rational knowledge production across all disciplines.

Defending Theses and Dissertations

Peer review takes many forms. It can happen informally when classmates trade drafts before submitting a term paper or when a friendly colleague agrees to read a scholar's latest article draft and offer suggestions. In fact, it is good practice for students and scholars alike to solicit feedback on their work before presenting it in a more formal setting. For many students, submitting a term paper or an essay for a grade will be the first and last stop along the presentation process. At some point, however, a student may get the opportunity to write a more substantive thesis and to participate in a formal thesis defense. This entails forming a committee of scholars, including the project mentor as committee chair and multiple outside readers. The committee reviews the finished work and then invites the author or authors to participate in a defense, or formal presentation and question-and-answer session.

The purpose of the defense is to subject the essay to peer review, to give the students an opportunity to present their research orally and in writing, to respond to questions and criticisms of a project, and to demonstrate their overarching competence with the historical topic and research process. Defenses are par for the course for graduate students, as they are required for certifying master's theses and doctoral dissertations. But they can be enormously rewarding for undergraduates, as well, who benefit from structured mentorship with a faculty member and gain early exposure to the advanced practices of an academic discipline. It is no wonder that undergraduate theses count among the high-impact experiences that enhance student engagement. Beyond the experience of completing a project and presenting it to a committee, thesis projects can form the basis, whether topically, thematically, or methodologically, for future graduate research.

Regardless of whether you are a graduate or an undergraduate student, defenses can elicit tremendous feelings of anxiety. With proper preparation, however, they can also be loads of fun. It begins with selecting a supportive and knowledgeable mentor and communicating with the mentor regularly. Mentors can be tremendously helpful at the beginning of a project, when their advice can help a student select a theme and define a research question, and they can be of obvious use when a student has a draft ready for review. Unfortunately, many students miss out on opportunities in the middle portion of a project. More than one mentor has complained of students vanishing for weeks or months at a time. It would be far better for students to stay in touch during those times, even when they are less satisfied with their progress. The mentor can be available to offer a word of encouragement or give practical tips for staying on track in each of the project's phases. At the same time, the students should communicate with the committee, since the committee members will have some final say in assessing the finished product. As the date of the defense approaches, we recommend that a thesis writer budget time so as to provide a penultimate draft about a month in advance to the mentor to allow for a final check for small issues or cosmetic matters and then to give the full committee the final version two weeks out to ensure that everyone has time to read the work carefully. Good mentors know when a work is ready to defend and should never send a student into a defense who is not likely to succeed. Such assurances can take a lot of the pressure off the student upon entering the defense chamber.

On the day of the defense, dress the part. Unless you are instructed otherwise, dust off your business attire and be prepared to exercise the same level of poise that you would for a job interview. But wear the most comfortable business shoes possible in case you find yourself standing at length. Create some note cards or brief slides to cue you on your presentation, but rehearse it beforehand so that you can run through it fairly comfortably and will not need to lean too heavily on your notes. If you stand to speak, remember not to lock your knees. And, above all, practice delivering your presentation with a positive attitude. Being professional does not mean being dour. A relaxed smile that appears from time to time conveys a friendly sense of confidence. The image that you wish to convey is that you are pleased to have the committee or the audience's participation in your defense and glad to share your work with them.

The structure of the defense itself varies from institution to institution. Some universities require public defenses, while others strictly forbid the involvement of outside spectators. The difference is significant because it dictates the demands on the student. In a formal public defense, the student should prepare a thorough oral presentation and be prepared for public comment, while a more private session may need only a brief overview of the main points and then expect a more detailed discussion with the committee. In any case, the presentation should focus on some or all of the following points:

- *A quick summary of how you came to the project:* What interested you from the outset in your research topic, and what larger questions spurred your initial curiosity?
- *An overview of your main research questions.*
- *The project's place in the literature:* The defense is not the place to rehearse your entire historiography, but it does serve to highlight the main currents into which (or against which) you are writing and to mention a couple of key works.
- *A discussion of your methods and theoretical framing:* Talk pointedly about how you carried out your project. Be more specific than saying that you used primary sources. Instead, identify the types of primary

materials you used, any special methods you used to investigate them (i.e., quantitative analysis, digital text mining, etc.), any theories that you relied upon to support your interpretations, and any challenges that you faced. Be sure to explain any special challenges you faced and the ways in which you may have limited your study, whether you confined it to a particular time period or geographical area or case study.

- *Your main conclusions and contributions:* Your presentation of the initial topic is your entry point to the discussion, and your conclusions mark the exit point. Be as specific as possible about your findings and the payoff or the ways in which your work contributes to the academic literature. This is also the place to qualify your study and to discuss potential implications beyond the defined parameters of your thesis.

Even in very short presentations, you should be able to cover these points. If possible, you can supplement parts of the presentation with slides illustrating key images or visual data, but do not include anything that is not relevant and indeed necessary to explaining the project. For longer presentations, it may also be a good idea to include a few choice examples, whether key anecdotes or explications of select primary texts. If you do not have time to mention specific cases, you can still keep them in reserve in case they become appropriate to a question from the committee or from the audience.

In the question-and-answer session, it is important to stand up for your conclusions, but not to get defensive about them. You should always expect pointed questions or suggestions from a committee, because their job is to provide constructive criticism. Do not take it personally. If you can address a committee member's concern, then do so in a calm and tactful way; otherwise, admit when you do not know something and be willing to accept a suggestion, either as an improvement on the present work or as an idea for future research. It is perfectly acceptable for you to ask clarification questions from committee members and to enter into a dialogue about particular points. As is the case for interviews, often the best sessions veer away from feeling like interrogations and become more like conversations between you and the committee.

At the end of the session, the committee may ask you to step out while they discuss the thesis. During this time, the members must determine whether the thesis merits a pass, how to score it in some cases, and then whether to recommend improvements or additions. While some theses pass outright, others get a conditional pass, meaning that the committee will sign the approval forms provided that the authors agree to make specific changes. This is by no means a bad outcome, but is part of the peer-review process. When you reenter the room, make sure that you come away with a firm understanding of the requested changes and make time to work on them right away. Finally, check with your department or university to learn about any required formatting rules for your thesis and incorporate those with your final changes.

Conference Presentations

Perhaps your defense experience will encourage you to take your research on the road. Historians working on new research often present their findings formally a variety of settings.

You may have already attended a sponsored lecture at your institution, where a visiting scholar presented his or her work before a public audience, or **seminars,** which are groups of meetings focused on selected topics that may include group readings or research presentations. Academics also gather in such collegial venues as **workshops,** which are meetings designed to impart new research findings or provide practical training that participants can apply in their fields. Then there are **symposia,** gatherings focused on discussions about a single, specific subject or theme.

Major disciplinary organizations usually host the largest **conferences,** usually on an annual basis, and it is here that scholars can share the findings of their latest research, solicit feedback on their work from the audience, and keep up to date on the most current research topics. Large conferences, such as the one held by the American Historical Association in January of each year, host thousands of historians, many of whom also come to participate in organizational activities, to meet with potential publishers at special book exhibitions, or to take part in the academic hiring process either as a candidate for a position or as a member of an institutional search committee. Much of the remaining action at conferences like the AHA happens in informal chats before sessions or over coffee or meals during breaks, when historians "talk shop," discuss their projects, offer feedback, share their ideas, and discuss potential collaborations for the future. The collegial interactions that accompany a tangible gathering at a conference also allow historians put faces to names when reading books, to build their collegial networks, and otherwise to foster the bonds that help promote the work of the historical community.

Large conferences host dozens or even hundreds of sessions. Most include at least one **keynote** address, which features an original lecture presentation from a senior member of the discipline, and then a number of **panel presentations,** featuring roughly three to four speakers delivering research findings on related topics. The panels often include a **commentator,** who provides an overarching comment on all of the papers, and a **moderator,** who keeps time and negotiates the question-and-answer session with the audience. Other sessions are more open-ended, **roundtable sessions** with speakers discussing or debating a single large research issue or question with, as the name implies, a round table, allowing them to face each other and discuss. Within each of these formats, papers can be either delivered fresh in front of the audience or **precirculated** and summarized in the presentation.

It is rarer for undergraduates to be accepted to formal organizational conferences, but there are plenty of smaller conferences that welcome students and some that are designed exclusively for graduate or undergraduate presenters. In consultation with your mentor, you may wish to apply for a presentation slot at a conference. It can be a very positive experience, since you would be sharing your work with scholars on the outside who may not be familiar with your work. That can be a great way to get different perspectives on your conclusions and hopefully secure both some encouragement and some helpful feedback. In most conference settings, the audience is friendly, understanding that most projects are delivered in progress rather than as finished pieces, and that there is interest all around in a candid and constructive session.

If you choose to present in a conference venue, you should first select a conference that fits your discipline and your topic area. Some conferences, like regional meetings hosted by the American Phi Alpha Theta Organization, are general meetings that cater to all topics. Others may designate particular focus on regional history or a specific theme. Once you have selected a meeting, you will need to apply to present within the group's designated time frame. You are looking to apply during the group's **call for papers**, which will usually be posted online and will describe the application process. Large conferences may issue their call for papers six months to a year in advance, while others may give a window of ninety days. The requirements also vary, with some requiring submission of full papers and others satisfied with an abstract or a prospective paper. Pay attention in the instructions to whether the organization wants full panel submissions, which would require you to find multiple scholars working on a similar topic, or if they accept **orphan papers** submitted on their own.

When deciding what to present, bear in mind that most panel presentations have rigidly prescribed time limits. The conventional rule is to limit speakers to twenty minutes, which translates to between ten and twelve pages of text typed, double-spaced. We recommend that you keep closer to ten pages so that you can speak at a normal rate. Ten pages is not a lot, and that means that you will need to be selective over what you present. It may be the case that you wish to present only a portion of your thesis or to use one narrower example to illustrate your broader argument. In that case, give your paper a different title than you give your thesis.

Many conferences allow you to use slides, but not all, so check in advance. When incorporating slides, use the principle of parsimony: less is more. If a slideshow contains the bulk of text from a presentation, then the scholar risks making himself or herself superfluous. You should use them only when they add something essential to the talk. They work best when you have important visuals to share, such as when analyzing a piece of artwork or discussing a statistical chart. In other cases, you may need them if you are employing quite a few foreign language terms or if you need to summarize the main points for an audience whose first language may not be English. For most history presentations, your talk alone will do the job.

The presentation itself follows many of the same rules that you observed for the thesis defense, with only a few minor exceptions. For one, it is acceptable to read a conference paper and in fact can be quite disastrous to try to memorize it or to wing it. One tip is to memorize only the first few sentences so that you can establish eye contact with the audience. Then, pace yourself while reading and look up at key moments to reengage the audience's interest. Because you will be reading from a podium, it is also important to make sure that your font size is big enough for you to read without stooping over the page and that your pages are in proper order, preferably paginated so there are no unfortunate breaks in continuity. Furthermore, you should write a paper to be read aloud differently than a normal paper. To help your audience stay on top of what you are saying, give stronger clues in the text as to your main points, such as "In this paper, I will make two key arguments," and so forth. Avoid long, complicated tapeworm sentences that snake around obscure terms. Make sure the audience can tell when you are quoting from a text and translate all foreign words. And, finally, practice staying within your time limit and work on keeping a careful rhythm and clear enunciation.

The audience questions are also similar to defenses, except that the time is shared with others on the panel. Sometimes questions are collected, so it is always a good idea to write down the questions and comments that you hear. It is also good to limit your responses so that your colleagues get their fair share. If a question is particularly complicated, you may give a brief answer and ask the audience member to chat afterward in more detail. For that matter, bring business cards if you have them and exchange liberally with colleagues at the panels you attend so that you may follow up with them after the conference and build your academic network or learn more about the feedback you received.

Publishing an Article

If your work makes a suitably original and significant contribution to the field, then you may wish to consider taking the last step of sharing your work, which is to publish it in an academic journal or edited volume. With a professional presentation, you reach a few dozen colleagues who attend your talk. With a defended thesis or dissertation added to your library's internal collection, you reach the students and faculty across an institution. But a journal article has the potential to reach an unlimited number of scholars around the world over an indefinite time period. In short, it offers the best chance of making a lasting, meaningful impact on the discipline. Of course, your decision to publish should be undertaken in consultation with a professional mentor who can help you assess the fitness of your work and assist you in finding an appropriate journal or other publishing opportunity.

Befitting its place as the pinnacle of scholarly sharing, publishing an article entails an especially rigorous peer-review process. After you and your mentors have made the decision to submit your piece (now called a manuscript) for publication, and after you have thoroughly reviewed and proofread the manuscript and ensured that it meets the requirements of the journal, including prescribed length, citation styles, and formatting, you will most likely submit the manuscript file through an online portal on the journal's website. The editors of the journal will then make an initial assessment to determine whether it fits the scope of the journal and whether the research warrants peer review. If so, they will notify you that the manuscript has been sent out to readers for what is ideally a double-blind peer review. You will not communicate with the readers and they will probably not know anything about you. At this point, when listing the piece on your curriculum vitae, you should list it as "under review" pending the outcome of the process.

Readers usually spend several weeks or a few months with a manuscript before returning a reader's report, in which they provide their assessment and make a recommendation on publication to the editor. The report will make three recommendations: to publish with no changes, not to publish, or to publish with revisions, which is known as "revise and resubmit." Sometimes readers do not agree, so it is up to the editor to decide based on the advice of readers whether to accept or reject a piece, or which revisions to ask of the author. In any case, you should be able to view the readers' reports and, in the case of revise and resubmits, respond to their recommendations. Even if a piece is rejected, the reports can be very helpful in thinking about how to proceed with your research and whether to revise and submit the manuscript to another journal. If the piece is rejected, try not to feel discouraged. As any faculty mentor can probably tell you, it happens a lot even to the best of us, and it is part of the process of maintaining rigorous standards in the field. You can thus see it as important constructive feedback aimed at making your work better.

In the case of a revision, keep close track of the content and structural changes you make to the manuscript, since you will want to provide a short list of the changes to the editors when you resubmit. The process might go back and forth a few times until an article is finally accepted and goes into a publication queue. From there, it can linger a little while, particularly for journals with long backlogs, and you may have to wait up to a year or longer to see it in print. In the meantime, when a piece is accepted, you may change the line in your vitae from "under review" to "forthcoming" and then remove that element and add a full citation when the piece officially appears in the journal.

Publishing is certainly a tantalizing outcome, but it is not an urgent priority for undergraduate or early career graduate students. Indeed, the

AHA Committee on Graduate Education identified pressures for graduate students especially to publish their work before graduation as evidence of a potentially unhealthy "premature professionalization," which may inhibit their "freedom to explore his or her profoundest intellectual passions."[23] The added caution is an important one and should remind us that our publications should stem from proper intellectual engagement, lest the motive to publish become another careerist box to check rather than a meaningful contribution to the field. If, however, a sense of genuine curiosity bears fruit and leaves you in a position to publish, then the result can also be a nice feather in your cap. For that matter, any effort to present the findings of your research is an opportunity to take part in the collective enterprise of historical discovery, but by showcasing your skills, it can also be a boon to your own academic and career plans. As you bring your project to a close in some fashion during the Presentation Phase, whether that is through an essay, a panel talk, a thesis defense, or even an article, there is always an added personal benefit. With that in mind, we turn now in the final chapter to a discussion of the ways that studying history and employing your skills to exploring the past can help you, regardless of whether history lies at the heart of your future.

APPLICATION EXERCISE

Prepare an oral presentation of fifteen or twenty minutes dealing with either a summary of your project or a single, self-contained component of the finished product. Even if you are not in a position to present your work in an official venue, you can still organize an informal event on your campus. If possible, invite outside students and faculty to attend and ask questions. Ask a faculty mentor for feedback on your presentation and talk with them about publishing opportunities connected to your research topic.

Notes

1   Francis Fukuyama, "The End of History," *The National Interest* 16 (1989): 3–18.

2   Francis Fukuyama, "Reflections on the End of History: Five Years Later," *History and Theory* 34, no. 2 (1995): 27–43, 28, 30.

3   Francis Fukuyama, "Against Identity Politics: The New Tribalism and the Crisis of Democracy," *Foreign Affairs* 97, no. 5 (2018): 90–114.

4   Francisco Martorell Campos, "El final de la historia a la luz de la utopía política. Entre Fukuyama y Jameson," *Política y Sociedad* 54, no. 2 (2017): 545–64.

5   Jordi Quoidbach, Daniel T. Gilbert, and Timothy D. Wilson, "The End of History Illusion," *Science* 339, no. 6115 (2013): 96–8, 98.

6   Ibid.

7   See David J. Staley, *History and Future: Using Historical Thinking to Imagine the Future* (Lanham, MA: Lexington, 2007).

8   Jo Guldi and David Armitage, *The History Manifesto* (Cambridge: Cambridge University Press, 2014), 8.

9   Deborah Cohen and Peter Mandler, "The History Manifesto: A Critique," *The American Historical Review* 120, no. 2 (2015): 530–42.

10   Guldi and Armitage, *History Manifesto*, 117.

11   Jean-Jacques Rousseau, *Emile, or On Education*, translated by Barbara Foxley (Auckland: Floating Press, 1921), 710.

12   Nancy A. Schaefer, "Y2K as an Endtime Sign: Apocalypticism in America at the fin-de-millennium," *Journal of Popular Culture* 38, no. 1 (2004): 82–105.

13   Timothy Snyder, *On Tyranny* (New York: Tim Duggan, 2017), 9.

14   Edward J. Watts, *Mortal Republic: How Rome Fell into Tyranny* (New York: Basic, 2018), 8.

15   Snyder, *On Tyranny*, 118.

16   Jeffrey Kluger, *Apollo 8: The Thrilling Story of the First Mission to the Moon* (New York: Holt, 2018); Robert Kurson, *Rocket Men: The Daring Odyssey of Apollo 8 and the Astronauts Who Made Man's First Journey to the Moon* (New York: Random House, 2018).

17   Margot Lee Shetterly, *Hidden Figures: The American Dream and the Untold Story of the Black Women Mathematicians Who Helped Win the Space Race* (New York: William Morrow, 2016).

18   Harriet Zuckerman and Ronald G. Ehrenberg, "Recent Trends in Funding for the Academic Humanities and Their Implications," *Daedalus* 138, no. 1 (2009): 124–46; Jürgen Mittelstrass, "Humanities under Pressure," *Humanities* 4, no. 1 (2015): 80–6; Mitch Smith, "Rural Students Ask, 'What Is a University without a History Major?'" *The New York Times*, January 12, 2019, accessed January 12, 2019, https://www.nytimes.com/2019/01/12/us/rural-colleges-money-students-leaving.html.

19   Nigel A. Raab. *Who Is the Historian?* (Toronto: University of Toronto Press, 2016).

20   Among the more recent titles, see George Anders, *You Can Do Anything: The Surprising Power of a Useless Liberal Arts Degree* (New York: Little Brown & Company, 2019); Helen H. Small, *The Value of the Humanities* (Oxford: Oxford University Press, 2016); Iain Hay, "Defending Letters: A Pragmatic Response to Assaults on the Humanities," *Journal of Higher Education Policy & Management* 38, no. 6 (2016): 610–24; Fareed Zakaria, *In Defense of a Liberal Education* (New York: Norton, 2015).

21   Raab, *Who Is the Historian?*, 107.

22   Justin Stover, "There Is No Case for the Humanities," *The Chronicle of Higher Education*, March 4, 2019, accessed January 10, 2019, https://www.chronicle.com/article/There-Is-No-Case-for-the/242724.

23 Thomas Bender, Philip M. Katz, Colin Palmer, and the AHA Committee on
      Graduate Education, *The Education of Historians for the Twenty-First Century*
      (Urbana: University of Illinois Press, 2004), 70.

Suggested Reading

Brands, Hal, and Jeremi Suri, eds., *The Power of the Past: History and Statecraft.*
    Washington, D.C.: Brookings Institution Press, 2015.
Evans, Richard J. *In Defense of History*. New York: Norton, 1999.
Hunt, Lynn. *History: Why It Matters*. Cambridge: Polity, 2018.
MacMillan, Margaret. *Dangerous Games: The Uses and Abuses of History*. New
    York: Modern Library, 2009.
Roth, Michael S. *Beyond the University: Why Liberal Education Matters*. New
    Haven: Yale University Press, 2014.
Wineburg, Sam. *Why Learn History (When It's Already on Your Phone)*. Chicago:
    University of Chicago Press, 2018.

10

History and Careers: What History Can Do for You

What we will do in this chapter:

➤ **REFLECT** on the connections between historical studies and career development.

➤ **DISCOVER** pathways to careers in history through graduate school, the academy, and beyond.

➤ **APPLY** career planning skills to developing a curriculum vitae.

In the late summer of 1786, the German novelist Johann Wolfgang von Goethe (1749–1832) departed from his adopted home city of Weimar on a two-year tour of the Italian peninsula. At the age of thirty seven, Goethe was already a well-established literary figure, but he had never before ventured from his homeland. Though the distances may not seem great today, Goethe experienced his journey as a monumental transformation. "There is nothing to be compared," he wrote years later, "with the new life which the sight of a new country affords to a thoughtful person. Although I am still the same being, I yet think I am changed to the very marrow."[1] It is scarcely a coincidence that soon after his return, Goethe completed his second novel, *Wilhelm Meister's Apprenticeship*, since hailed as one of the first great *Bildungsromane*, or novels of self-discovery.

The fruits of Goethe's personal discoveries live on today. The same ideas of *Bildung*, of cultivation of the self through experience and learning, have become an indelible part of modern higher education.[2] They manifest themselves perhaps visibly in the study-abroad experience. Like Goethe, thousands of university students undertake semesters in locales far from home. While the overall percentages of students who study abroad remain relatively small, the experience has grown steadily as part of a university curriculum, and rightly so. If one of the purposes of a university education is to broaden horizons and see oneself in a new light, then what better way than by plucking students from their familiar surroundings and setting them in a new environment, among those who speak a foreign tongue and who act and think differently? Studies show that students fully expect to be transformed through their experience, and they cite "personal growth" as a primary motive.[3] Like Goethe over two centuries earlier, today's students want to feel the experience in their bones.

What we might miss when we think about personal metamorphosis as a journey is the degree to which it is also an internal process. Indeed, *Bildung* is also a feature of the classroom, and this is why universities are structured as curricula. Derived from the Latin word *currere*, to run, the university curriculum is conceived as a set of courses that "run" together to shape the whole person as a single, comprehensive experience. No subject and no course really should constitute an isolated learning opportunity. Rather, the courses that comprise an undergraduate or graduate transcript should coalesce, with domains of inquiry that come together to inform a broader understanding of the world and skills that reinforce and complement one another.

Research is one of these skills. From the beginning, this book has described research as a process, following a sequence and drawing upon a battery of skills to add new knowledge to a field of study. But it would be just as well to think of research as a journey whose steps may be metaphorical but whose capacity to transform is no less potent than any physical voyage. In the last chapter, we considered how the fruits of your research might contribute to the advancement of scholarship and to our understanding of history. Now it is time to think about how the outcomes of your studies can benefit you in terms of your future education, your career, and your life as a whole.

History as a Primary Field of Study

It is a true delight for us to chat with a prospective university student who is considering history as a course of study. Secondary school students and their parents often tour university campuses, attend sample lectures, and meet with faculty. During these meetings, students tell us something about why they are interested in history, whether they are fascinated with a particular period or simply love reading, writing, and narrativity. We answer the questions they have about curricula, coursework, and grades. And, inevitably, someone in these meetings, usually a parent, asks the same particular question, "What jobs do you get with a history major?"

In some ways, this seems a perfectly reasonable question. Higher education is expensive, and it is hard to deny that universities are pricing themselves out of the market for abstract goodness. At the same time, career choices can seem dicey. There really do not seem to be very many historians running around out there. Evening television choices offer no end of cop, doctor, and lawyer programs, but not so many gripping dramas about the glamorous lives of academics. Just as outside observers have questioned the value of history and humanities research, so too have they associated the corresponding degree programs with vanity majors and cul-de-sac career pathways. Implicit in a student or parent's seemingly innocuous question about "getting jobs" is a plea for assurances that history is not a one-way ticket to a future mix of idealistic poverty and chronic underemployment.

Unfortunately, such fears are grounded on a number of misconceptions. Having taught thousands of students and seeing the outcomes that they have achieved, we see a different picture. In fact, we would argue that "what jobs do you get with a history degree?" is very much the wrong question to ask for at least three key reasons.

The "Horizon" Problem

The question that everyone loves to ask is flawed first of all because it misunderstands the connections between academic degree programs and careers. It assumes, incorrectly, that there is always a direct relationship between a course of study and a specific line of work. Such thinking conceptualizes degrees as some form of vocational training, which for many bachelor's degrees is simply not the case. To explain further, it might be helpful to make a distinction between two types—to use US parlance—of **academic majors**, which are clusters of courses within a degree program focused on one field of study. On the one hand are the majors that entail some sort of certification for a specific type of work, such as certified public accounting, nursing, or social work. We might think of these types of programs as *pipeline majors*, because they lead directly to a relatively narrow range of professional employment options. Most programs, however, and certainly most liberal arts programs, are more what we might call *horizon majors*, because they hold the potential for use in a wide variety of employment sectors and career types. When meeting with groups of secondary school students and parents, one of the ways we make this clear is to play a little game we call "Guess My University Major." In this "game," we show a listing of career outcomes from real students who have attended our institutions and ask the group to hazard a guess at what majors the students had completed. Here is a sample:

Air traffic controller	Documentary filmmaker	Minister
Assistant professor	Editorial assistant	Physician
Attorney	High school principal	Public information officer
Campaign manager	Insurance actuary	Regional bank manager
Dentist	IT director	University Dean of Students

As you may have guessed, this is a trick question, because the answer is that all of these students were history majors who studied with us in US universities. This sample shows why it is so difficult to provide a short answer to the "what jobs do I get?" question, because the possibilities are so extensive. Notice that none of the listings include professional historians (though we have produced our fair share). As it turns out, most history majors never work in history. In fact, many of the positions listed here may not have even occurred to many students or parents as career options. The examples here stem from personal experience, but there is national data to support our observations. The American Academy of Arts and Sciences produces a very helpful set of "humanities indicators" designed to help raise awareness of the possibilities for careers for liberal arts students. The data they provide show a similarly wide-ranging distribution of career outcomes in the management, business, education, media, and service sectors, among others.[4]

The outcomes for horizon majors like history should by no means discourage a student from choosing a pipeline major. In fact, both have their advantages and disadvantages. One of the benefits of a pipeline major is that there is a clear career goal to guide a course of study. The disadvantage, of course, is that the career outcomes are only meaningful if there are enough positions available; otherwise, you may find yourself retraining for a different line of work. Furthermore, finding the comfort of a "sure thing" career is not the same thing as finding one that you enjoy. If you are the sort whose ambition it is to be a healer and to help others, then a nursing program makes perfect sense, but if you are studying nursing simply for a guaranteed paycheck, then you may not be satisfied with your career and once again feel compelled to retrain.

With a horizon major, there are many more possibilities for finding a career with the working conditions and the outcomes that best suit you. Because the skill set is more transferable, it can also be easier to reinvent yourself and switch careers over time as desired. The downside, of course, is that your career path is not so clearly laid out before you, and it may demand more proactive work on your part to discover the possibilities and prepare for success. That can be very intimidating for many students, but the success of so many who have come before should give you courage. And the data look promising, too. According to American Academy, the rates of unemployment for humanities students with a bachelor's degree stood at roughly 4 percent in 2015, on par with social sciences, life sciences, and physical sciences majors, and less than half a point away from business and engineering degree holders.[5] Earnings are solid, as well, with humanities graduates in the United States earning median salaries within five to ten percentage points of most social and natural science, business, and health science graduates, and surpassing those in arts and education.[6]

The "Get" Problem

The second problem with the "what jobs do I get?" question concerns the verb "to get." In fact, one does not "get" a job or career from any course of study. One has to prepare to earn a position. This may seem like quibbling, but our experience suggests that it can have a significant psychological impact on student attitudes. Each May and June, we see scads of new first-year university students undergoing orientation for the following academic year. At the end of the standard icebreaker exercises and campus tours, there is a final session dedicated to choosing a schedule for the fall semester and, implicitly, choosing a major or primary course of study. At that particular moment, we see tremendous anxiety as students and parents confront the future. They treat this is a momentous decision, because they need a career, and they believe that they need a course of study that fits that career. Sitting at the computer arranging their schedule, they select a career that they have heard of and find the degree program that apparently "gets" them there. Maybe they want to be a physician, and because they heard at school that the MCAT entrance exam for medical school in the United States has a lot of biochemistry, they decide to major in biochemistry. Waves of relief spread across their faces as they confirm their fall schedule and dust off their hands, grateful that they will not have to think about that again for the next three years.

We have seen a lot of students set aside their career anxieties once starting their studies. It seems that for every student who interrogates us about careers with a history degree, there is an empty career fair or unfilled internship. This is not a symptom of laziness, since the students work hard in their studies; rather, it is a symptom of a passive approach to career planning. If students believe that their majors will "get" them a job, then they may lean too much on the promise of an academic major. A biochemistry major cannot by itself guarantee high marks on the MCAT exam if the student has not prepared for it, nor can it carry him or her through an interview with a medical school. The data suggest that humanities students can actually match or even outperform many other majors on the MCAT, or the GMAT exam for Masters in Business Administration programs, or the LSAT for law school, partly because the humanities skill set is ideal for some of the exams, but also because they plan and prepare in advance.[7] Choosing a major is thus not the same as "getting" a job.

The "Hammer" Problem

The jobs question implies that university majors are like tools, and in some ways, this is a fine analogy. University curricula should be useful, and like a tool, you should be able to carry them with you throughout your life. The problem, which forms the third reason why the jobs question is the wrong one to ask, is that we are thinking of the wrong tool. Imagine that your major is like a hammer. Just as a hammer is an indispensable part of a good toolkit, so too is a university degree essential. Hammers are rugged and will last virtually forever. But hammers only do one thing: they drive nails. If you think of your major simply as a pathway to a specific career, then you are similarly restricting the possibilities.

What if we thought differently about the history major? What if we likened it not to a hammer, but to a multipurpose tool, like a Swiss army knife? As the name suggests, the main tool in a Swiss army knife is the blade, which is designed primarily for cutting. The knife is analogous to the way your major helps you prepare for a professional career. Beyond the knife are various other tools, such as screwdrivers, bottle openers, saws, pliers, and many more. These tools, even though they are still secondary to the knife, nevertheless come in handy. They are thus akin to the parts of the major that we tend to ignore through our fixation on specific careers. If we can set aside our common belief that the expense of university tuition makes professional and nonprofessional considerations mutually exclusive, then we can begin to conceive of our educational goals with more imagination and to find that they have incredible value beyond the transient walls of the office cubicle.

Ask any historian what sorts of noncareer outcomes attach to the study of history, and you will get an ear full. Here we will name one prime example, which relates to history as preparation for informed citizenship. It is easy to overlook such a contribution, but it is simply wrong to think that humans instinctively possess the healthy habits that make it possible to live in an open and democratic society. In his 1966 book, *The Arrogance of Power*, J. William Fulbright, chairman of the US Senate Foreign Relations Committee, former Rhodes Scholar at the University of Oxford, and a 1925 graduate in history from the University of Arkansas, reflected on his country's foreign policy. He focused on its dangerous conflation of raw power with virtue and the absence of meaningful dissent in the face of harmful policies abroad. With the Vietnam War heating up and a polarized electorate emerging, Fulbright argued that universities were partly to blame, because they had turned away from their ideals. In a statement sharply at odds with today's careerist and market-based notions of the university, he explained:

> Only insofar as the university is a place where ideas are valued above their practical application, in which there is greater interest in contributing to the sum of human knowledge than in helping a government agency to resolve some practical problem, is the university meeting its academic responsibility to its students and its patriotic responsibility to the country.[8]

Fulbright knew very well that the nation stood to benefit from the university's mission of "cultivating the free and inquiring mind," and he outlined two ways in which universities could use that mission to "enrich the life of the individual" and promote the responsible exercise of global influence.[9]

One was to promote tolerance of thoughtful dissent as a normal feature of public life. "Freedom of thought," he explained, "diminishes the danger of an irretrievable mistake and it introduces ideas and opportunities that otherwise would not come to light."[10] Another was the ability to "liberate our imaginations" in order to transcend facile ideologies and thereby "acquire some understanding of the world-view held by people whose past experiences and present circumstances and beliefs are radically different from our own."[11] Only then could we approach the meaningful questions of our time, about the antecedents of war, the pathways to peace, and the ways to sustain mutual understanding.

These two contributions are integral elements of engaged citizenship, and both are strengthened through historical study. The skills you have learned in the course of your historical reading and research are what make possible the critical inquiries that inform national debates and community discussions. The knowledge gained from history raises awareness about the roots of our own societies while shaping humane perceptions of foreign cultures. Fulbright would likely have agreed that every insight that we gain about our neighbors, allies, and rivals enhances our national security and makes possible a more peaceful world.

If academic majors are like Swiss army knives, then we must remember that no two types of Swiss army knives are alike. Shop for one, and you will see that they all have different sets of tools. Some have rulers, others have corkscrews, and a few have, you guessed it, hammers. Academic fields are much the same. You should select the one that is right for you. Only now you can disregard a single career outcome as a primary criterion and base your choice on the content of the field, on what you want to know, and on what you want to learn how to do. You should focus on what interests you. An engaging field is one into which you are likely to put more time and energy and in which you will perform at a higher level. Your grades will be better, and the knowledge and skills certified by the diploma will be stronger.

The Right Question to Ask

With our eyes opened and our perspectives duly enhanced, we can now turn to the proper question for assessing what history can do for you: *How do I make the most of my history degree?* This question recognizes that a course of study should entail tangible benefits, but it suggests an active rather than passive relationship between student and curriculum. It allows you to think about your own actions and suggests the need for raised awareness about how the lessons and activities within each individual course coalesce to produce overarching outcomes.

A more nuanced question merits a more nuanced answer. With proper faculty mentorship and forethought, there are many steps that you can take to elicit the full benefit from both your major field and from your broader curriculum. Here we might identify ten possibilities:

1 *Find your niche:* Undergraduate learning entails a transition from the breadth of secondary learning to the depth of graduate study, moving toward specializing in a particular field of knowledge. You must consequently balance breadth and depth in order to maximize your curriculum. As you progress, embrace the advantages of core learning and be mindful of how the fundamentals inform advanced learning (an idea at the heart of this book). At the same time, gradually increase your level of specialization. Finding your niche means honing your general skills but also letting your interests, talents, and experience guide you toward more focused outcomes and expertise. If you find yourself particularly interested in British history, then focus more of your advanced coursework on that field. If you come to like digital history, tailor your research in that direction, and learn more about the relevant computer applications and procedures.

2 *Make bold choices:* When selecting courses, it is sometimes wise to blend tougher subjects with more manageable ones. But you should also challenge yourself. Do not avoid seemingly difficult courses solely to protect your standing or grade point average. Think about how a recommendation letter on your behalf might read. Would you prefer it to say that you always played it safe or that you were not so easily intimidated by new subjects or daunting projects?

3 *Deepen your knowledge:* When we take a passive stance toward a course syllabus, we tend to allow the readings and assignments contained within to define the limits of our engagement with a subject. A more effective strategy is to take an active role, and never to allow yourself to feel bored in a course. If you want to know more, go to the library and read more outside materials. Try not to think of your course grade as the final measure of your performance, but set yourself to the task of learning as much as you can about a topic and letting your knowledge speak for itself.

4 *Cultivate your skills:* This book has been all about identifying and improving basic skills in order to build better advanced skills. From here, you should seek every chance to practice what you have learned, both within classes and through peripheral coursework and extracurricular activities. If you want more training in critical thinking, take a logic course or enroll in a statistics course to enhance your quantitative prowess. Moreover, you should look for opportunities to develop new skills beyond the major that might inform you career prospects. Pursue software certifications online if that helps, or if you are interested in a career in business, take a course or two in management or accounting.

5 *Communicate with faculty:* Professors are specialists in their respective fields and can connect you with a variety of opportunities

related to the field. For this reason, you should at a minimum know a thing or two about your professor's expertise and experience and be on the lookout for mentoring opportunities. Meanwhile, you should stay plugged in to your institutional program. Watch for their announcements, follow them on social media, and attend special events.

6   *Build networks:* Beyond your institution are alumni and professionals who can help you make the most of your degree. Reach out and connect with as many of these individuals as possible. When you have a chance to correspond with a career practitioner in a field that interests you, ask him or her about his or her own pathways to success and solicit feedback on your work. Get to know alumni from your institution working in the career sectors that appeal to you. They may one day open doors for you. And once you have succeeded, pay the favor forward to the next generation.

7   *Seek experiences:* The scope of learning within a degree program always transcends the course curriculum. To make the most of it, you must get out there and collect meaningful experiences. Study abroad, find an internship, volunteer, participate in a student group, or take part in other activities that allow you to cultivate and apply your learning.

8   *Know how to talk about your learning:* This may seem obvious, but you may be surprised to see how many students make their way through university without a clear sense of what they have learned or of how to leverage it to meet their own goals. The key is to know how to spell out and explain the overarching lessons and skills that you have acquired over years of study. It is not enough, for example, to say that you have practiced critical thinking. Instead, describe what critical thinking is and how you have specifically used it in your own research.

9   *Practice parallel career development:* Horizon majors like history may not necessarily align with specific careers, but they can certainly inform career development. So, treat career development and academic planning as parallel processes and locate the places where the two overlap. While exploring majors, also explore career options. When honing your academic abilities, try to spot the points of intersection with career-specific skills. When pursuing an extracurricular experience, be mindful of how it can also be useful for the needs of different professions. Think beyond the immediate context of an internship, for example, and also consider what you are actually doing. Are you researching? Are you working with the public? Back on campus, take advantage of every career-building offering at your institution. Learn interview skills, network with professionals at career fairs, and talk with guest speakers from various fields.

10. *Showcase your accomplishments:* One last way that you can make the most of your studies is to track the outcomes. That may involve building a portfolio to highlight particular skills, maintaining a professional social media presence on sites like LinkedIn, and keeping reflections on the challenges you have faced and the ways that you have grown over the years. Finally, as we will discuss at the end of this chapter, you should also maintain a résumé or curriculum vitae that attests to your accomplishments as a student.

REFLECTION EXERCISE

To what extent are you "making the most of your major or degree"? Using the suggestions above, assess the ways in which you have already acted proactively, and then identify the ways you could improve further your level of engagement. Brainstorm with peers some other ways you can maximize the value of your degree.

History as a Career

At the beginning of this book, we likened the study of history to swimming in a great sea. Since we all have a connection to the past in one way or another, we all swim together. Thus, the discipline of history holds something for everyone, and not every history student must pursue it as a career. As we have made abundantly clear, the study of history offers strong career prospects along a number of pathways. However, for those who come to love history and wish to make a career of it, there are also a number of possibilities.

Among the more traditional careers for history majors who wish to apply their learning directly are the legal and teaching professions. History is ideal preparation for success in law school, partly because the law itself is a historical entity, with a body of rules and practices built over time. But it also matters that the work of the attorney mirrors so closely the research of the historian. Specifically, legal work requires a great deal of synthesis, of stitching together disparate opinions and case law to form legal arguments. These practices are very similar to the type of syntheses that historians create when they blend primary sources to depict a historical event or compose an analysis of a complex historiography. Teaching history or social studies, meanwhile, is another obvious choice because it demands professionals who not only can practice good pedagogy but also know something about the subject matter. Both are time-honored choices with practitioners who owe a great debt to their history degrees.

A wholly different and growing sector of employment relates to the broad field of **public history**, which involves sustained connections between the work of the historian and a nonspecialist audience. Public historians have specialized training in communicating with and engaging the public, and prepare themselves to work in a variety of contexts. The field can lead to work in government agencies, libraries, parks, and museums and can include work in curation, exhibit design, historical interpretation, and historical conservation. Other possible outcomes include working in popular book publishing, children's and teen's nonfiction, documentary filmmaking, and Web and video game design.[12] Every historian should in practice work with the public in one way or another, but the unique needs of public communication have created a fast-growing niche for those who choose to specialize in the public and nonprofit sectors. A long-term commitment to public history careers may require at least a master's degree, whether the usual Master of Arts in a historical research field with practical experience in public history or a specialized master's degree in public history, museum studies, or cultural resource management.

Since this is a book about the "essential skills" that shape advanced research techniques, it stands to reason that we should say something about academic professions. When compared with other career outcomes in the corporate, public, legal, and education sectors, the range of professions available to research-oriented historians is smaller, but there are a number of possibilities nonetheless. In fact, many of these get unduly overlooked by faculty and students in PhD programs. Although a growing number of commentators have promoted the value of the so-called **alternative academic** (or **alt-ac**) opportunities for history doctoral students, many continue to treat these as secondary outcomes.[13] This is a mistake, because beyond the professoriate, there are some terrific careers in academic publishing, consulting, archives, and research libraries. Moreover as Michael Lesiuk has observed, "Many businesses have realized that humanities scholars offer a unique skill set that can be trained or modified to adapt to very different industries."[14] Students considering pursuing doctorates in the field would be well served to consider these sorts of positions as desirable primary outcomes rather than mere fallback positions, while graduate programs could certainly do more to prepare students to succeed in these fields, including developing specialized courses and relevant internship programs.

Choosing an Academic Career in History

The professoriate, of course, can also be an enormously rewarding career. For those in full-time positions, the pay is generally above the median for humanities earners, the hours are long but flexible, and the working conditions ideal for those who love researching and teaching history. Academic historians can make important contributions to their field, and they often derive great satisfaction from their impact on the intellectual and professional development of their students. Finally, there is something to be said for coming to work each day at the university campus or for the opportunities to travel to research sites and conference venues.

Unfortunately, there are some real drawbacks to academia, and students interested in the professoriate should think very carefully before making a commitment. The most significant problem is the shortage of positions. Newly minted history PhDs usually seek **tenure-track** lines, which are positions at universities leading to tenure, which guarantee a higher salary, a measure of job security, and academic freedom. Unfortunately, the number of tenure-track positions has dwindled in recent decades. In the United States, the American Historical Association tracked fewer than 600 advertised positions in history in 2016–2017. Meanwhile, the American Association of University Professors estimates that up to 73 percent of all faculty positions in all fields were off the tenure track in 2016.[15] The trends in the United Kingdom are equivalent, exacerbated by the introduction of a policy in 2011 that reduced the amount of funding allocated from government budgets for teaching and replacing it with income from student tuition fees, which increased dramatically. Although the security of tenure was abolished in the 1980s, British universities do offer permanent, "open-ended" contracts, but these applied to only 66 percent of academic staff in 2016.[16]

The daunting tenure-track numbers do not mean it is impossible to work as an academic historian. Because demand for higher education instruction remains high, there are other full-time, non-tenure-track positions available, including clinical professorships or professorships of practice, which emphasize teaching over research. For a great many others, there are short-term visiting appointments and contractual adjunct appointments that may pay an annual salary or that pay a set amount for each class. While a number of faculty and unions, especially the University and College Union in the UK, have called for stronger salaries and working conditions, the adjuncts with whom they work often do not have the same possibilities to participate in academic governance activities, so their say in how their positions are treated is limited. As a result, a student considering a career in the field should be aware that the market for academics is highly competitive and that a position is not guaranteed. At a minimum, new academics should be prepared to be active on a national or international job market and be flexible as to where they live and in what type of institution they practice their profession. That being said, for those lucky enough to secure a position, it is possible to have a very satisfying research and teaching career at all levels of the profession, whether one is appointed at a community college, a small liberal arts institution, or a large private or public research university.

If you are genuinely interested in an academic career, we encourage you to talk to your faculty mentors and adjuncts in your institution about their own experiences and to be mindful of both the potential benefits and the challenges that confront the profession. When considering applying for graduate school, it is also wise to consider separately the Master of Arts from the PhD, or Doctor of Philosophy degree. Since master's programs usually take no more than two years, they can be a very good educational investment. Particularly when funding is available, a master's degree can provide an intellectually satisfying advanced education while retaining the broad characteristics of the "horizon" bachelor's degree. That means you can finish an MA relatively quickly and use the specialized training to enter a wide variety of fields.

The real decision point is between finishing an MA and starting a PhD program. On the one hand, a doctoral degree is very employable. The American Academy of Arts and Sciences reports that in 2015 history majors who went on to earn advanced degrees had unemployment rates below 3 percent.[17] On the other hand, finishing a PhD can take between three and five years beyond the master's degree, a significant increase in the investment of time and money. Good doctoral programs will often provide tuition funding and a living stipend for well-qualified students in exchange for teaching courses, but the stipends are low, meaning that students either must take extra loans or otherwise lose out on years that they could otherwise be earning higher salaries elsewhere. Thus, even though the range of potential employment remains very strong, the horizons are a little smaller, meaning the positions that justify the time and expense of a doctoral program are fewer than those for an MA. For this reason, it is usually relatively easy to recommend an MA program or even to apply for a PhD program that includes an MA as part of the process, but when the time comes to decide whether to continue beyond the MA, a student should consult with their mentors and consider their options very carefully. In general, if you have demonstrated a great deal of ability and potential as a research historian, and if you are open-minded about the career possibilities, then these may very well be good reasons to continue.

The Graduate School Experience

Undergraduate programs combine a bit of breadth into their matrix, but graduate programs are all about depth. In history, students apply to graduate programs to work in very specific fields, broken down in many cases by region, time period, and methodology. A student, for example, may seek to complete an MA in twentieth-century American cultural history or in medieval Europe with a focus on the religious history of the Iberian Peninsula. When seeking a suitable program, a potential graduate student should look for universities whose programs include a desired specialty. If your skills and experience are suited for a focus on sub-Saharan Africa, then you need to make sure that the school to which you apply has at least one specialist (and preferably more) in that field. Moreover, if you know something about your preferred graduate research topic, your top choices will lie with schools whose faculty have overlapping interests.

Once in the program, graduate students pursue depth by choosing a primary field at the MA level and at the PhD level by selecting a primary field and up to three secondary fields. Each field is supervised by a faculty member, with the primary field being directed by the student's doctoral adviser. The fields often are chosen with an eye toward building a student's expertise and profile as a researcher and a teacher. For instance, if a student's first field is in modern British history, then it may make sense to complete secondary fields in modern and early-modern continental Europe and then do some work on a fourth field in a specific methodology or thematic specialty, like intellectual history or diplomatic history.

For each of their fields, students take a selection of graduate seminars focused on discussions of themes or topical readings. Unlike undergraduate lecture courses, graduate seminars include a dozen or more monographs and a substantial writing requirement. Through their seminars, students prepare lists of readings in each field in consultation with their field supervisors, and after completing their prescribed graduate hours, they take a battery of comprehensive examinations to prove their expertise. The process varies, but generally students take a written test in which they respond to a typically historiographical question (e.g., "How have historians explained the outbreak of the American Civil War?" or "How have historians debated the reasons for the rise of the Nazi state?") in a lengthy and detailed essay lasting hours or days. The written exam is followed by an oral exam, which addresses any questions or deficiencies from the written exam. Students who pass their "comps" are then admitted to the status of doctoral candidacy and designated as "ABD," or "All but Dissertation."

Along the way, graduate students learn the advanced methods of history and demonstrate their competencies by producing original research directed by their graduate adviser, who works very closely with the student from beginning to end. In many programs, students spend two years completing and defending an article-length master's thesis on a single research topic. The PhD includes an additional one or two years of coursework, and, after that the student passes the comprehensive exams, the requirement of a doctoral dissertation. Traditional dissertations are book-length theses that almost always include archival research and must make a substantial contribution to a historical topic. It sounds a bit daunting, but doctoral candidates come to their dissertations after years of reading in the field and training in historical methods. Although the task is far more involved and more advanced than the undergraduate thesis, the process follows the steps we have described here, so students who begin to master the "essential skills" are well armed for the travails of advanced research.

Entering the Professoriate

While they are finishing courses and working on their dissertations, doctoral students spend time preparing for their careers, which in many cases means developing as teachers. One of the difficulties that confronts an ABD doctoral candidate is the prospect of writing a dissertation while designing new history courses, but the experience prepares them for balancing the duties required of new professors. As they near completion, doctoral candidates enter the academic job market, which traditionally begins in the fall as institutions post positions they expect to fill for the following academic year. In the United States, selected candidates often take part in an initial screening interview online or at the annual AHA Convention, and then a handful are invited for an on-campus visit to deliver a teaching demonstration or formal presentation of their research, known as a "job talk."

New tenure-track professors enter their new position with the rank of Assistant Professor. Their workload is divided into what James M. Banner, Jr. has called the "Academic Trinity," referring to teaching, research, and service obligations.[18] The teaching load includes a set number of courses for each quarter or semester, usually between two and four courses per semester depending on the institution (a 2/2 or 4/4 teaching load), which at some strongly teaching-oriented schools (like community colleges) may stretch to 5/5. The research portion of the position is measured in terms of productivity, whether in progress toward a published book or articles or applications for research grants. Finally, because universities are ostensibly governed by their faculty, the service requirement includes participation in faculty governance: working on various committees or on disciplinary association boards. For more senior professors, the "Academic Trinity" becomes the proverbial Four Horsemen of the Apocalypse, as the three traditional work areas are joined by a fourth: administration, which includes work as department chairs, college deans, or university provosts.

From the first day of their appointment, assistant professors are on a **tenure clock**, which is a fixed amount of time that they have to earn tenure. Six years is a normal time frame, though that can vary by institution and can be paused for parental leave or illness. By the end of that time period, assistant professors must apply for tenure and show they have met the standards set by their departments and universities. History in particular is a book field, and the research requirements include the publication of a monograph, often based on the dissertation. Tenure candidates are also expected to demonstrate teaching excellence and a record of institutional and professional service. For assistant professors who meet the requirements, the granting of tenure often accompanies promotion to the rank of Associate Professor. Unless extraordinary circumstances intervene, tenure is granted for the duration of a faculty member's career, although future work can lead to further promotions to the rank of full Professor and on to any distinguished professorial ranks. For those whose qualifications do not merit tenure, the university usually ends the contract with an additional year to find a position elsewhere. The vast majority of tenure cases are successful, but even in the rare instances in which they are not, they do not preclude an academic from going on to earn tenure at another institution, and in many cases a little extra time is all that is needed.

Tenure is not a protection against hard work. Newly tenured historians suddenly find that their workload increases, as they launch a new book project amid rising service and administrative expectations. It is not uncommon for tenured and tenure-track professors to work an average of sixty hours or more each week teaching classes, assisting students, grading assignments, completing committee work, and of course writing books and articles and keeping up to date on the reading in their fields.[19] Nevertheless, tenure is extremely important not only for individual scholars but for the institutions to which they belong and to the whole enterprise of scholarship. Tenure guarantees academic freedom, which means that scholars have the liberty to pursue their research topics wherever it may take them without fear of retribution from those who may disagree or be angered by the results. There is also a comfort in knowing that a position is protected from those who discount the value of a field of study. We have gone to great lengths in this book to reaffirm the broad worth of history, for example, but tenure is an important safeguard against the capricious whims of politicians and pundits who may seek to deny funding for research that has no clear market value. Although tenure remains much misunderstood outside the world of academia, it is vital as both a license and an obligation to engage in rigorous, honest, and valuable academic research.

DISCOVERY EXERCISE

Conduct informal interviews with at least two history graduates, with at least one working in an academic and another in a nonacademic profession. Ask them about their career journey from graduation to career and about the ways they use their history learning in the careers today. Finally, talk to them about your own plans and write a short reflection piece discussing how the conversation informs the way you see your future in your current area of study and in your prospective career.

Building a Curriculum Vitae

Having practiced the essential skills for historians and learned about the range of academic, personal, and career possibilities before you, it is at last time to think about the next steps for your own future. This calls for you to reflect a great deal, but it also demands a clear accounting of your university accomplishments. One key way in which you can showcase your qualifications and the products of your work is to maintain a résumé or curriculum vitae, often called a CV for short. Résumés and CVs are much the same, but the former often focuses on both accomplishments and skills tailored to the requirements of a specific position or line of work. A curriculum vitae, which literally means "course of life," covers a wider range of accomplishments, but includes no details about specific activities. Every historian and every history student should keep an updated CV as a showcase of their professional activities, positions, and recognitions.

Essentially, CVs are organized lists of activities. They usually have three main layers, differentiated with different font sizes or styles. The first, which is composed in the largest font and set in bold style, is the list of headings identifying broad areas of activity like "education" or "research." Then follows the subheadings for classes of activities within the broad area, usually marked with a slightly smaller font or with a bold or italics style. Under the "research" heading, for example, subheadings can include "publications" and "presentations." Beneath the subheadings are the activities themselves, listed in a plain, body-sized font.

Like an essay, CVs are read from top to bottom and from left to right. The two vertical organizing principles are significance and time. You want to start at the top of the page with the most important types of activities and then list the individual accomplishments in reverse chronological order. Do not start a CV with your hobbies or athletics; rather, begin with your overarching education credentials and then move to specific, meaningful academic achievements: awards, grants, presentations, and so on. The top of each of your lists should state your current or most recent activities, and then work backward down the page toward older ones.

There are no hard rules for the horizontal arrangement of your entries, but each should name the accomplishment or activity and the relevant dates, usually limited to years. Whereas résumés include short descriptions of activities, CVs are usually content with a simple line identifying the activity itself. If you held an officer's position in a club, you can indicate the title of the position, the name of the organization, and the years you held the position. If you won a grant or fellowship, you can name the title of the award, the name of the organization bestowing the award, sometimes the amount of the award, and the year in which you received it. For theses, publications, and conference presentations, provide a full citation in Chicago style. Make sure that you properly align each horizontal line with their neighboring lines above and below and that you are consistent with the spacing between lines and between sections.

With the basic principles in mind, you can arrange your CV to fit your specific accomplishments. At the very top and center of your CV, we suggest you place your name and contact information. There is some debate about whether to include a photograph, but most do not, and you probably should omit it. List your education next, providing the type of degree earned or expected (collegiate level or higher only), the majors, minors, or primary fields of study, the year of expected graduation, and the current grade point average or academic ranking. Awards, grants, and fellowships can follow, and then publications or presentations. Graduate students can then list the courses they have taught, and then all students should list their memberships and service activities. There is no need to list individual courses or assignments in courses; they belong in a university transcript or portfolio. And do not include skills unless you have formal certifications. The one exception is foreign language. If you have any significant language training (at least two years or more of study), list the language along with the level of proficiency in speaking, reading, and writing, including if available any international certifications of fluency.

If you are an undergraduate student or beginning graduate student building a CV from the ground floor, it is acceptable to include important achievements from previous schooling, such as a major award from high school or an undergraduate thesis from your undergraduate years. As you become more experienced, you will probably want to shed those earlier accomplishments. Graduate student CVs carry no vestiges from high school, and new professors lose the entries from their undergraduate days. This does not diminish their value but allows you to place proper emphasis on more recent activities.

You should start keeping a CV from the earliest possible moment, even if your achievements seem a bit thin at first. Over time, you will enjoy watching it grow as you become more accomplished and document the ways you have strived to meet your long-term goals. With the skills you have learned in these pages, and with a project guided by this book, you will hopefully soon have another tangible entry on your CV. It may be but a single line on the page, but with any luck, it will mark a significant step on the path to your future.

APPLICATION EXERCISE

Visit your university's career development office or go online and view samples of professional curriculum vitae. Take note of the lists of content items and the language used to describe specific accomplishments, and pay attention to such stylistic issues as the use of fonts, headers spacing, and alignments. Then, create your own curriculum vitae or polish up an existing one. Share your finished CV with members of your class and offer constructive feedback on the CVs of your peers.

Notes

1   Johann Wolfgang von Goethe, *Letters from Italy*, in *The Works of Goethe*, vol. 2, edited by Nathan Haskell Dole et al. (Boston: F.A. Nicolls, 1902), 247.

2   Peter Watson, *The German Genius: Europe's Third Renaissance, the Second Scientific Revolution, and the Twentieth Century* (New York: Harper Perennial, 2010), esp. 740–2.

3   J. Zimmermann and F.J. Neyer, "Do We Become a Different Person When Hitting the Road?: Personality Development of Sojourners," *Journal of Personality and Social Psychology* 105 (2013): 515–30.

4   American Association of Arts and Sciences, "Humanities Indicators III-3a: Occupational Distribution of Holders of Terminal Bachelor's Degrees in the Humanities, 2015" 2018, accessed January 10, 2019, https://www.humanitiesindicators.org/content/indicatordoc.aspx?i=281.

5   American Association of Arts and Sciences, "Humanities Indicators III-3f: Unemployment among People with a Terminal Bachelor's Degree, by Gender and Undergraduate Major, 2015" 2018, accessed January 10, 2019, https://www.humanitiesindicators.org/content/indicatordoc.aspx?i=10922.

6   American Association of Arts and Sciences, "Humanities Indicators III-4p: Median Earnings of Humanities Majors as a Share of Median Earnings in Other Selected Fields, by Age, 2015," 2015, accessed January 10, 2019, https://www.humanitiesindicators.org/content/indicatordoc.aspx?i=10931.

7   American Association of Arts and Sciences, "Humanities Indicators III-5d: Medical College Admission Test Mean Score, by Examinee's Field of Undergraduate Study, 1991–2009," 2011, accessed January 10, 2019, https://www.humanitiesindicators.org/content/indicatordoc.aspx?i=300; "Humanities Indicators III-5b: Graduate Management Admission Test Mean Total Score, by Examinee's Field of Study, 2000–2009," 2011, accessed January 10, 2019, https://www.humanitiesindicators.org/content/indicatorDoc.aspx?i=298; "Humanities Indicators III-5f: Law School Admission Test Mean Score, by Examinee's Field of Undergraduate Study, 1996–2009," 2011, accessed January 10, 2019, https://www.humanitiesindicators.org/content/indicatordoc.aspx?i=302.

8   J. William Fulbright, *The Arrogance of Power* (New York: Random House, 1966), 40.

9   Ibid.

10 Ibid., 31.

11 Ibid., 167.

12 Thomas Cauvin, *Public History: A Textbook of Practice* (New York: Routledge, 2016).

13 Leonard Cassuto, "The Alt-Ac Job Search: A Case Study: How to Prepare a PhD for Faculty and Non-Faculty Jobs," *The Chronicle of Higher Education*, November 23, 2015, accessed January 10, 2019, https://www.chronicle.com/article/The-Alt-Ac-Job-Search-A-Case/234295.

14 Michael Lesiuk, "'Small Bets' and the PhD Process: Alt-Ac Careers for Humanities PhDs," *English Studies in Canada* 39, no. 4 (2013): 17–20.

15 American Association of University Professors, "Data Snapshot: Contingent Faculty in U.S. Higher Ed," October 11, 2018, accessed January 10, 2019, https://www.aaup.org/sites/default/files/10112018%20Data%20Snapshot%20Tenure.pdf.

16 Higher Education Statistics Agency, "Higher Education Staff Statistics: UK, 2016/2017," accessed January 18, 2019, https://www.hesa.ac.uk/news/18-01-2018/sfr248-higher-education-staff-statistics.

17 American Academy of Arts and Sciences, "Humanities Indicators III-3g, Unemployment among People with an Advanced Degree, by Gender and Undergraduate Major, 2015," accessed January 10, 2019, https://www. humanitiesindicators.org/content/indicatordoc.aspx?i=10923.

18 James M. Banner, Jr., *Being a Historian: An Introduction to the Professional World of History* (Cambridge: Cambridge University Press, 2012), 97.

19 Laura McKenna, "How Hard Do Professors Actually Work?" *The Atlantic*, February 7, 2018, accessed January 10, 2019, https://www.theatlantic.com/ education/archive/2018/02/how-hard-do-professors-actually-work/552698/.

Suggested Reading

Banner, James M., and John R. Gillis, eds. *Becoming Historians*. Chicago: University of Chicago Press, 2009.

Banner, James M., Jr. *Being a Historian: An Introduction to the Professional World of History*. Cambridge: Cambridge University Press, 2012.

Basalla, Susan, and Maggie Debelius. *"So What Are You Going to Do with That?": Finding Careers Outside Academia*, 3rd ed. Chicago: University of Chicago Press, 2014.

Kelsky, Karen. *The Professor Is In: The Essential Guide to Turning Your Ph.D. into a Job*. New York: Three Rivers, 2015.

Peters, Robert. *Getting What You Came For: The Smart Student's Guide to Earning an M.A. or a Ph.D*. New York: Farrar, Straus and Giroux, 1992.

GLOSSARY

academic majors: prescribed clusters of courses within a degree program focused on one field of study.

active learning: an approach involving self-awareness and engaged participation in the pursuit of new knowledge or skills.

active reading: an approach to texts using a high level of metacognitive self-awareness to discern an author's intentions and respond to a sophisticated message.

ad hominem **fallacy:** an error in critical thinking that occurs when one evaluates an argument based on the perceived identity or qualities of the person making the argument.

alternative academic (or alt-ac): career pathways and opportunities for holders of advanced graduate degrees lying outside tenure-track professorships.

altruism: an ethical orientation privileging the needs of others when determining right and wrong.

anachronism: a person, place, thing, or idea invoked outside of its proper historical context.

Annales School: a school of historiographical thought first appearing in France in the mid-twentieth century that broadly favored long-term structural studies of history, along with an emphasis on mentalities.

annals: a collection of recorded facts and observations grouped by year.

anthology: collections of writing, such as essays, on a related set of topics.

archival turn: a scholarly movement beginning in the late twentieth century that raises questions about the guiding assumptions behind the preservation and cataloguing of information.

argument: in a critical thinking exchange, a position asserted with supporting premises or evidence.

article: a short piece of original research usually published in an academic journal.

bandwagon fallacy: a critical thinking error that occurs when an arguer attempts to suggest that the strength of others' opinions affirms the strength of a conclusion.

BCE (Before Common Era): a secularized version of the older Western date-keeping abbreviation BC ("before Christ") that refers to all dates preceding the year zero.

bibliography: a formatted list of sources consulted for a research project.

Boolean search: a feature allowing for the use of delimiters such as "and" and "not" to narrow down a large set of records from a keyword search.

call for papers: an invitation to submit proposals, presentations, of manuscripts for an academic meeting or publication.

call number: a designation derived from a classification system that identifies the location of a book or other information item within a library.

CE (Common Era): a secularized version of the older Western date-keeping abbreviation AD ("anno Domini") that refers to all dates falling after the year zero.

Cliometrics: a term describing the quantitative historical approaches that became common in the late twentieth century.

collection: the artifacts, books, journals, media holdings, and other information or display items held within a library or museum.

commentator: an invited scholar tasked with offering reflections and criticism on a lecture or panel presentation.

conference: an academic meeting featuring scholars in a primary or secondary disciplinary field gathered for the purpose of presenting and disseminating new research findings.

correlation: a statistical relationship among two or more measured phenomena.

critical thinking: an active, rational, and defensible thought process that aims to solve a problem or make a decision.

crowd-sourcing: in academic publishing, a writing technique in which multiple, anonymous authors contribute to the production of a text and offer feedback.

cultural turn: a movement beginning with late-twentieth-century historiography that sought to historicize the development and transformation of shared cultural meanings.

data visualization: representations on a computer that enable people to see patterns or connections within and among data.

database: collections of data organized to facilitate searches using multiple identifying characteristics.

deduction: an approach to knowledge that conceives general principles and tests them against observations of specific phenomena.

deliverables: the outcomes identified from the results of a research project.

deontological ethics: an ethical principle that favors the rightness of actions as more important than the rightness of outcomes.

digital positivism: the belief that digital information is superior to information delivered through other means.

discovery phase: the component of the research process involving the analysis of primary evidence with the goal of responding to a **research question** and resolving a **research problem**.

egoism: an ethical orientation in which the needs of the self are paramount for determining right and wrong.

empiricism: a theory that emphasizes the value of knowledge derived from the physical senses.

ethical reasoning: a process of analyzing, evaluating, and constructing arguments about right or wrong actions and decisions informed by moral principles.

ethics: a branch of philosophy dealing with systems, principles, and conceptions of right and wrong.

evidence: material derived from empirical observation that supports or proves an argument or conclusion.

explicit premise: a supporting claim that is directly stated in an argument. See also **premise**.

extant: referring to past sources that remain available in the present.

external funding: grants or other resources provided by individuals or agencies outside the researcher's home institution.

fallacy: any error resulting from a violation of the principles of critical thinking.

fallacy of inappropriate authority: an error of critical thinking in which an argument appeals to a source of authority that lacks the relevant expertise.

fallacy of the dichotomous question: an error of critical thinking that limits the answer to a question to two opposing semantic categories that limit the full range of possible outcomes.

federated searching: the act of using multiple linked databases to return a single set of results from a query.

finding aids: a search tool providing the location, description, and use regulations of a source in an archive.

genealogy: refers to the study of family lineages, and also used to describe ideas or trends that unfold not in direct succession, but as a complex set of relationships spread unevenly across time.

historical analogy: the act of comparing episodes or elements from the past to circumstances in the present.

historical contingency: the notion that trends, ideas, or beliefs are dependent upon the specific context in which they are formed.

historical continuity: the notion that trends, ideas, or beliefs are relatively unchanging or tend to stay stable over long periods of time.

historical research: a process of identifying, analyzing, evaluating, and synthesizing information from and about the past in order to answer historical questions and resolve historiographical problems.

historical thinking: a process in which one thinks about or with history in order to make sense of the past, present, or future.

historicism: a school of historical thought stressing the uniqueness of specific moments in the past and the capacity of scholars to comprehend past eras through the study of their particular contexts.

historiography: the study of historical scholarship and writing. Also refers to the body of secondary literature about a historical topic.

hypothesis: a preliminary conclusion based on initial experience and research.

impact factor: an attempted quantitative measurement of the scholarly significance of an academic journal derived from the average of citations for recent articles in the journal over a designated time period.

implicit premise: a claim supporting an argument that is not directly stated in the argument but that may be suggested in the wording or structure of the argument. See also **premise**.

in-text searching: a system for finding information within a text that converts every word into an identifier to enable precise searching.

induction: an approach to knowledge that observes particular phenomena in order to establish general conclusions or principles.

information literacy: competency with finding, identifying, assessing, and utilizing information to answer questions and solve problems.

interdisciplinary: research or teaching whose questions or methods draw upon the practices or approaches of more than one academic field.

interlibrary loan: a service that allows library patrons to request items from other libraries and have them delivered to their home institutions.

internal funding: research resources provided by a researcher's home institution.

keynote: a featured lecture or presentation at an academic meeting.

keyword: in an information search, a term that identifies or describes a text or other information source that can be used to locate its record in a library or archive.

majors: see **academic majors.**

mean value: the average of all the numerical values in a series.

median value: the number marking the halfway point in a sequential series of numerical values.

meta-searching: see **federated searching.**

metacognition: an individual's awareness and self-conscious application of his or her own internal thought processes.

metanarrative: overarching accounts of historical periods, places, and events that frame a variety of smaller histories on related topics.

microhistory: a historical approach that seeks to answer larger questions about past eras through in-depth studies of a single individual, place, or event.

modal value: the number that occurs most frequently in a set of numerical values.

modeling: describes the ways in which data and the resulting interpretations are organized and presented using digital means.

moderator: a scholar at a lecture, panel, or roundtable session tasked with managing the presentations and audience discussions.

monograph: a book or other major piece of scholarly writing treating a single topic.

moral absolutism: an ethical principle that asserts the absolute rightness and inviolability of established rules for right and wrong.

moral relativism: an ethical principle that asserts that rules of right and wrong are not absolute but depend on factors external to the moral system.

network analysis: a historical research approach, often aided by digital means, that explores the underlying connections among distinct groups.

open access: in academic publishing, a description of a journal or other scholarly work published online and available without cost or subscription.

operationalize: in goal planning, the act of expressing plans as concrete actions that can be accomplished in a defined period of time.

opinion: in a critical thinking exercise, a position adopted on an issue or a question without supporting premises or evidence.

orphan paper: a prospective research presentation submitted for inclusion in an academic meeting without prior arrangement for participation on a panel.

paleography: the study of ancient and historical writing.

panel presentations: a small group of scholars presenting research or discussing issues connected to a related topic or theme.

paraphrase: to reiterate the content and underlying ideas of a text entirely in one's own words.

peer review: a research activity in which specialists in a researcher's field read a prospective work to assess its accuracy, methodological fitness, scholarly significance, and adherence to ethical standards.

plagiarism: the act of representing as one's own the words or ideas of another person.

precirculated: describes research presentations submitted to participants in advance of an academic meeting.

premise: in critical thinking, a rational claim that supports or proves a larger argument or conclusion. See also **explicit premise** and **implicit premise.**

presentation phase: the component of the research process involving the delivery, revision, and reception of findings from the **query phase** and **discovery phase** of a project.

presentism: applying the standards of one's own time period when analyzing or evaluating the past.

primary sources: artifacts, texts, or other sources derived from or directly connected to the era, event, person, or place under study.

principal investigator (PI): a senior or lead researcher on a scholarly project team.

provenance: referring to the place of origin of a historical text or archaeological artifact.

public history: a subfield of history concerned with sustained connections between the work of the historian and a nonspecialist audience.

query phase: the component of the research process involving an examination of a body of existing scholarship designed to determine the completeness of available answers to an academic question and define problems that frame new research.

range: a statistical measure of the distance between the smallest and the largest numbers in a data set.

rationalization fallacy: an error of critical thinking that represents weak or false reasons as strong reasons to support an argument.

rebuttal: in critical thinking, a cogent argument responding to an objection raised against an argument.

reference section: area of a library containing the (mostly noncirculating) tertiary sources, dictionaries, almanacs, and other sources providing factual data and brief overviews of information.

reliability: a statistical measure of the consistency of results from a statistical analysis.

research problem: any error, gap, omission, or unanswered question in a body of academic literature that defines the objectives of a scholarly project and helps determine the relative value of its contribution to an academic discipline or discussion.

research question: the articulation of the desired information or interpretation that serves as the starting point of a scholarly project.

reverse outlining: a process of active reading in which a reader identifies the main elements of a text in order to analyze and evaluate its essential structure and main ideas.

roundtable sessions: an open-ended, usually less formal discussion of an issue or a theme at an academic meeting.

second-order knowledge: in historical thinking, the processes, problems, and protocols that historians observe to interpret the substantive components of the past.

secondary sources: accounts or representations of a subject created by those who did not live during the time period or who did not directly experience the events related to the topic.

semantic fallacy: any error of critical thinking characterized by arbitrary uses of language or linguistic categories to define the outcomes of research.

seminar: a meeting within a series focused on studying and discussing a particular topic, question, or set of sources.

situational ethics: a view of right and wrong stating that the adherence to moral principles is contingent upon the prevailing circumstances.

SQ3R Method: a system of active reading developed by Francis P. Robinson involving "scanning, questioning, reading, reciting, and reviewing" a text.

stemmed search: see **truncated search.**

subject heading: a designated word or phrase that defines a group of works and can be used to locate their records in a library or archive.

substantive concepts: in historical thinking, it refers to the ideas, beliefs, and concepts that existed in the past but whose meaning and forms can change over time.

substantive knowledge: in historical thinking, it refers to factual or quantifiable information about history, such as the concrete names, dates, and events of the past.

S-RUN-R Method: a system of active reading developed by Nancy Bailey that calls for "surveying, reading, underlining, note-taking, and reviewing" a text.

symposium: academic meeting focused on discussions about a specific subject or theme.

teleological ethics: an ethical principle that favors the rightness of outcomes as more important than the rightness of actions.

tenure-track: describes an academic position that holds the opportunity of tenure at the end of a probationary period.

tenure clock: a predetermined amount of time granted to new professors during which they are expected to meet the requirements for tenure at an academic institution.

tertiary sources: academic scholarship synthesizing mostly secondary sources. Includes reference works such as encyclopedias and historical dictionaries.

text mining: intensive searches, usually with the aid of computers, of large bodies of texts for very specific sets of information.

topic sentence: an opening sentence in a paragraph that identifies the issue addressed in the paragraph.

topical paragraph: a paragraph whose contents deal entirely with a single issue.

truncated search: a feature allowing the use of a shortened keyword to return records related to variations on the keyword.

validity: an estimation of the degree to which a statistical analysis properly measures the object it intended to measure.

workshop: an academic meeting usually designed to impart new research findings or provide practical training that participants can apply in their fields.

zeitgeist: the "spirit of the times," referring to the mind-set and attitudes of a given time period.

INDEX